No $\dfrac{822.}{99287}$

to Observe'

Reimagining Ireland

Volume 62

Edited by Dr Eamon Maher
Institute of Technology, Tallaght

PETER LANG

Oxford • Bern • Berlin • Bruxelles • Frankfurt am Main • New York • Wien

Whitney Standlee

'Power to Observe'

Irish Women Novelists in Britain, 1890–1916

PETER LANG

Oxford • Bern • Berlin • Bruxelles • Frankfurt am Main • New York • Wien

Bibliographic information published by Die Deutsche Nationalbibliothek.
Die Deutsche Nationalbibliothek lists this publication in the Deutsche
Nationalbibliografie; detailed bibliographic data is available on the Internet at
http://dnb.d-nb.de.

A catalogue record for this book is available from the British Library.

Library of Congress Control Number: 2014952715

ISSN 1662-9094
ISBN 978-3-0343-1837-2 (print)
ISBN 978-3-0353-0680-4 (eBook)

Cover image: Sarah Cecilia Harrison, *Portrait of the Artist*, 1900,
Dublin City Gallery, The Hugh Lane, Ireland/Bridgeman Images.

© Peter Lang AG, International Academic Publishers, Bern 2015
Hochfeldstrasse 32, CH-3012 Bern, Switzerland
info@peterlang.com, www.peterlang.com, www.peterlang.net

This publication has been peer reviewed.

Printed in Germany

For my husband
Todd Standlee
who made it possible

Contents

Acknowledgements

I would like to express, first of all, my deep gratitude to the Arts and Humanities Research Council for funding the doctoral research on which this book is based. I am also grateful to the British Association for Irish Studies and the International Association for the Study of Irish Literature, both of which have provided support for the project.

The book would not have been possible without the invaluable guidance provided over the years of its gestation by Frank Shovlin, to whom I will forever be indebted for his support and encouragement. I am sincerely grateful to Marianne Elliott, Diane Urquhart and Lauren Arrington – all of the Institute of Irish Studies, University of Liverpool – for their advocacy and assistance. I am indebted to John Wilson Foster, who has encouraged me to pursue the road less travelled and who, through his pioneering work into Irish literature, has laid the foundations for those of us who have followed in his wake. In mentioning Jack Foster, I must also direct my thanks to a number of researchers who have helped me, either directly or indirectly, either through personal encouragement or the example of their work, including James H. Murphy, Heidi Hansson, Margaret Kelleher, Shaun Richards, Laura Izarra, Kathryn Laing, Matthew Campbell, Naomi Doak, Aurelia Annat, Scott McCracken, Theresa Wray, Beth Rodgers, Tina O'Toole, Rolf Loeber, Magda Stouthamer Loeber, Lisbet Kickham, Tony Murray, Eve Patten, Mary S. Pierse, Julie Anne Stevens, Patrick Maume, Bronwen Walter, Ellen McWilliams, R. F. Foster, Claire Connolly, Peter van de Kamp and all those who are working to illuminate and expand our knowledge of Irish women's literature. Thanks to both Ellen McWilliams and Tony Murray for making me feel like a welcome part of the Irish in Britain group.

I also wish to acknowledge the staff of the Special Collections and Jo Ashley, the subject librarian for Irish Studies, at the Sydney Jones Library, University of Liverpool and the staff at the following libraries and archives:

the Jesuit Archive in Dublin, and particularly Damien Burke, who allowed me to share his office and a space heater during a particularly cold and snowy week in Dublin; the John Rylands Library Deansgate and the John Rylands University Library, Manchester, with special thanks to Janet Wallwork, who shared her knowledge of Katharine Tynan with a true generosity of spirit; the National Library of Ireland; the Firestone Library at Princeton University; Trinity College Dublin Library; Marsh's Library, Dublin; Roscommon Public Library; the Bodleian Library, Oxford; and the British Library, London. I would also like to extend my profound gratitude to Mark Blundell, who contributed days of his time, numerous cups of tea and a corner of his living room at Crosby Hall to assist me with my research into his great grandmother's work.

I cannot neglect to mention the early and ongoing support of the two men who, by being enthusiastic and gifted lecturers, kindled my interest in Irish literature in my undergraduate days, Dr Scott Brewster and Professor Michael Parker. At the University of Worcester I have received consistent and invaluable encouragement from colleagues such as Jill Terry, David Arnold, Barbara Mitra, Jean Webb, Luke Devine, Andreas Mueller, Nicoleta Cinpoes, John Parham, Peter Cann and Simon Hardy.

As always, thanks to my extended (and extensive) family for their support and understanding, especially my mother for her daily emails which always express her unwavering belief in me, my father, stepfather, stepmother, sisters and parents-in-law for their interest in the project, and to my sons, Ryan and Nathan Standlee, for just being.

Finally, words cannot express how much I owe to Simon Barton, Jimmy Fennessy, Kati Nurmi, Niall Carson, Ciaran O'Neill and Anna Pilz – thanks Niall, Ciaran and Anna for reading and commenting on this work. All were once my colleagues and are now like family. I could not have done it without them.

Arts & Humanities
Research Council

Introduction: Irish Women, British Politics, and the Novel

> 'M. E. Francis,' otherwise Mrs Francis Blundell, is like so many of the younger writers of to-day, Irish.
>
> — SIR WILLIAM ROBERTSON NICOLL, 'New Writers,'
> *Bookman* (1894)[1]

> Mrs Thurston, the author of *The Circle*, the novel which has been so much talked about, is one of the numerous young Irishwomen who have made a name for themselves in the literary world.
>
> — 'A Rising Novelist', *Tatler* (1903)[2]

> I think it is pretty generally recognised to-day that one of the most effective, if not quite the most effective, vehicles for conveying ideas to the general public is the novel. Few, at all events, will deny that it may be a most powerful means of propaganda.
>
> — STEPHEN J. BROWN, 'Novels of the National Idea,'
> *Irish Monthly* (1920)[3]

Three decades into the twentieth century, the ardent Irish nationalist Daniel Corkery produced a list of those writers among his compatriots who had chosen to live and work outside of Ireland. In expounding on what he identified as a peculiarly Irish tendency, Corkery suggested that the exodus of literary talent from his homeland was nearly absolute. Most

1 Sir William Robertson Nicoll, 'New Writers', *Bookman* 6/35 (August 1894), 138.
2 Clipping, 'A Rising Novelist', *Tatler* (18 February 1903), n.p., Katherine Cecil Thurston Papers, National Library of Scotland, Acc. 11378, Box 9.
3 Stephen J. Brown, 'Novels of the National Idea', *Irish Monthly* 48/563 (May 1920), 254.

of Ireland's actively professional writers were at that time living elsewhere, he asserted, and those few who remained in the country tended to be either less committed to the pursuit of writing, or more amateurish in stature. 'It is to be noted that whereas most of those expatriate writers live by the pen,' Corkery wrote, 'there are hardly more than one or two of the home-staying writers who do so, so that in a way we have no home-staying *writers* at all'.[4] In offering as evidence of his contentions a list of literary exiles that included James Joyce, Austin Clarke, Sean O'Casey, Liam O'Flaherty, George Moore and George Bernard Shaw, Corkery made a compelling argument that there was indeed an ongoing and troubling haemorrhage of native literary talent from Ireland.

This proclivity was not in any regard new, however. It had been in evidence for decades by the time of Corkery's writing and was attributable to the fact that the Irish literati had been disillusioned with the 'depressed' state of the Irish publishing industry [since] the nineteenth century'.[5] The preferred site of relocation for Irish authors was very often the nearest point of expatriation: Britain. The magnetic attraction that London in particular held for Irish writers is exemplified in the letters and diaries of Katharine Tynan, who, when embarking on a visit to the English capital in 1884, wrote to her mentor Father Matthew Russell, the editor of the Jesuit-owned periodical the *Irish Monthly*, to request a letter of introduction into a literary household: 'You will understand that I am very anxious to make some literary friends,' Tynan confessed. 'To get into a London literary circle is my earthly ambition'.[6] By the end of that same year, Tynan had become characteristically dismissive about Dublin and the prospects for publishing there: 'I should not go to [the Dublin publishing house M. H. Gill &

---

4   Daniel Corkery, *Synge and Anglo-Irish Literature* (Cork: Cork University Press, 1931), 4.

5   Rolf Loeber and Magda Stouthamer Loeber, 'Literary Absentees: Irish Women Authors in Nineteenth-Century England', in Jacqueline Belanger, ed., *The Irish Novel in the Nineteenth Century* (Dublin: Four Courts Press, 2005), 169.

6   Letter from Katharine Tynan to Matthew Russell (24 January 1884), papers of Father Matthew Russell, Jesuit Archive, Dublin, Folder J27/73.

Son] unless as a dernier resort,' she commented to Russell when considering options for the publication of her first volume of poetry:

> You must not think me presumptuous when I say that publishing in Dublin would not please me very much. I have always thought that to publish there is almost to ensure that the book shall be still born. Tell me anyone whose book published by Gill has had a vogue outside Ireland, and I am ambitious enough to wish for a larger audience than the Ireland of *to-day*.[7]

As a middle-class Catholic and the daughter of a farmer, Tynan may have come from a more modest background than did her contemporaries William Butler Yeats and George Moore, yet she viewed late nineteenth-century Dublin in much the same manner as they did: as a literary backwater.

The exodus Corkery referred to may have been longstanding and had its viable reasons for existing, yet there is an element of his list of exiles which remains unexplained: its gendered one-sidedness. His is a roll call which strongly indicates that the tradition of leaving Ireland for the sake of literary endeavour was a peculiarly masculine phenomenon. Expanding Corkery's list still further to incorporate other prominent exemplars of the practice such as Thomas Moore, Oscar Wilde and Samuel Beckett, it becomes apparent that, in popular conception, Ireland's literary exiles have been envisioned as predominantly or even exclusively male. If it was indeed the case that it was solely men who were leaving the country to forge their writing careers, however, the literary exodus would have been distinctly at odds with the prevailing gendered divide in Irish emigration. Between 1891 and 1921, more than half – approximately 53 per cent – of emigrants from Ireland were female.[8] Where Britain was the intended destination, Irish women not only outnumbered their male counterparts but were more numerous than any other ethnic group. Over the course of the entire 150-year period between 1850 and the turn of the twenty-first century, it was in fact Irish females who continually constituted 'the largest migrant

---

7   Letter from Tynan to Matthew Russell (8 December 1884), Russell Papers J27/73.
8   Pauline Jackson, 'Women in Nineteenth-Century Irish Emigration', *International Migration Review* 18/4 (Winter 1984), 1007.

group to come to Britain'.[9] These figures are commensurate both with Irish
literacy rates, which climbed from 53 per cent in 1851 to 88 per cent in 1911,
and with a sharp decline in marriage rates in Ireland over the same period,
indicating that, lacking viable or advantageous marital prospects, women
were leaving Ireland in pursuit of the jobs they required, and were better
equipped than ever before to enter the professions rather than follow the
traditional routes of mill work or domestic service.

Katharine Tynan's name may at first appear to be a gendered anomaly
among the larger list of literary exiles, but, in actuality, she was far from
atypical. Just as wider trends saw women emigrating from Ireland in greater
numbers than men in the decades that surrounded the turn of the twentieth
century, the same statistics appear to have applied to the gendered divide
among literary emigrants. While actual figures are difficult to ascertain, the
1890s marked a significant point of entry for Irish women onto the British
publishing scene, and the proliferation of these authors did not escape the
notice of contemporary commentators. Sir William Robertson Nicoll,
editor of the *Bookman*, a magazine which reported on publishing trends and
thus one of those best placed to comment on the industry, noted in 1894,
for instance, that the Laois-born author M. E. Francis (Mary Sweetman
Blundell) was, 'like so many of the younger writers of to-day, Irish'. Nearly
a decade later, the *Tatler* suggested that the trend continued to hold true:
about Katherine Cecil Thurston, a Cork native, a reviewer commented
that she was 'one of the numerous young Irishwomen who have made a
name for themselves in the literary world'. Evidencing the inclination for
emigration to Britain among female authors in his 1916 bibliography of
Irish fiction, Stephen J. Brown managed to place more than a dozen Irish
women novelists in England at the turn of the century alongside an only
marginally greater number of male writers in similar circumstances, and
this despite the relative scarcity in the volume of biographical details for

9   Mary J. Hickman and Bronwen Walter, 'Deconstructing Whiteness: Irish Women
     in Britain', *Feminist Review* 50 (Summer 1995), 6.

female writers.[10] More recently, in a brief review of Irish women whose literary careers were forged in Britain during the nineteenth century, Rolf Loeber and Magda Stouthamer Loeber name nearly thirty prominent Irish women who were both domiciled and publishing novels in England over the course of the 1800s.[11]

More than twenty years ago, Ann Owens Weekes suggested that Irish women's writing was 'an uncharted tradition.'[12] Shortly thereafter, the historians Margaret MacCurtain, Mary O'Dowd and Maria Luddy created 'An Agenda for Women's History in Ireland', in which they asserted that the 'whole idea of female literacy leads one to investigate the contribution made by women to literature and culture in the [nineteenth] century'. Drawing attention to the fact that studies to that point had overwhelmingly favoured the work of just three Irish women writers – Lady Morgan, Maria Edgeworth and Lady Gregory – MacCurtain, O'Dowd and Luddy noted that work on and about female authors from Ireland had fallen well short of comprehensive; that there were, in fact, 'many other women who also made an impact on the Irish literary scene'.[13] Weekes subsequently published *Unveiling Treasures: The Attic Guide to the Published Works of Irish Women Literary Writers* (1993), a volume which attested to the depth of material remaining to be explored, and works such as James H. Murphy's *Catholic Fiction and Social Reality in Ireland, 1873–1922* (1997) and Kathryn J. Kirkpatrick's *Border Crossings: Irish Women Writers and National Identities* (2000) provided additional detail into the nature and extent of Irish women's literary work. The scarcity of women writers in the Irish literary canon was the instigation for MacCurtain, O'Dowd and Luddy to join with Angela Bourke, Siobhán Kilfeather, Gerardine Meaney, Máirín Ní Dhonnchadha and Clair Wills in editing the controversial fourth

---

10 See Stephen J. Brown, *Ireland in Fiction: A Guide to Irish Novels, Tales, Romances and Folk-Lore* (Dublin and London: Maunsel, 1916).

11 See Loeber and Loeber, 'Literary Absentees', 167–186.

12 Ann Owens Weekes, *Irish Women Writers: An Uncharted Tradition* (Lexington: University Press of Kentucky, 1990).

13 Margaret MacCurtain et al., 'An Agenda for Women's History in Ireland, 1500–1900', *Irish Historical Studies*, 28/109 (May 1992), 35–36.

and fifth volumes of *The Field Day Anthology of Irish Writing*, published
in 2002, which were devoted solely to charting the tradition of Irish wom-
en's writing. These two most recent volumes of *The Field Day Anthology*
remained divisive for years after their publication, in part because so little
scholarly attention had been paid to a number of the women writers whose
work was featured in their pages that their inclusion had still to be fully
justified. In the ensuing years, studies such as Lisbet Kickham's *Protestant
Women Novelists and Irish Society 1879–1922* (2004), Mary S. Pierse's five-
volume *Irish Feminisms: 1810–1930* (2010) and Tina O'Toole's *The Irish
New Woman* (2013) have emerged to evidence the prominence and proliferation of Irish women's writing in the period. Alongside such works, John
Wilson Foster's *Irish Novels 1890–1940: New Bearings in Culture and Fiction*
(2008) and Murphy's *Irish Novelists and the Victorian Age* (2011), while not
specifically conceived to rescue women's novels from obscurity, collaterally
unearthed substantial amounts of previously un- or under-studied work
by Irish women, providing additional bases on which to build this critical
heritage. Loeber and Loeber's directive for research to be undertaken on
nineteenth-century Irish women writers who lived and worked in England
appeared in 2005. Since then, however, Heidi Hansson's *Emily Lawless
1845–1913: Writing the Interspace* (2007) remains the sole full-length text
to have been produced on an Irish female writer of the nineteenth century
who lived and worked in Britain.[14] This critical neglect is almost certainly
due to the difficulty that presents itself in accessing texts by, and compil-
ing biographies for, writers whose works and lives have long lain dormant.

---

14   It should be noted, however, that two studies of Katharine Tynan and her work were
     published in the 1970s. See Marilyn Gaddis Rose, *Katharine Tynan* (Lewisburg:
     Bucknell University Press, 1974) and Ann Connerton Fallon, *Katharine Tynan*
     (Boston: Twayne, 1979). Two doctoral theses on Katherine Cecil Thurston have been
     completed since 2007, suggesting that academic interest in her work is increasing.
     See Caroline Copeland, 'The Sensational Katherine Cecil Thurston: an investigation
     into the life and publishing history of a "New Woman" author' (unpublished PhD
     thesis: Edinburgh Napier University, 2007) and Alan Thomas Bergin, 'Masquerade,
     Self-Invention and the Nation: uncovering the fiction of Katherine Cecil Thurston'
     (unpublished PhD thesis: NUI Galway, 2014).

It is precisely the aim of this study to answer the calls for research by scholars such as the Loebers, MacCurtain, O'Dowd and Luddy, and to continue the ongoing project of filling the critical gaps to which the debates surrounding the fourth and fifth volumes of *The Field Day Anthology* allude. This study focuses on Irish women writers who were living and working in Britain during the period 1890 to 1916, the closing years of Ireland's long nineteenth century. It begins from a point of supposition that the Irish female writer living in Britain during this period inhabited a unique migrant position: almost without exception well educated and of relative financial privilege, these women do not readily fit into existing conceptions of the wider Irish diaspora, which was primarily an outward dispersion of the unskilled labouring classes.[15] Neither do they occupy a space analogous to that of male literary exiles, the majority of whom would have carried with them on their journeys out of Ireland a foreknowledge of their own creative agency and potential. As Ellen McWilliams has noted, exile had long been viewed by male writers as 'a key facet in the making of the author-intellectual'.[16] For men, the literary legacy of exile existed; for women, it did not. The writers covered by this study therefore represent a unique group unto themselves, with distinct social and professional imperatives. The project undertaken herein is threefold. Loeber and Loeber have noted that the 'relative obscurity of Irish women authors in England is partly due to insufficient historical excavation of their lives', and thus a significant part of the task has been to uncover as much biographical detail on these authors as possible.[17] Secondly, the work here has been limited to the study of novels for the simple reason that the novel was by far the most popular format for literature at the turn of the twentieth century. Those novels written about Ireland and the Irish have been prioritized, with a view to

---

15 For a discussion of the class distribution and skills thresholds of the majority of Irish migrants over the course of the eighteenth, nineteenth and early twentieth centuries, see Andy Bielenberg, 'Irish Emigration to the British Empire, 1700–1914', in Andy Bielenberg, ed., *The Irish Diaspora* (Harlow: Peason, 2000), 226.

16 Ellen McWilliams, *Women and Exile in Contemporary Irish Fiction* (Houndmills, Basingstoke: Palgrave Macmillan, 2013), 18.

17 Loeber and Loeber, 'Literary Absentees', 168.

understanding how the country, its people and, most importantly, its politics are portrayed by the Irish female writer viewing her homeland from a distance. Thirdly, it has been the focus of this project to place each of the works in its relevant historical context, using both archival and published information to locate the texts as closely as possible to the personal and public circumstances of the respective authors.

This is, for most of its length, a study of the lives of, and novels written by, a sample group of authors from various family, political, religious and class-based backgrounds. In the pursuit of accuracy, it has been limited to those writers who could be placed, without doubt, in Ireland through most of their formative years and in England for the majority of the period between 1890 and 1916, at which time they must also have been publishing texts. Due to the established parameters of the study, it has necessarily been confined to writers for whom a substantial amount of biographical detail could be located. The act of placing these limiters on the research has meant the exclusion of authors whose work would otherwise have fallen under its scope, including, most notably, B. M. Croker (Bithia Mary Sheppard Croker) and Ella MacMahon, for whom extensive efforts to locate detailed and accurate biographical information have thus far proved unsuccessful. In some cases, an author has been chosen as the preeminent Irish example of a category or genre of authors – for instance, the New Woman writer George Egerton (Mary Chavelita Dunne) over other Irish exponents such as Sarah Grand (Frances Elizabeth Clarke McFall) and 'Iota' (Kathleen Mannington Caffyn). Despite the appeal of Grand's texts, she was deemed less representative than Egerton due to the fact that she spent only the first seven years of her life in Ireland, was not of Irish parentage and did not consider herself to be Irish; Iota was set aside in favour of Egerton because her most influential text, *A Yellow Aster* (1894), was written during the period she was resident in Australia. There is also a rich tradition during the era of novels written by Ulster women, but only one of these authors, Charlotte Riddell, emerged on the list of verifiable long-term emigrants to England, and her sole novel to be published during the established timeframe was issued very early in the period (in 1892). That this type of detail has not been forthcoming is almost certainly due to the readily recognizable dearth of research into the lives and work of nineteenth and early twentieth-century Ulster women writers – Naomi Doak refers to it as the most 'prominent hiatus in Irish literary history' and points to John Wilson Foster as the only researcher to have consistently made efforts to redress this critical imbalance. The work of Riddell, Beatrice Grimshaw and F. E. Crichton alone are sufficient evidence that a full-length study of pre-partition writing by women from the north of Ireland is long overdue.[18]

What remains is a cross-section of six high profile writers who lived and worked in England through all or the greater portion of the period 1890 to 1916: Emily Lawless (1845–1913), L. T. Meade (Elizabeth Thomasina Meade Toulmin Smith, 1844–1914), George Egerton (1859–1945), Katherine Cecil Thurston (née Madden, 1875–1911), M. E. Francis (1859–1930) and Katharine Tynan (1859–1931). This list includes two Catholics, two Protestants, one writer born of mixed Protestant and Catholic parentage, and another who converted from Catholicism to Protestantism. There are three middle class women in the group, two from the landed class, and one whose family's upper middle class status was in rapid decline during the years of her upbringing. Taken together, they represent some of the most popular, prolific and critically acclaimed authors of the period. Lawless was the daughter of Lord Cloncurry of Lyons House, Kildare, whose Irish novels sparked political debate and were read and discussed by, among many others, the Prime Minister William Ewart Gladstone; Egerton, who was raised primarily in and around Dublin, was the author of several experimental, proto-feminist texts which earned her both notoriety and a place among the Decadents and New Woman writers of the *fin de siècle*; Thurston, from Cork, produced novels which enjoyed worldwide popularity on a scale which dwarfed the success of other Irish writers of the era; L. T. Meade, another County Cork native, was a literary innovator who wrote more than 250 novels and remained among the most admired authors of girls' fiction for decades; Francis, of County Laois, was one of the most well-respected Catholic writers of her day whose novels gained the admiration of both the reading public and literary critics; and Tynan, from Clondalkin

18 Naomi Doak, 'Ulster Protestant Women Authors: Olga Fielden's *Island Story*', *Irish Studies Review* 15/1 (2007), 37.

in County Dublin, who managed to produce approximately 100 novels alongside her copious journalistic work and numerous volumes of poetry, memoir and short stories, was a co-founder of the Irish Literary Revival.[19] Between them, this group of women wrote more than 400 novels. By the middle of the twentieth century, their works, almost without exception, had been forgotten.

The feminist critic Elaine Showalter referred to the similarly extensive and inexplicable abandonment of nineteenth and early twentieth-century women's texts when she began her research into British women's writing in 1965. At that point, Showalter notes, 'Virginia Woolf's letters and diaries were scattered and unpublished [...] No one edited women's studies journals, or compiled bibliographies of women's writing.'[20] By the 1970s, this critical neglect was being overturned and the process of resurrecting the reputations of unjustly forgotten American and British women writers was set in motion by the new feminist critics. Among those that Showalter herself singled out for comment and commendation was George Egerton, who subsequently became the subject of various scholarly studies in which she was only very rarely identified as an Irish writer. Egerton's case is indicative of a practice that has been exercised repeatedly in relation to Irish women writers whose careers were forged in England. The 'insufficient historical excavation of their lives' to which Loeber and Loeber have referred has meant that there has been a tendency to define these women as natives of the nation in which they lived, rather than the nation from which they emerged.[21] As a result, many Irish women writers, and most particularly those whose writing careers were forged prior to the founding

19   In 1908, W. B. Yeats publicly credited her with being one of the triumvirate who embarked on a venture 'to reform Irish poetry' and thereby kindled the Literary Revival. The other two, according to Yeats, were Lionel Johnson and himself. See W. B. Yeats and Lionel Johnson, *Poetry and Ireland: Essays by W. B. Yeats and Lionel Johnson* (Dundrum: Cuala Press, 1908), 3.

20   Elaine Showalter, 'Twenty Years On: A Literature of Their Own Revisited', *NOVEL: A Forum on Fiction* 31/3 (Summer 1998), 399.

21   Loeber and Loeber, 'Literary Absentees', 167–168.

of the Irish Free State in 1922, have for years been placed under the vague heading of 'British'.

Alongside these issues of misidentification, the recovery of Irish women's writing of the nineteenth and early twentieth centuries has not continued apace with that of their American and British counterparts. The situation which confronts the scholar researching such texts and their authors today is much the same as that which Showalter experienced during her research in the 1960s and 1970s. At the National Library of Scotland, Katherine Cecil Thurston's copious letters, personal papers, photographs, keepsakes and manuscripts – comprising thirteen boxes in total – continue to be unmediated and uncatalogued. Many of the pages of the copy of L. T. Meade's earliest novel, *Ashton-Morton* (1866), held at the Bodleian Library in Oxford remained uncut 150 years after it was printed. A First World War diary written by Katharine Tynan – as valuable in its way as are the volumes of memoir she published during her lifetime – is held in the John Rylands library in Manchester, yet has never been made available in print. M. E. Francis's personal papers – which include photographs, personal letters and an incomplete but important manuscript recounting her reminiscences of Catholic elite society in Brussels during the 1870s – are still held in the private collection of her great-grandson, who has received only two requests for access to them during his lifetime. Egerton herself left a large quantity of letters from and to some of the most famous personalities of her day – including George Bernard Shaw, Oscar Wilde, Charles Stewart Parnell, W. B. Yeats, Ellen Terry, Seumas O'Sullivan, Austin Clarke and W. Somerset Maugham. Although the bulk of these are held at Princeton University and the National Library of Ireland, and can, as such, be readily accessed, most are unpublished, unstudied and unremarked upon. In the cases of some of the writers in question, personal papers are virtually or wholly non-existent. Emily Lawless asked that her letters, papers and manuscripts be destroyed after her death, an act her brother faithfully but regrettably carried out. Very little of what must have been the active and abundant correspondence of L. T. Meade survives, despite the fact that she was not only an in-demand author working regularly with several publishing houses and contributing to various periodicals, but was also the editor of *Atalanta* magazine and appears to have mentored and befriended many of its contributors, who included Tynan, Francis, H. Rider Haggard, Grant Allen, John B. Yeats, Angela Brazil and the prominent suffragists Millicent Garrett Fawcett and Evelyn Sharp.

The period between 1890 and 1916, the point at which one of the most critical political crossroads in Anglo-Irish relations was reached and also an imperative turning point for the women's rights movement, provides a particularly fruitful source for this study. For Ireland, the years surrounding the turn of the twentieth century marked an era of intense change – a point at which the progress of ordinary parliamentary politics appeared to have stalled and those political energies were being redirected into the burgeoning Gaelic Revivalist movement in sport, language and literature. Yeats famously referred to the downfall of the Irish Parliamentary Party leader Charles Stewart Parnell in 1890 as the moment at which '[a] disillusioned and embittered Ireland turned from parliamentary politics' and began the 'long gestation' of an event, the Easter Rising of 1916, which would lead to its political independence.[22] Central to that gestation, Yeats was to assert, was the formation of a new type of movement intent on developing a 'modern literature of Ireland'.[23] Such a view of the period was not, as has often been suggested, 'largely an invention of Yeats'.[24] The idea of a sudden political stasis occurring with the fall of Parnell, and of a literary movement arising to fill its place, had become part of the common parlance almost immediately after Parnell's death in 1891. By 1894, Katharine Tynan was remarking in an interview that, '[f]or the first time Irish literature has a chance, owing to the present lull in politics. Political strife has strangled literature in Ireland. The Irish Literary Society started at a very fortunate time'.[25] In the same year, William Patrick Ryan produced a study of the Irish Literary Revival in which he anticipated in that movement almost precisely the type of embryonic potential as would Yeats years later:

22   Quoted in R. F. Foster, *Modern Ireland 1600–1972* (London: Penguin, 1988), 431.
23   Foster, *Modern Ireland*, 431.
24   Sean McMahon, *A Short History of Ireland* (Dublin: Mercier Press, 1996), 136.
25   Percy L. Parker, 'Katharine Tynan at Home', *Woman's Signal* 2 (11 January 1894), 17.

The Irish literary movement, of which so much has been heard of late, has now passed its decade. In the stress and tension of political interests it remained too long unnoted in the background. It is now of nationwide importance, great in its possibilities of good for Ireland, and, mayhap, not without promise of wider influence.[26]

It is apparent from these comments that those involved in the Literary Revival – as Tynan, Ryan and Yeats were – had by the early 1890s already pre-defined the era ahead of them as one in which literature would act as an expedient tool to remedy Irish political inefficiencies. In many ways, they were not wrong in doing so. Cultural movements such as the Literary Revival did indeed do their part to redefine popular conceptions of Irishness and invigorate the country's politics in the run-up to the Easter Rising. It is almost certainly no mere coincidence, for example, that both the founder of Sinn Féin, Arthur Griffith, and one of the leaders of the Easter Rising, Patrick Pearse, were devoted to Revivalism and involved in literary pursuits of their own. Though it has often been dismissed as arrogance on the poet's part, Yeats's lyrical question, 'Did that play of mine send out/Certain men the English shot?' is a more logical one than is often supposed. It was indeed Yeats's (and, it must be remembered, Lady Augusta Gregory's) rebellion-themed play *Cathleen Ní Houlihan* which was being revived at the Abbey Theatre in Dublin during Easter week, 1916. There is abundant evidence, in fact, which attests to a degree of truth in the assertion of political influence in Ireland being exerted by literature. Likewise, it is undoubtedly true that parliamentary politics in the years surrounding the turn of the twentieth century lacked both the vigour and the minor successes that had marked the tenure of Parnell and his interventionist followers.

More questionable, however, is the contention that the products of the Revival were the only texts which harboured the potential to alter the course of Ireland's political future. Such an emphasis has undoubtedly had the residual effect of obscuring a consideration of popular fiction, and the 'social and cultural illumination' it provided to its many thousands of readers, from the discourse surrounding the relationship between Irish literature

26   William Patrick Ryan, *The Irish Literary Revival* (New York: Lemma, 1970 [1894]), v.

and politics.[27] The idea that the 'long gestation' from 1890 to 1916 represented a form of political void for Ireland is also inherently problematic. In reality, this space of time was to be a significant and ultimately decisive period in Anglo-Irish relations which was only partially invigorated by the arrival of a 'modern literature' to Ireland. As R. F. Foster has asserted, the wholesale adoption of a Yeatsian version of events 'distorts the continuing power of the constitutional political movement, ignores the context of the First World War and the contingent nature of the 1916 rising'.[28] In addition to the overarching contexts to which Foster refers, and contiguous with the advent of the Literary Revival, organizations had begun to spring up across the country which indicated a gradually intensifying sense of nationalist insularity and the emergence of a renewed and fortified strain of Celtic Irishness. Douglas Hyde, whose lecture 'On the Necessity for De-Anglicizing the Irish People' in 1892 in some regards heralded these types of ideological shifts, collaborated with Eoin MacNeill in the founding in 1893 of The Gaelic League, a 'unique pressure group' dedicated to the reinstatement of the Irish language to the Irish people.[29] In 1900, a new political organization dubbed *Cumann na nGaedheal* ('Party of the Irish') was established by Arthur Griffith, a former editor of the *United Irishman* and founder of the Celtic Literary Society. Originally intent on promoting pacifist principles, *Cumann na nGaedheal* sought to draw attention to Ireland's cultural, national and – by limiting its membership to 'persons of Irish birth or descent' – ethnic differences from Britain.[30] Five years later, the party was undergoing a change in name to Sinn Féin ('Ourselves Alone') and a hardlining of its policy. Sinn Féin would increasingly advocate an Irish-Ireland ethos that sought to exclude any and all British trade, goods or influences – whether those were educational, cultural, financial or political – from Ireland. Substantiating this new stringency, at the first

27   John Wilson Foster, *Irish Novels 1890–1940: New Bearings in Culture and Fiction* (Oxford: Oxford University Press, 2008), 19.
28   R. F. Foster, *Paddy and Mr Punch* (London: Allen Lane/Penguin, 1993), 229.
29   Foster, *Modern Ireland*, 447.
30   Foster, *Modern Ireland*, 457.

annual Sinn Féin Congress held in the Round Room of the Rotunda in Dublin on 28 November 1904, a speaker named John Sweetman – a cousin of the novelist M. E. Francis – 'proposed a resolution declaring that the people of Ireland were a free people, and that no law made without their authority was binding on their consciences'.[31] With Sweetman's speech – which was, in essence, an Irish Declaration of Independence – the rhetoric of a new type of rebellion was begun in earnest.

Meanwhile, Irish nationalists had found themselves with adequate reason, in the run-up to the Easter Rising, to lose faith in parliamentary politics. The first Home Rule Bill for Ireland had failed to pass Parliament in 1886; its second and third incarnations were introduced in the House of Commons in 1893 and 1912 respectively. The 1893 bill was defeated by a wide margin in the House of Lords. By 1913, the new bill, having twice been ratified in the House of Commons, was twice summarily thrown out by the Lords. New legislation meant, however, that the Lords could not quash the legislation if it continued to pass the Commons, and implementation of Home Rule thereby became inevitable. During the intervening period between the bill's introduction and the day on which it was finally carried, 25 May 1914, two militant organizations – the pro-union Ulster Volunteer Force and the pro-republican Irish Volunteers – were formed, raising the spectre of civil war in Ireland.[32] With the onset of the First World War in August of 1914, however, the implementation of Home Rule was shelved and the threat of internal Irish hostilities temporarily averted. While the preoccupations of Parliament turned from the situation in Ireland to the situation in Europe, it remained the case that nothing had been resolved in or for Ireland. The fate of Ulster still hung in the balance; Irish nationalists were left without their promised measure of self-government. Tensions in Ireland continued to simmer. A frustrated republican faction eventually

---

31   'The National Council. Boycott of Non-Irish Goods', *Irish Independent* (29 November 1904), 5.

32   Hundreds of articles concerning the 'imminent' civil war were published in Ireland during 1913 and 1914. See, for instance, 'The Threatened Civil War', *Irish Independent* (20 January 1914), 6; 'Civil War Imminent', *Irish Independent* (21 March 1914), 5; and 'Mr F. E. Smith & Civil War Cry', *Freeman's Journal* (2 May 1914), 9.

staged the Easter Rising in 1916, and set Ireland on its violent path towards independence.

Over the course of the same period, female commentators on political issues and women's organizations with political motives emerged as ever more influential civic forces. *Inghinidhe na hÉireann* ('Daughters of Ireland'), Ireland's first 'autonomous all-female organisation', was formed in 1900.[33] Fuelled by anti-Boer War sentiment and faced with an impending official visit to Ireland by Queen Victoria, Maud Gonne and her *Inghinidhe na hÉireann* (INE) followers joined forces to organize an overtly nationalist counter-celebration during the period of the Queen's visit to Dublin. Referred to as a 'National Children's Fete' or 'Patriotic Children's Treat', the INE's efforts drew the students and faculties of an estimated sixty 'Convent, Christian Brothers and National schools' to Dublin on 6 July 1900, and approximately 30,000 children attended the celebrations at Clonturk Park. Described by one newspaper as 'one of the most remarkable Nationalist demonstrations ever held in Dublin', it was an unmitigated success which served to raise Gonne's profile exponentially and launched her on her self-professed mission to become Ireland's Joan of Arc and lead the country to freedom from British rule.[34] The existence of *Inghinidhe na hÉireann* – which endured until 1914, when it was absorbed by another women's organization, *Cumann na mBan* ('League of Women') – and the prominence of Gonne in the nationalist movement at large signalled that a new form of politically active Irish womanhood, whose revolutionary potential had been glimpsed very briefly two decades earlier in the successful but prematurely truncated political campaigns of the Ladies' Land League, might be emergent. The early, professed intentions of Sinn Féin to commit to feminist ideals, also a founding principle of its forerunner *Cumann na nGaedheal*, was likewise evidenced by the presence of Jenny Wyse Power on its board of delegates at the Rotunda Congress in 1904.

33   Ann Matthews, *Renegades: Irish Republican Women 1900–1922* (Cork: Mercier Press, 2010), 9.

34   'Remarkable Demonstration in Dublin. English Rowdyism Smartly Punished', *Southern Star* (Cork) (7 July 1900), 3.

Despite this, however, unionist and Protestant women would continue throughout the period to have a more straightforward relationship to politics than did their nationalist and Catholic counterparts. Unionist suffrage societies existed, but there were no nationalist equivalents. The Ladies' Land League had earlier been suppressed not by the British government but by its male contingent, and in its wake women were, in the main, debarred from membership in the National League. Catholic women, many of whom held nationalist sympathies, were not brought into the suffrage movement in significant numbers.[35]

The emergence of some Irish women onto the political scene indicates, nonetheless, that the 'Irish Question', as the debate surrounding Ireland's movement towards political autonomy was popularly known, was not the only topic to be vehemently or even violently contested on an almost daily basis. The same twenty-six year interval between 1890 and 1916 constituted a large portion of the pivotal period leading towards women's suffrage in Britain and Ireland, during which the roles of women were being debated in the vastly different arenas of politics, the popular press and literature. This was an era in which journals, periodicals and newspapers were saturated with articles concerned with the 'Woman Question', which focused on the rights of women and ran contiguous to disputes over Ireland and its fate. The roots of the Woman Question's genesis can be traced as far back as the 1840s, when it emerged as a notable topic of discussion in periodicals and newspapers. Issues surrounding it would become increasingly prominent during the 1870s, when the movement to repeal the Contagious Diseases Acts of the 1860s gained momentum and women's rights began to appear more regularly as a theme in popular fiction.[36] That decade saw a limited

---

35 See Senia Pašeta, *Irish Nationalist Women 1900–1918* (Cambridge: Cambridge UP, 2013), 89–90.

36 Sally Ledger writes that the Contagious Diseases Acts of the 1860s 'had been passed with the aim of curbing the transmission of venereal disease from prostitutes to men [...]; under the terms of the Acts, women suspected of prostitution could be forcibly detained and treated in a "Lock Hospital" for up to three months. The Acts of course failed to control the spread of sexually transmitted diseases, because whilst they sought to check and control diseased women, they left their (equally diseased) male clientele

number of periodicals publishing self-consciously political feminist fiction, among them the *Englishwoman's Domestic Magazine*. Between January 1874 and December 1875, for example, the *Englishwoman's Domestic* serialized a novel, *Forgotten Lives*, by Francis Derrick (Frances E. M. Notley), which argued that

> In no country in Europe are there so many poverty-stricken, helpless, unskilful, uncared-for women as in this great England. The reason is obvious. Men legislate selfishly, regarding all questions from only a masculine view, hence they have fallen into cruel blunders, not perceiving that, 'The woman question is the man's,' and injury to one is hurtful to the other.[37]

Derrick's explicitly feminist themes were something of an anomaly in the 1870s, but from the time of the publication of Olive Schreiner's novel *The Story of an African Farm* in 1883 until the mid-1890s, fiction concerned with promoting the variety and spectrum of women's rights, eventually dubbed 'New Woman' literature, was increasingly popular.

As has been noted, three women born in Ireland – George Egerton, Sarah Grand and 'Iota' – were among the most prominent of the New Woman writers, indicating a disproportionate degree of involvement on the part of an Irish female contingent in contemporary debates surrounding the rights and roles of women. Irish women were not, however, only making their mark on the suffragist and feminist side of these arguments. In June of 1889, the month in which Henrik Ibsen's *A Doll's House* premiered on the London stage and in its wake the term 'New Woman' began to gain currency, an anti-suffrage lobby was organized by the novelist Mrs Humphry Ward and the names of its all-female adherents appended to an article in the *Nineteenth Century* magazine.[38] Among the women who

---

free to re-infect anyone with whom they came into contact'. Sally Ledger, 'The New Woman and feminist fictions', in Gail Marshall, ed., *The Cambridge Companion to the Fin de Siècle* (Cambridge: Cambridge University Press, 2007), 158.

37 Francis Derrick, 'Forgotten Lives', *Englishwoman's Domestic Magazine* 119 (1 November 1874), 229.

38 Sarah Grand has frequently been credited with coining the phrase 'the New Woman' in 1893, but it is evident that the concept had been named and was circulating in the

supported 'An Appeal Against Female Suffrage' were several whose names had been connected, in very public ways, to Ireland and its political struggles. These included the educational reformer Lady Frederick Cavendish, who had remained supportive of her husband's reformist politics for Ireland even after his assassination by radical Irish nationalists in the Phoenix Park in Dublin in 1882; Lady Randolph Churchill, who openly supported her Orange card-playing husband in his anti-Home Rule politics; and, most notably, the Irish author Emily Lawless, whose recent work of non-fiction, *Ireland: The Story of the Nations* (1887), had actively and with undisguised skepticism addressed the issue of Home Rule for Ireland.[39] In 1911, Millicent Garrett Fawcett, the president of the National Union of Women's Suffrage Societies and co-founder (in 1871) of Newnham College Cambridge, would note the irony of such signatories to the appeal by stating that '[s]everal of the ladies who signed the *Nineteenth Century* protest were at that moment in 1889 taking an active part for or against the main political issue of the day, the granting of Home Rule to Ireland; and yet, they were saying at the same time that women had not the material to form a sound judgment in politics'.[40] Not only the existence of such a list but the prominence of its positioning in one of the most widely read periodicals of the period is, as Fawcett indicates, deeply paradoxical, for it strongly indicates the degree to which disenfranchised women felt inclined and at liberty to exercise their political influence through unofficial channels. One of the most important of these outlets, it might be persuasively argued, was the novel. By 1893, what was viewed as a new generation of 'Wild Women' – or 'Shrieking

---

popular press several years prior to this. The first mention of the phrase 'the New Woman' being used in the mainstream British press in this context is in a reference to the character of Nora Helmer in Ibsen's *A Doll's House* just days after the farewell performance of that play's inaugural run in London. See 'To-Day's Tittle Tattle', *Pall Mall Gazette* (1 July 1889), 6.

39   See 'An Appeal Against Female Suffrage', *Nineteenth Century* 25/148 (June 1889), 781–788 and Emily Lawless, *Ireland: The Story of the Nations* (London: T. Fisher Unwin, 1887), 413–414. Incidentally, Lucy Cavendish was also the Prime Minister W. E. Gladstone's niece.

40   Millicent Garrett Fawcett, L. L. D., *Women's Suffrage: A Short History of a Great Movement* (New York: Dodge Publishing, 1911), 45.

Sisterhood' or 'Revolting Daughters', as they were alternately known –
had been definitively re-christened with the 'New Woman' label by the
popular press, and this terminology soon became shorthand not only for
a 'type' of emancipated woman but also for the feminist fiction produced
by such women and their supporters during the 1890s. For several years,
this fictional genre exercised the imaginations of an extensive readership,
and stimulated an unprecedented degree of debate concerning women's
roles in society.

As with the Home Rule Bills for Ireland that had stalemated in the
House of Lords in 1886 and 1893, bills intended to grant women the vote
were repeatedly introduced in Parliament and just as frequently stymied by
the 'inbuilt Tory majority in the Upper House' until the power of the Lords
was eventually curtailed in the second decade of the twentieth century.[41]
Further evidence that Irish nationalist organizations were (or could appear
to be) anti-feminist in intent can be found in the fact that Parliamentary
devotees of the Home Rule cause for Ireland played their part in hindering the movement for women's suffrage. From the 1880s, Irish nationalist
members of Parliament, fearful of upsetting the balance in a House of
Commons whose members were only then beginning to lean in favour of
Home Rule by introducing the unknown quantity that women represented
into the electorate, often actively sided against or abstained from taking
part in balloting on measures which would have extended the franchise
to women.[42] Meanwhile, the New Woman writing in Britain would suffer
its own form of Irish defeat when a newly conservative atmosphere befell
the British publishing industry in the mid–1890s. Long associated with
Oscar Wilde and his Decadent cohort, the New Women would share in
Wilde's demise when he was convicted of eight Acts of Gross Indecency
in the spring of 1895. Although this might have proved only a temporary

41   Les Garner, *Stepping Stones to Women's Liberty: Feminist Ideas in the Women's
      Suffrage Movement 1900–1918* (Cranbury, New Jersey: Associated University Presses,
      1984), 7.
42   See Pašeta, *Irish Nationalist Women*, 88.

setback for feminist fiction, the onset of the Boer War in 1899 was to deal it a final deathblow.

The woman's movement, like the Irish Home Rule movement which was both interconnected with and in some regards actively antagonistic to it, reached a point of relative inertia in the decades which bookended the turn of the twentieth century. Whereas debates on the issue of women's suffrage had been regular fixtures in Parliament since 1869, and there had been thirteen such deliberations on the floor of the House of Commons between 1870 and 1890, the waning in political interest concerning the initiative is evidenced by the fact that only four such debates occurred between 1890 and 1908. The Boer War ended in 1902, but the movement for women's suffrage would not be substantially reenergized until the second decade of the twentieth century. As the progress of the women's suffrage initiative through Parliament slowed, the women's movement gradually altered. The New Woman was replaced by the figure of the militant suffragette, who was even more widely vilified than her 'revolting' precursor. Much like the Irish drive towards political autonomy, from 1910 onwards the woman's movement would rapidly shift away from the realms of the literary, the rhetorical and the parliamentary to become actively and violently oppositional.

Emigration to England in the decades leading to the Easter Rising often resulted in a head-on confrontation with what had become the prevailing debates of the period. Yet because the Irish and Woman questions were being asked about, rather than posed to, women and the Irish, they attempted to exclude Irish women from their solutions by the very terms in which they were proffered. Due to their political disenfranchisement, Irish women, it might be said, were doubly debarred from engaging in the resolution to these professed 'problems'. As such, these remained, from a rhetorical standpoint, questions to be asked and answered exclusively by British men. Each of the women writers to be examined in this study nonetheless managed to circumvent the terms of their exclusion by engaging publicly in these debates, albeit to varying degrees and with what were at times widely divergent viewpoints.

In some respects, this tendency towards political commentary is hardly surprising. Once in England, an educated Irish woman seeking a literary career would have avoided the debates surrounding the Irish and Woman Questions only with difficulty. If she lived in or spent large portions of time in London, she would quickly have become immersed in a world replete with women's clubs and debating societies, a place where social philanthropy was the order of the day. So ubiquitous was the women's club that nearly every professional author of the period could claim an allegiance to one or another of them: Thurston, Tynan and Francis attended the Lyceum Club, which invited women writers and illustrators into its membership, Egerton belonged to the Ladies' Athenaeum Club for professional women, and Meade was a member of the pro-suffrage Pioneer Club. Women writers often felt inclined to reveal their political opinions in interviews and discursive writings as well as through open activism, and it is relatively easy to locate evidence that, for instance, Meade and Tynan were dedicated suffragists, Lawless was at one point avowedly anti-suffrage, and that Tynan and Francis professed their allegiance to Revivalist pursuits by joining the Irish Literary Society in London. Several of the writers in this study signed political petitions; all made public speeches. Women were not, it seems, excluding themselves from debating politics in either their private or their public lives, and it only remains to be answered whether or not this trend towards political commentary and activism continued to be exercised when it came to the writing of their novels. The fact that these texts, published almost exclusively in England, Scotland and the United States, were intended for an English-speaking readership that included Britain, Ireland and an array of colonies current and former, meant that the degree of influence that might be exercised was potentially vast and wide-ranging.

In his own musings on the subject of literature and emigration, Daniel Corkery was moved to wonder whether 'national literature' – literature for the consumption and edification of the Irish people – could be produced from a space of expatriation.[43] The emphasis for Corkery was on the overtly political aspects of the work in question, and so too would it be for many earlier Irish commentators, particularly in those turbulent years immediately prior to Ireland's independence from Britain. In attempting

---

43   Daniel Corkery, *Synge and Anglo-Irish Literature*, 4.

to answer 'The Question of Irish Nationality' in 1912, the man who would four years later become the first comprehensive bibliographer of Irish fiction, Stephen J. Brown, had posited the Irish writer living in England as one of those best placed to view and convey the political differences between the two nations: 'anyone who has power to observe, and who has lived in both countries in more or less intimate relations with their peoples knows that a deep gulf still separates the two', he asserted. Brown proceeded in the same article to contend that the 'contrast has been best drawn in the form of fiction, in such books as [...] M. E. Francis's "Frieze and Fustian," and "North, South and Over the Sea," [and] Katherine [sic] Tynan's novels of English and Irish country life'.[44] Writing in the *Irish Monthly* eight years later, at a point in which Ireland's status as a nation hung delicately in the balance, Brown identified the novel as one of the most potent political tools then available: 'I think it is pretty generally recognised to-day that one of the most effective, if not quite the most effective, vehicles for conveying ideas to the general public is the novel', Brown would assert, adding that '[f]ew, at all events, will deny that it may be a most powerful means of propaganda'.[45] After citing Charles Reade, Benjamin Disraeli, Charles Dickens and Harriet Beecher Stowe as evidence of those who had exercised such novelistic influence to great effect, Brown would contend that the 'contrast of temperaments' between the Irish and English had been best exemplified during his era by, among others, the novels of M. E. Francis, and that texts such as hers had the potential to prove more useful to the cause of nationalism than many other more overtly political Irish works, including those by William Carleton and Patrick Pearse.[46] In these articles, Brown draws consistent attention to novels written by Irish women domiciled and working in Britain, asserting that these authors could and did use their texts to exercise their political influence.

44 Stephen J. Brown, 'The Question of Irish Nationality', *Studies: An Irish Quarterly Review* 1/4 (December 1912), 645.

45 Stephen J. Brown, 'Novels of the National Idea', *Irish Monthly* 48/563 (May 1920), 254.

46 Brown, 'Novels of the National Idea', 260.

This book is in its most distilled essence an exercise in testing the hypothesis that Irish writers exiled to Britain enacted a 'power to observe' the political situation – gendered, national and cultural – in and between their native and adoptive homelands. It provides a detailed insight into the lives and works of the most high profile women writers of the period who occupied this cultural location, and ventures out from a logical point of assumption that Irish women writing from an English location were placed in a complex cultural locus that afforded an insight which was at once both familiar and foreign. Emily Lawless, L. T. Meade, George Egerton, Katherine Cecil Thurston, M. E. Francis and Katharine Tynan have been chosen as the subjects of this study because it is their lives which have been most readily traceable: the excavation of their biographies has been made easier by the fact that each writer was a subject of interest in the press between the years 1890 and 1916. At the same time, the extent of their visibility in the contemporary press indicates their suitability as subjects of study by reflecting a proportionate degree of public interest in their works, their opinions and their lives. This study is unique in its project of venturing as closely to those lives as possible and in the contention that it is only through a comprehension of all the factors that came to bear on the production of their texts that we can understand the distinctive challenges these women faced (as Irish writers, women writers, exiled writers) and gain a more thorough appreciation of their literary achievements. In exploring the works and lives of Irish women authors living and working in Britain between 1890 and 1916, this study adds both substance and nuance to the relatively thin forces of criticism on Irish women's writing of the period. It also adds much-needed flesh to the bones of our understanding of six women who emerge in these pages not only as writers of interest because they afforded unique perspectives on their personal circumstances, but as writers of importance because they were competent, confident and, more often than not, compelling commentators on the cultural and political situations in which they were embedded.

A View from 'Both Sides': Emily Lawless's Rebellion Novels and the Irish Question

The book is slanderous and lying from cover to cover, and it is slanderous and lying on a preconceived purpose so mean that only the daughter of an Irish landlord could pursue it.
— Review of Emily Lawless's *Hurrish,* the *Nation* (1886)[1]

Miss Lawless is the sister of Lord Cloncurry, a militant Irish landlord, but in the broad sense she can scarcely be anything but an Irish nationalist.
— KATHARINE TYNAN HINKSON, Review of Emily Lawless's *Maelcho, Boston Literary World* (1894)[2]

The titles of two of Emily Lawless's most important works offer clues to the degree to which her emigration from Ireland permeated both her consciousness and the themes of her literary output. In them, she places herself in positions which act in opposition to one another: in her early historical novel about the Elizabethan campaign to halt the Tyrone rebellion, *With Essex in Ireland* (1890), she situates herself alongside an English interloper on Irish soil; in her later poetic volume, *With the Wild Geese* (1902), she aligns herself with Jacobite soldiers exiled from their Irish homeland to fight for continental armies. Both of these positions can be seen as accurate representations of Lawless's own relationship to Ireland. As an Anglo-Irish woman who was sympathetic to nationalist interests at the same time that

---

1   'Hurrish', the *Nation* (20 February 1886), 3.
2   Clipping from *Boston Literary World* (1 December 1894), n.p., Emily Lawless Papers, Marsh's Library (Dublin), Z2.1.15/27.

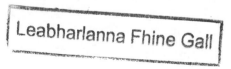

she remained avowedly unionist, her position in relation to Ireland was similar to that which she asserted the Earl of Essex held: one of simultaneous insider and outsider status, from which it was possible to view 'both sides of a question'.[3] Like her imagined soldierly comrades in *With the Wild Geese*, she also found herself in exile from a country for which she held great affection, but to which she felt she could not return. The differences between these titles and their metaphorical locations illustrate the complexities of the personal and political positions Lawless occupied at various points in her life, and her titular shift from trespasser in Ireland to exile from Ireland suggests that, in the twelve years between the writing of *With Essex in Ireland* and *With the Wild Geese*, she moved ideologically nearer to a sense of her own Irish identity even as she was in the process of distancing herself geographically from her homeland.

As these titles further suggest, Lawless's texts are haunted by the remnants of an Irish past which is both communal and personal. Overtly preoccupied by the history of her homeland, the pathos of which can be seen to trouble and fascinate her in equal measure, her writings are also and similarly bound to her family's history, which was marked by its own forms of political dissension and emotional upheaval. Born in 1845 at Lyons House, near Hazelhatch, County Kildare, one of her family's two stately homes, Emily Lawless was the eldest daughter and fourth child of Edward Lawless, the third Lord Cloncurry, and his wife Elizabeth.[4] On her mother's side, she was descended from a long and distinguished line of the Kirwan family, one of the fourteen ancient tribes of Galway. On her father's side, however, the family's fortunes and aristocratic status were more tenuous, having been acquired a mere three generations prior to her birth and in circumstances that remained highly contentious during Lawless's lifetime.[5]

At the height of her literary fame, the Irish nationalist MP John Gordon Swift MacNeill would reignite a century-old controversy which

---

3   Emily Lawless, *Ireland: The Story of the Nations* (London: T. Fisher Unwin, 1887), 209.
4   The Lawless's other home was Maretimo, Blackrock, County Dublin.
5   Heidi Hansson, *Emily Lawless 1845–1913: Writing the Interspace* (2007), 16.

surrounded the Lawless family's acquisition of the Cloncurry title in 1789.
MacNeill's 1894 volume, *Titled Corruption*, was written as a means of questioning the legitimacy of certain members of the aristocracy – Lawless's
brother, Valentine, being one – who had voted against the second Home
Rule Bill for Ireland in 1893.[6] In his book, MacNeill used the writings and
testimony of Henry Grattan, William Brabazon Ponsonby and John Philpot
Curran as evidence that Lawless's great-grandfather, Nicholas Lawless –
whose father had made the family's fortune by working his way up through
the ranks of, and eventually marrying into, a woollen merchants' business –
had converted to Protestantism on spurious terms and had bribed his way
into the peerage. Condemning her family, MacNeill did not spare Lawless
herself. Noting that, in the first of her Irish-set novels, *Hurrish* (1886), she
had referred 'slightingly [to] the lowly antecedents of some Irish members' of Parliament, he called attention to the hypocrisy of Lawless's attitudes by reminding his readers that her own great-grandfather had been
'the son of [a] woollen-draper's errand-boy'.[7] As MacNeill's attack on the
Lawless family suggests, the controversies and schisms that surrounded
the Cloncurry title were more intricate than even the inherent duality of
their Anglo-Irishness conveys. The first Lord Cloncurry was not only, as
MacNeill asserted, widely known to have purchased his peerage, but was
generally regarded by his contemporaries as a pro-Union sycophant who
had converted to Protestantism solely for the purpose of furthering his
own already substantial financial interests.[8]

6   See also Patrick Maume, 'Emily Lawless's *Maelcho* and the Crisis of Imperial Romance',
     Eire-Ireland 41/3–4 (2007), 245–246.
7   J. G. Swift MacNeill, Q. C. M. P., *Titled Corruption* (London: T. Fisher Unwin,
     1894), 67.
8   MacNeill, *Titled Corruption*, 67. See also G. O. Sayles, 'Contemporary Sketches
     of the Members of the Irish Parliament in 1782', *Proceedings of the Royal Irish
     Academy. Section C: Archaeology, Celtic Studies, History, Linguistics, Literature* 56
     (1953/1954), 243; Edith M. Johnson, 'Members of the Irish Parliament, 1784–1787',
     *Proceedings of the Royal Irish Academy. Section C: Archaeology, Celtic Studies, History,
     Linguistics, Literature* 71 (1971), 213; and John William Fitzpatrick, *Life, Times, and
     Contemporaries of Lord Cloncurry* (Dublin: James Duffy, 1855), 231–232.

In stark contrast, his son Valentine Browne Lawless would, upon assuming the Cloncurry title, become both a United Irishman and noted enemy of the Union who was twice imprisoned in the Tower of London for his political activism. Valentine Browne Lawless's life was not, however, without its own scandals. In 1811 he divorced his first wife, Elizabeth Georgiana (née Morgan), after having successfully sued her lover for £20,000 in damages for adultery.[9] Edward Lawless, the eldest son of Valentine Browne Lawless's second marriage to Emily Douglas, assumed the title of third Lord Cloncurry upon his father's death in 1853. With his accession came a return to the devout unionism and the type of political indiscretion exemplified by his grandfather. The most infamous act of his political tenure came when he resigned his position as a deputy lieutenant of the city of Dublin in protest over the appointment to a counterpart post of William Lane Joynt, the serving Lord Mayor of Dublin, who, in Cloncurry's opinion, was an 'ultra-Radical electioneering agent'.[10] Newspapers throughout Great Britain and Ireland published reports on the incident, some of which referred derogatorily to Cloncurry as both an 'unsupported ultra-Tory' and 'the titled grandson of a Liberty tradesman'.[11] As these descriptions indicate, press opinion ran overwhelmingly in favour of Lane Joynt, who subsequently sued Edward Lawless for libel. Two years later, in April of 1869, Edward Lawless committed suicide by throwing himself from an upper storey window at Lyons House.

Emily Lawless was twenty-four years old at the time of her father's death. An inquest confirmed that it followed at least three years of severe mental illness, the symptoms of which indicate that he suffered from paranoid schizophrenia.[12] These findings might have exonerated the family from the legacies of Edward Lawless's recent political embarrassments had his son Valentine, the fourth Lord Cloncurry, not become in his wake one of the most infamous evicting landlords of the Land War era.

---

9   See 'Trial of Sir J. Piers', *Morning Post* (London) (24 February 1807), n.p.
10 'The Right Hon. The Lord Mayor and Lord Cloncurry', *Freeman's Journal* (14 March 1867), 1.
11 'The Right Hon. The Lord Mayor and Lord Cloncurry', 1.
12 'The Late Lord Cloncurry. The Inquest', *Freeman's Journal* (6 April 1869), 4.

By 1881, the actions of the newest Lord Cloncurry had caused him to be so reviled that his tenants were burning him in effigy at Abingdon in County Limerick.[13] Consistently leasing his lands for sums twenty to fifty per cent in excess of Poor Law Valuations, he was in court time and again during the 1880s and 1890s to defend his actions. As late as 1892, the Evicted Tenants' Commission was launching inquests into his affairs.[14] Although his stance would eventually alter with the changing times, and he would become a senator in the Irish Free State after its formation in 1922, Valentine Lawless remained one of Ireland's most reviled landlords throughout the period of his sister's writing career.

It is almost certainly no coincidence that Lawless's first novel, *A Chelsea Householder*, was published in 1882, the same year that mass evictions occurred on her brother's estates. The debts her family had incurred as the result of mortgages taken out in the post-famine era, and the depletion of income from their estates which resulted from the reduction in rents which followed these evictions, undoubtedly instigated financial concerns for the family. As an unmarried woman until then wholly supported by profits from the Cloncurry estates, Lawless was almost certainly embarking on an attempt, through her turn to professional writing, to achieve a modicum of financial independence.[15] Perhaps as a result of the controversies which surrounded her brother's actions, she would spend increasingly more time away from Ireland over the course of the 1880s, yet her affection for her homeland remained undimmed and many of her family ties continued to be very close. She was deeply devoted to her mother, who Lawless's close friend, the novelist Margaret Oliphant, once described as 'the only true and perfect democrat' she had ever known. Although Elizabeth Kirwan Lawless hailed from a family of 'high Tories', she was, according to Oliphant, a political dissenter among her relations who had 'left family politics far behind in the openness of her sympathies and her

---

13   *Nenagh Guardian* (4 June 1881), 4.
14   'The Evicted Tenants' Commission', *Freeman's Journal* (3 December 1892), n.p.
15   For additional information concerning the debts incurred by the Cloncurry estates, see Terence Dooley, 'The Mortgage Papers of St Patrick's College, Maynooth. 1871–1923', *Archivium Hibernicum* 59 (2005), 120.

soul'.[16] Lawless's mother remained, however, 'strongly opposed to Home Rule and all the follies connected with that conception', a stance similar to her daughter's.[17] Having acted as her mother's near-constant traveling companion since the late 1870s, Lawless admitted that her mother's death in 1895 came as a 'crushing' blow.[18]

She would also share an intense bond with her brother, Frederick, who was two years her junior. The relationship between the siblings would, over the course of the late nineteenth and early twentieth centuries, be made even more intimate by their mutual grief over the death of a favoured younger brother, Denis, and the suicides of two of their three sisters.[19] Frederick, for his part, would fill scrapbooks with the dozens of clippings about his sister and her work that he collected from newspapers and magazines, and also inserted his own affectionate comments and reminiscences into the margins of her books.[20] On Lawless's death in 1913, he would add a poignant, handwritten note to his own copy of *With Essex in Ireland*, in which he wondered why 'the dear sister [should] be taken, and stupid me left lamenting?'[21] It would later be his fate to become the last of the Cloncurry Lords. After his elder brother Valentine died without a male heir in 1928, the unmarried Frederick assumed the title of fifth Baron Cloncurry. With his death a year later the title became obsolete. It had endured just over a century.

The intermingling of affection for and disaffection with her family and her home is apparent in the actions Lawless took and attitudes she

16   M. A. Oliphant, 'A Noble Lady', *New Review* 14/82 (March 1896), 244.

17   Oliphant, 'A Noble Lady', 246.

18   Letter from Emily Lawless to W. E. H. Lecky (13 May 1895), Lecky Correspondence, Trinity College Dublin, MSS 1827–1836/2474.

19   See Robert Hogan, *Dictionary of Irish Biography* (London: Aldwych Press, 1996), 687. The deaths of all of these siblings had occurred by the year 1906, when *Whitaker's Peerage* lists only five remaining Lawless brothers and sisters out of the original nine. See *Whitaker's Peerage, Baronetage, Knightage and Companionage for the Year 1906* (London: Whitaker's, 1907), 208.

20   Frederick Lawless's notebooks, scrapbooks and collection of his sister's published works are held in the Lawless Papers, Marsh's Library, Dublin.

21   Held in the Lawless Papers.

expressed both personally and publicly. In a 1905 letter, for instance, she would reveal the degree of her attachment to her homeland by writing to a friend to suggest that a piece of poetry was flawed because it made the mistake of 'putting Heaven into the chief place instead of Ireland. That it may be the better place of the two I am willing to admit, but the latter has at present more of my affections, so I had to leave it the place of honour'.[22] Nonetheless, when she was eventually free after her mother's death to make her own living arrangements, she chose to settle in England. She never married, but spent the final fifteen years of her life in Gomshall, Surrey, living in a house – built in 1897 and designed by Edward Lutyens – that she and her long-term companion, Lady Sarah Spencer, had built to 'their own desires'.[23] Yet the name that Lawless chose for that home, 'Hazelhatch', paid conspicuous homage to the region of Kildare in which she was raised, and she would attempt to recreate the landscape of her mother's native west of Ireland by transplanting the flora she collected from the Burren and Connemara in her English garden.[24] Her fiction would enact a similar process of re-envisioning her homeland. Although in her early career she would write three English-set novels – *A Chelsea Householder* (1882), *A Millionaire's Cousin* (1885) and *Major Lawrence, F. L. S.* (1887) – after 1890, Lawless never again turned to sources outside Ireland for the inspiration for her fictions.[25]

She was an avowed unionist, yet her political opinions appear to have been as complex as was her family history, and there is abundant evidence in her writings to suggest that, like her cousin Sir Horace Plunkett, she was sympathetic to the plight of the Irish peasantry and to the emotional appeal of Irish nationalism. She admitted to having been strongly

22   Edith Sichel, 'Emily Lawless', *Nineteenth Century and After* 76/449 (July 1914), 87–88.

23   Sichel, 'Emily Lawless', 97.

24   The garden was designed by Gertrude Jekyll.

25   For additional details about Emily Lawless's life, and a complementary reading of her work, see Hansson's meticulously researched *Emily Lawless 1845–1913: Writing the Interspace* (2007), to which this work is indebted for drawing attention to a number of sources about Lawless.

influenced in early life by her grandfather's militant stance against the Union, and in 1901 wrote a thinly veiled account of her inordinate pride as a youth in the knowledge that he had been imprisoned in the Tower of London for his rebellions against the Crown.[26] Over time, however, she found it increasingly difficult to regard Britain as she had when she was young – as 'the Great Bully, the Supreme Tyrant, red with the blood of Ireland and Irish heroes'.[27] Much of her prose writing, fictional or otherwise, reveals that she instead viewed her homeland largely through the lens of the committed historian, and came to believe that its current troubles were, as she deemed they had been throughout its turbulent past, as much due to internal strife as they were a result of external forces: 'she would have liked to be able to be a Home Ruler,' her friend Edith Sichel wrote, 'but she did not regard her countrymen as ripe for self-government'.[28] There is also an indication that she had in common with many unionists a fear that Home Rule would mean Rome Rule, and in the history of Ireland she came to write in 1887 she would express her objections to what she viewed as the increasing tendency to bring 'the priest into politics'.[29] Doing so, Lawless believed, had the detrimental effect of 'accentuating the religious side of the contest' between unionists and nationalists.[30]

At the same time, she involved herself, albeit tenuously, in that movement which would become synonymous with the drive towards nationalism: the Irish Literary Revival. A friend of Lady Augusta Gregory, Lawless acted as one of the first guarantors of the Abbey Theatre alongside such disparate fellow patrons as John O'Leary, Timothy Healy, Douglas Hyde and John Dillon.[31] On visits to Gregory's marital home, Coole Park, she also came in close contact with, and developed a far from cordial relationship to,

---

26   See Emily Lawless, 'Of the Personal Element in History', *Nineteenth Century* 50/297 (November 1901), 794.
27   Emily Lawless, *A Garden Diary* (London: Methuen, 1901), 68.
28   Sichel, 'Emily Lawless', 87.
29   Lawless, *Ireland: The Story of the Nations*, 384.
30   Lawless, *Ireland: The Story of the Nations*, 385.
31   Lady Augusta Persse Gregory, *Our Irish Theatre: A Chapter of Autobiography* (New York and London: G. P. Putnam's Sons, The Knickerbocker Press, 1913), 17.

W. B. Yeats. In her diaries, Gregory would recall that, during their mutual stays at Coole, Lawless repeatedly took the poet to task for his impracticality, not only as this trait manifested itself in his lack of knowledge on the scientific and historical matters in which she herself was interested (she was a keen amateur entomologist and historian), but also with regard to his finances: 'The British, perhaps the commercial, side of the first holder of the [Cloncurry] title, the blanket manufacturer,' Gregory would suggest, 'made [Lawless] indignant that [Yeats] was not writing articles every week that would enable him to support his family'.[32] The two 'always turned to a subject they could not agree on', Gregory claimed, and this despite the fact that he 'admired *Essex* and she his poems'.[33] Gregory herself was less appreciative of Lawless's literary output than was Yeats. Unlike him, she at first found little to admire in *With Essex in Ireland*, and maintained an active dislike for Lawless's oft-praised *Maelcho* (1894) throughout her lifetime. By 1929, however, she had come to believe that much of Lawless's writing was nationalist in tone, and that at least three of her poems – 'Munster Forest', 'The Clare Coast' and 'After Aughrim' – had 'given her a lasting place in the memory of the country'.[34]

Lawless's fictional project, as she herself once described it, was to vivify history and make it relevant to the present: 'To induce history to live and move, to induce its men and women to walk and talk, to live, breathe, sigh, weep, and laugh for us, in their habit as they existed,' she asserted, 'is the aim of every good writer, and ought to be the aim of every good reader'.[35] She nonetheless comprehended the difficulty of such a project in terms of its accessibility to readers. A shared joke that spanned the generations, she believed, was among the most effective tools in uniting the readers of

---

I am indebted to Anna Pilz for drawing my attention to the passages from Gregory's autobiographical writings and journals that deal with Lawless.

32 Lady Augusta Gregory, *Lady Gregory's Journals: Volume Two, Books 30–44, 21 February 1925–9 May 1932*, ed. Daniel J. Murphy (Gerrards Cross: Colin, Smythe, 1987), 424.

33 Gregory, *Lady Gregory's Journals: Volume Two*, 386.

34 Gregory, *Lady Gregory's Journals: Volume Two*, 541.

35 Lawless, 'Of the Personal Element in History', 797.

her day with the actors of history, but humour was not, she acknowledged, an instrument that lent itself well to the Irish historical subject matter with which she often dealt: 'the truth is, Irish history does not seem to be quite fair game for any little sport of the kind,' she wrote. 'Its record is too dark [...] Men laugh who win, and the winning days for Irishmen have been a long time on the road'.[36] Realizing this, she would apologize to her readers for the excessive 'gloom' of her novel *Grania: The Story of an Island* (1892), and for the way in which *Maelcho*, originally conceived as a 'lively' adventure tale, grew 'grimmer' and 'more lugubrious' as it progressed.[37] Her novels are not, however, without that humour to which Lawless refers, although she is careful to achieve it largely at the expense of male characters who either are, or act as tropes for, English or Anglo-Irish men, including the bigoted Hal Harvey in *With Essex*, the indolent Murdough Blake in *Grania*, and the self-aggrandizing Hugh Gaynard of *Maelcho*.

The earliest of her Irish works, *Hurrish* (1886), deals centrally with the subject of the Land Wars in which her brother figured so prominently.[38] It was also the work which evoked the most starkly varied responses among her Irish readers. Among its most vehement critics was a commentator in the *Nation*, who referred to it as 'slanderous and lying from cover to cover, and [...] slanderous and lying on a preconceived purpose so mean that only the daughter of an Irish landlord could pursue it'. Among the Irish Literary Revivalists it also aroused conspicuous censure. Lady Gregory criticized its 'patronizing tone' and Yeats, too, joined the dissenting side, later suggesting that her fiction was repeatedly marred by her tendency to depict the relationship between her Irish and English characters in a

36   Lawless, 'Of the Personal Element in History', 797–798.
37   Emily Lawless, *Grania: The Story of an Island*, 2 vols (London: Smith, Elder, 1892), 1: 'Dedication', and Emily Lawless, *Maelcho: A Sixteenth-Century Narrative*, 2 vols (London: Smith, Elder, 1894), 1: 'Dedication'.
38   For a more detailed discussion of the Lawless family during the Land War era, see Whitney Standlee, 'The "Personal Element" and Emily Lawless's *Hurrish* (1886)' in Heidi Hansson and James H. Murphy, eds., *Fictions of the Irish Land War* (Oxford: Peter Lang, 2014), 19–40.

stereotypical manner which emphasized a sense of Irish inferiority.[39] The *Dublin Evening Mail*, in contrast, would assert that *Hurrish* was of nearly unprecedented political importance – 'as opportune to English politics of the day as the publication of Mrs Stowe's famous novel was to the discussion of the American slavery question' – a review which indicates that, in line with Stowe's *Uncle Tom's Cabin* (1852), a novel credited with turning popular opinion in America against slavery despite its controversial portrayals of African Americans, *Hurrish* acted to expose injustices at the same time that it reinforced stereotypes of servility and impotence.[40]

In portraying, in *Hurrish*, a struggling and largely ingenuous Irish peasantry with viable reasons for remaining distrustful of British law, Lawless envisioned her themes and characterizations in a manner more apt to influence a British readership than an Irish one, and responses to the novel suggest that she not only reached this target, but swayed opinion in a way she almost certainly did not intend. Among those who were taken in by the message that *Hurrish* conveyed, and understood it as relevant to contemporary politics, was the Prime Minister William Gladstone. A passionate admirer of the novel, Gladstone in fact used it as part of his justification for advocating Home Rule, believing that it acted to explain and justify, more forcibly and convincingly than any other text he had read, Irish distrust of British authority.[41] As Gladstone's advocacy indicates, the question of the legitimacy of British law in Ireland is central to *Hurrish*, and this tendency to interrogate the validity of Britain's governance of her homeland would permeate all of Lawless's Irish novels, to greater and lesser degrees.

A glance towards Lawless's personal affiliations illuminates this narrative preoccupation. Of these, two of the most important were the historian W. E. H. Lecky and Plunkett. The intimacy of her acquaintance with Lecky is evidenced by the fact that they were not only regular correspondents, but

39 Gregory, *Lady Gregory's Journals: Volume Two*, 416. See also W. B. Yeats, *Uncollected Prose*, John P. Frayne, ed., (London: Macmillan, 1970), 369.

40 Clipping from *Dublin Evening Mail* (1886), Lawless Papers.

41 W. E. Gladstone, 'Notes and Queries on the Irish Demands', *Special Aspects of the Irish Question: A Series of Reflections in and since 1886. Collected from Various Sources and Reprinted* (London: J. Murray, 1892), 151.

that he had also proofread both *Ireland* and *Maelcho* prior to their respective publications and had reviewed her work enthusiastically.[42] R. F. Foster describes Lecky as '[i]n Irish terms, always nationally minded, never nationalist; a liberal Unionist', a political stance Lawless appears to have found complementary to her own.[43] She was an unabashed admirer of Lecky's scholarship, and was particularly impressed by the final volume of his important work, *History of England in the Eighteenth Century* (1878–1890), a text generally acknowledged to be more sensitive to Irish interests than antecedent histories. Writing enthusiastically to Lecky after her first reading of the book, Lawless hailed Lecky's ability to remain impartial on Irish issues, despite his challenging subject matter: 'wretched as the story is, and blackened as one supposed it to be'.[44] With Plunkett, she regularly debated Irish politics, and found such commonality with his viewpoints that she read, critiqued and even suggested the title for his *Ireland in the New Century* (1904), a volume he had originally intended to call *With the Tame Geese* in homage to her.[45] During their long association, Plunkett's political allegiances would undergo a dramatic and significant modification: a Unionist MP for South Dublin from 1899–1900, by 1911 he regarded himself as a Home Ruler.[46] Such affiliations suggest that Lawless's own version of unionism was, in common with Lecky's, of the liberal variety.

Over the course of her writing career, Lawless also developed friendships with women whose working lives and personal circumstances were markedly dissimilar to her own, and, through them, gained a different perspective on women's issues. These included, most notably, the historian, philanthropist and novelist Edith Sichel, whose many social projects

---

42 See letters from Emily Lawless to W. E. H. Lecky (24 August 1889) and (n.d.) Lecky Correspondence, Trinity College Dublin, MSS 1827–1836/2476 and 2482, and W. E. H. Lecky, 'Noticeable Books: *With Essex in Ireland*', *Nineteenth Century* 28/162 (August 1890), 236–251, in which Lecky praises both *Hurrish* and *With Essex*.

43 R. F. Foster, *Modern Ireland 1600–1972* (London: Penguin, 1988), 85.

44 Letter from Emily Lawless to W. E. H. Lecky (30 December 1890), Lecky Correspondence, Trinity College Dublin, MSS 1827–1836/639.

45 Letter from Horace Plunkett to Lawless (3 October 1902), Lawless Papers.

46 Foster, *Modern Ireland*, 426.

included the establishment of a vocational training program for girls from the impoverished Whitechapel district of London, and Margaret Oliphant, an industrious author who, after several of her male relatives failed to provide for their families, acted as the primary breadwinner for a sizable contingent of her extended relations. As a result of her new familiarity with the alternative experiences of women such as Sichel and Oliphant, Lawless eventually softened her stance against women's suffrage and came to support working women's right to vote, stating on the subject that, although she had 'no sympathy with the Suffragette methods' and had 'personally no wish for a vote', 'the helplessness of great bodies of women-workers even against *admitted* wrongs, simply because there is no one whose *interest* it is to speak for them' had convinced her that, for some women at least, suffrage was a necessity.[47]

Although this alteration to her stance on suffrage would not come until a point significantly after her novel *Grania* was written, narrative clues suggest that her ideas on the subject were already undergoing a transformation by the time of the book's composition. The only of Lawless's post-1890 novels to feature a female protagonist, *Grania* echoes and emphasizes ideas concerning women's agency and potential that she had previously hinted at in *Hurrish*. In the earlier novel, her landowning character, Pierce O'Brien, shares a number of recognizable similarities to her brother Valentine, both in his experiences and in his attitudes towards his tenantry.[48] A kindly but misguided landlord, O'Brien is described in the novel as having the type of brains which are not 'the sort best suited for the work that they had undertaken' – a narrative comment which enacts a subtle but recognizable criticism of her brother's similar land management policies and suggests that the author herself recognized how to manage the land and its people more effectively than do the fictional and actual landlords to which she refers.[49] In *Grania*, she conveys a more overt critique of the failure to

47   Sichel, 'Emily Lawless', 98.
48   For a detailed discussion of the parallels which are drawn in the novel between Pierce O'Brien and Lawless's brother, see Standlee, 'The "Personal Element" and Emily Lawless's *Hurrish*', 30–31.
49   Lawless, *Hurrish*, 1: 112.

recognize the deficiencies of men, and the capabilities of women, with regard to the governance of Irish land.

Set in a wholly Irish-speaking community, *Grania* represents Lawless's acknowledged attempt to democratize Irish society by avoiding 'that brogue' which, she claimed, was 'a tiresome necessity always' in Irish fiction.[50] Yet despite her efforts to elide outward markers of difference between her characters, her narrative acts as confirmation that disparities will endure and social hierarchies emerge even in the most isolated and microcosmic of societies. In Lawless's text, Grania is a young native of the Aran Island of Inishmaan who is dissatisfied with the terms of her existence. Not only by subtitling her novel 'The Story of an Island' but also through textual evidence, Lawless demonstrates that woman and island are analogous in both position and predicament: they share a similar dislocation and disenfranchisement. Throughout the narrative, Lawless's characterizations act to disturb traditional notions of gender and to interrogate the placements of women in society. This is most notably evidenced by the ways in which she creates male characters who are uniformly weak and incompetent in comparison to their female counterparts: Grania's father, unable to overcome his heartbreak after his wife's death, is incapable of caring for his daughters; the indolent Shan Daly allows his wife and children to starve while he spends his days drinking at the ruined ancestral home ('the villa') long ago left empty by Inishmaan's landlord, Lynch Bodkin; and Bodkin himself is an absentee landowner whose financial imprudence suggests wider and ubiquitous patterns of patriarchal neglect. Yet, while Lawless demonstrates that Grania is consistently able to fill the voids of responsibility left by these men, and is also physically stronger than the majority of men on the island, it is in fact Grania's fiancé Murdough Blake – a man who is averse to labour and, like many of his male counterparts, prone to drink to excess – who is repeatedly posited as the island's heir-apparent to the position abdicated by Bodkin.

The notion that Lawless intended Grania's fiancé as a representative of a new and emerging form of social aristocracy on the island is emphasized

50   Emily Lawless, *Grania*, I: 'Dedication'.

by the connections she creates between him and the villa, a building to which he holds the keys and is said to have a 'prescriptive right'.[51] That Murdough is also doomed to re-enact a similar form of undeserved and misused power to that wielded by the Big House's previous inhabitant is reinforced by the parallels Lawless draws between the characters and settings of her novel and those in the most famous Big House tale in the Irish literary canon, Maria Edgeworth's *Castle Rackrent* (1800). Like Sir Patrick Rackrent – the character who in Edgeworth's novel starts Castle Rackrent on its road to ruin – Bodkin is said to have been a profligate, indebted drunkard who continues to be admired by his former tenantry for the very reasons that have led to his downfall: namely, his ability to ignore his financial troubles and his inexhaustible appetite for alcohol. The heirloom cracked punch bowls which in both novels symbolize the damaged (and damaging) legacies of the Ascendancy provide a more specific link between Lawless's and Edgeworth's texts, while the crumbling structures of the buildings themselves indicate the diminishing fortunes and disintegrating authority of the class to which both Rackrent and Bodkin belong. Yet it is through her choice of 'Murdough' as the name of Bodkin's successor that Lawless draws the most readily recognizable correlation between the characterizations in *Grania* and those in *Castle Rackrent*, in which Sir Patrick's heir had been called 'Murtagh'.

Murdough's emergence as the island's new aristocracy may act to defy conventional notions of social class, but through him Lawless simultaneously suggests the persistence of discriminatory patriarchal and property-based hierarchies even in societies where economic resources are standardized. The most vivid portrayal of this idea comes when Grania – preparing to make her way to the neighbouring island of Inishmore to summon a priest for her sister, Honor, whose death is imminent – arrives at the villa to plead with Murdough to accompany her on the journey. At the entrance to the Big House – a space from which she, as a woman, has always been excluded – Grania stands on the lowest stair and Murdough comes to occupy the position on the landing above her. Looking upwards,

Grania experiences a sudden and debilitating realization of her position in relation to him. She has, Lawless writes,

> a feeling of being there a suppliant, a beggar – of being at a disadvantage, she could not tell how or why. Probably it was something in their mutual attitude which suggested it. She had never in her own person known the feeling of being a suppliant, for in her time there had never been any gentry on Inishmaan, and she and Honor stood quite on the summit of such social altitudes as she was acquainted with. All the same, she did know it instinctively, and it arose without any bidding now. This fine young man standing at rest upon the top of the steps – at his own hall door, as it were – the girl – herself – with her petticoat over her head, appealing from below. Where had she seen those two figures that they seemed so familiar?[52]

Here, Lawless indicates that Grania's familiarity with her position as suppliant, motivated by Murdough's stance above her and in front of the Big House, is a legacy of feudal fealty which inheres in her behaviour. Grania's subsequent act of climbing the stairs to stand equal with Murdough can be interpreted as one in which she crosses the metaphorical boundaries of patriarchal authority. By consistently questioning and undermining this authority through her narrative critique of Murdough, Lawless demonstrates at the novel's close that Grania's enduring faith in him is illusive. Even more importantly, by portraying Grania being pulled to her death by a mass of seaweed she believes is Murdough come to save her, she suggests that Grania's inability to wrest herself from his metaphorical grasp – and all that his grasp has come to represent – is what brings about her heroine's demise.

The closing images of *Grania* enact a subtle but recognizable commentary on the transience and endurance of power, and the prevailing and misplaced reliance on those men who hold it illicitly. Ideas surrounding the governance of Ireland surface with regularity in her Irish novels, but she deals with contemporary politics most explicitly in her historical novels, all of which are set against the backdrop of insurgence in Ireland. Each of her rebellion novels enacts a commentary on Irish politics in the respective eras in which Lawless was writing. The first of these, *With Essex in Ireland*,

52   Lawless, *Grania* 2: 226–227.

was published two years prior to *Grania* (in 1890), and is Lawless's fictional treatment of the Tyrone rebellion and the campaign led in 1599 by Robert Devereux, the Earl of Essex, to quell it. It was written and published during the period 1889–1890, at a point immediately prior to the downfall of Parnell and at a juncture when the Home Rule movement had reached a relative stasis under the new Conservative government. Three years earlier, Lawless had written a history of Ireland in which she had titled the chapter which dealt with Essex's time in Ireland 'The Essex Failure', and admits to having borrowed the term 'failure' from the majority of historians' assessments of the campaign. Her evaluations of both the man and his mission were, however, more favourable than those that preceded her, as the summation she offers in that chapter makes clear:

> Essex's very virtues and better qualities, in fact, were all against him in this fatal service. His natural chivalrousness, his keen perception of injustice, a certain elevation of mind which debarred him from taking the stereotyped English official view of the intricate Irish problem; an independence of vulgar motives which made him prone to see two sides of a question – even where his own interests required that he should see but one – all these were against him; all tended to make him seem vacillating and ineffective; all helped to bring about that failure which has made his six months of command in Ireland the opprobrium ever since of historians.[53]

Expanding on these sentiments to construct a revisionist fictional history of Essex's campaign when she came to write *With Essex*, Lawless chose to concentrate on his 'virtues and better qualities' rather than his failings.

Gladstone was again enthusiastic about this novel, and it is not difficult to conjecture the qualities in *With Essex* which would have appealed to him. In it, Lawless portrays Essex as a man who, much like Gladstone himself, endeavours to make his more lenient views of the Irish situation understood by his English contemporaries, alienates many in his own country by doing so, and labours under the watchful eye of a long-serving Queen. His willingness to compromise with the rebel Hugh O'Neill, the Earl of Tyrone, despite the latter's violent tactics, has obvious analogies to Gladstone's treatment of Parnell, notwithstanding the Irishman's

---

53 Lawless, *Ireland: The Story of the Nations*, 209.

controversial political alliances and manoeuvrings which, at a number of key points, found little favour with Gladstone's British compatriots. Although in ensuing decades the mythologizing of Parnell would tend to elide the more contentious episodes of his career, it must be remembered that by the apex of his political associations with Gladstone, Parnell had been accused publicly of, among other things, supporting Fenianism and sanctioning the Phoenix Park murders.

Like the politics of its day, Lawless's work abounds with misunderstandings and conflicts between its Irish and English factions. Travel westward to and through Ireland, whether the traveller comes as friend or foe, becomes the modality, in all of her Irish texts, by which English perceptions of the Irish are transformed. The characters whose viewpoints of Ireland she endorses always mimic those she had come to advocate herself as an Irish woman in Britain: those who have extensive experience of life on both sides of the Irish Sea and whose sympathies are aroused by the sufferings of Ireland even as they reinforce the advantages of the country remaining an English protectorate. Essex adheres closely to this paradigm: in an early passage which asserts his affection for the country while also drawing on oft-repeated stereotypes of Ireland as a weak and feminized land, he arrives in Dublin viewing Ireland not as a traitorous territory to be conquered by force, but as a lover to be wooed back into the arms of 'her' protector.[54]

In contrast, Essex's secretary Henry 'Hal' Harvey, the novel's unreliable narrator, is blinded by a misguided self-confidence and arrogance, and Harvey's consistent misjudgements permit Lawless to interrogate and confront the views he expresses. The text challenges, for instance, Harvey's assertion that the Irish are 'as inferior to us by nature as they are by birth and breeding', using Essex as the means by which his views are exposed as flawed and dogmatic: '[it is little] we know of such matters or can so much as guess at the thoughts of others, especially of those we despise', Essex states, 'contempt being as it were a natural veil or blinder of the eyes, hindering us from guessing how they whom we scorn do in their turn regard us.'[55]

54   Emily Lawless, *With Essex in Ireland* (London: Smith, Elder, 1890), 9.
55   Lawless, *With Essex in Ireland*, 162–163.

Initially likening the Irish to 'savage beasts', Harvey concludes that 'there is but one way of dealing with this country, and that [is] to slay without ruth or remorse', although he blanches when a subsidiary character, Colonel Sethcock, boasts of his part in a previous campaign of slaughter and devastation in the country.[56] Captain Charles Warren is a liberal counterpart to both Harvey and Sethcock who recognizes the shared history of the two islands and suggests about the Irish that, 'if they are papists, marry, why so were our own fathers or grandfathers, so that seems scarce sufficient reason for treating them like beasts'.[57] In demonstrating a range of responses to the Irish situation which confronts her English characters, Lawless both conveys and interrogates stereotypes of Irish savagery which continued at the time of her writing to be deployed by commentators such as Sir Robert Peel, who as late as 1886 was suggesting that without British governance Ireland was doomed to become a 'savage wilderness'.[58]

Essex's journey is represented as both geographical and psychological, and his growing discontent and disorientation mirror images of the increasingly strange and inhospitable landscape through which he travels. Movement westward is demonstrated to lead to both hell and Connaught, the latter a space where Essex finds himself at 'the very gates of Hell, if no i' th' inside of Hell itself'.[59] When he is forbidden by the Queen to return to England, his angry response reiterates and reinforces his figurative location: 'Keep Essex in Ireland! Keep him in prison! Keep him in Hell!'[60] At the same time, the act of moving westward and the interaction with the Irish people it allows are transformative: whereas Harvey initially deems Essex's favourable opinions of the Irish 'fantastical', proximity forces him into grudging agreement with his leader.[61] Witnessing Irish foot soldiers ('kernes') demonstrating remarkable powers of perception, he

56 Lawless, *With Essex in Ireland*, 67 and 69.
57 Lawless, *With Essex in Ireland*, 69.
58 *Lloyd's Weekly Newspaper* (20 June 1886), 1.
59 Lawless, *With Essex in Ireland*, 191.
60 Lawless, *With Essex in Ireland*, 260.
61 Lawless, *With Essex in Ireland*, 164.

acknowledges that they 'are in truth humans like ourselves', and this realization humbles him.[62]

Essex defies his orders from Elizabeth and leads his army on a route that takes them away from Tyrone and his rebel troops, yet the implication remains that he is powerless to chart a metaphorical new course in Ireland. While he often displays strong pro-Irish sentiments – conveying, for example, the opinion that Ireland needs to be healed, rather than brought to heel – these are just as consistently challenged by his inability to identify the requisite cultural affinities which might reconcile the Irish and English.[63] The 'best way of dealing with this people has not been found', he asserts, although he is unable, himself, to think of any solution to the Irish problem which confronts him.[64] Essex, as Lawless constructs him, is a man increasingly aware of his own impotence but motivated in his 'failure' by an affection for and burgeoning understanding of Ireland and the Irish; who says about the country that he 'would gladly serve it, were it for any time or in any office, if I could thereby hope to bring it peace and prosperity at the last'.[65]

His inability to subdue the Irish rebellion leads him, however, to wonder if his longing for leniency is 'some womanish weakness or folly that I carry from my mother', and he thereafter resolves to be more ruthless.[66] The repercussions of his more aggressive stance are swift and brutal, as Sir Henry Harrington's troops are resoundingly defeated by the Irish, and Essex learns that the surviving soldiers from Harrington's division have fled in terror.[67] By presenting this as the most decisive defeat of Essex's campaign and the one which literally divides his army, Lawless demonstrates the deficiencies of a 'masculine' approach to the Irish situation and thereby privileges, to borrow her own terminology, 'womanish' compassion in dealings with the Irish.

62   Lawless, *With Essex in Ireland*, 164–165.
63   Lawless, *With Essex in Ireland*, 173.
64   Lawless, *With Essex in Ireland*, 174.
65   Lawless, *With Essex in Ireland*, 173.
66   Lawless, *With Essex in Ireland*, 180.
67   Lawless, *With Essex in Ireland*, 180.

When, too late, Essex concedes that any Englishman who attempts to rule Ireland is doomed – stating that there 'breathes not, I believe, upon earth at this moment that man whose virtue or prudence could carry him in safety through [Ireland's] intricacies' – his words effectively justify the truce he has agreed with Tyrone.[68] His most costly mistake is not, however, this armistice, which Lawless demonstrates to be negotiated chivalrously on both sides, but his belief that he can remain loyal to the Queen and win the affections of the Irish at the same time. By recognizing the complexities of the Irish problem, sympathizing with the appeals of the 'other' island and dividing his allegiances between Ireland and England, Essex has tried and failed to woo two mistresses. In his eventual recognition of the futility of the task which he has been set, he expresses the difficulties he has faced in terms which assert the impossibility of serving England and Ireland simultaneously. Anyone who undertakes such a project, he claims,

> must be pitiless as Nero, yet must no trace of blood be found on his hands. He must give ear to all petitioners, and promise to redress all wrongs, yet must he do nothing […] He must know every wound and bleeding sore with which this wretched country bleeds to death, yet must be content to staunch none of them, for that were costly, and money is of all things that which her Majesty least loves to see shed in Ireland.[69]

Famines, mass emigrations and violent disputes over land render Lawless's reference to the crown's reluctance to offer monetary aid to Ireland as relevant in its nineteenth-century context as in its sixteenth-century setting.

Lawless conspicuously avoids confronting the deaths of Essex and his ideals within the confines of her narrative. The reader, however, recognizes that the prognosis is not good. In Harvey's last glimpse of his master standing on the deck of a ship as he sails towards England, his eyes are drawn to 'the very whiteness of [Essex's] neck where it rose above his armour', and

---

68 Lawless, *With Essex in Ireland*, 235.
69 Lawless, *With Essex in Ireland*, 236.

to the man behind him who holds a sword aloft.[70] The reader is thereby offered a vision of a man who is both literally and metaphorically cast adrift between a country whose affections he has not been permitted to win but which he has no desire to master by force, and another whose people he can neither placate nor their opinions alter. More importantly, it is an image of Essex with the blade poised to fall, suggesting that he, like every other Englishman who attempted to situate himself in a position politically between England and Ireland – including, as time would prove, Gladstone himself – was doomed by a complex and brutal history to fail.

In *With Essex*, the conciliatory stance Lawless's main character is shown to take towards the Irish situation reflects the political context in which she was writing, a point at which the Union between Ireland and Britain was markedly more stable than it had been under the deposed Liberal government headed by Gladstone. Lawless's next novel of Irish rebellion, *Maelcho: A Sixteenth Century Narrative* (1894), written in a distinctly altered political climate, takes an altogether different standpoint on the Irish situation. *Maelcho* was composed in 1893–1894, a period when Gladstone had returned to the Prime Ministerial post and a second Home Rule Bill was being debated, voted on and (eventually) defeated in Parliament. Although on its surface a sympathetic portrayal of Ireland in the midst of rebellion, *Maelcho* foregrounds characters whose disparate racial and religious backgrounds emphasize the multiplicity of Irish identities, a narrative tactic which casts doubt upon the notion that a consensus of thought and opinion might be reached amongst the Irish, and by extension implicitly queries the viability of Irish self-government.

With *Maelcho*, Lawless's focus turned to the Desmond Rising and the period in Ireland twenty years prior to the events fictionalized in *With Essex*, and through this new subject matter a distinctly more pessimistic vision of the fate of Ireland would emerge. At the same time, she offers readers a view of the other side of the 'Irish Question' by choosing a succession of Irish characters as her focalizers. This shift in narrative focus from alien to native viewpoints almost certainly accounts for the fact that her fellow

---

70   Lawless, *With Essex in Ireland*, 292.

Irish author (and English resident), Katharine Tynan, a confirmed Home Ruler, praised *Maelcho* unequivocally, in one publication referring to it as a 'great and noble book'; in another calling it 'the finest historical romance we have yet had'.[71] Yeats, too, valued the novel highly and included it in an 1895 list of 'the best hundred books' in Irish literature.[72] The *Irish Daily Independent*, meanwhile, suggested that the book 'ought to make rebels' and wondered how 'the writer of this book can be anything but disaffected to the English rule in Ireland', the reviewer's evident dismay suggesting his/her familiarity with Lawless's familial and political affiliations. Such foreknowledge had been evidenced throughout her career in reviews of her work, which often referred to her status as 'the daughter of an Irish landlord' and sister of a 'militant Irish landlord', indicating that commentators consistently came to her work with preconceived expectations of what they were going to find.[73]

Other reviews, however, would indicate the wider interpretive scope the novel afforded. '[T]he narrative wrings the heart of the reader for the wrongs of Ireland,' a reviewer in London's *Daily News* would suggest, adding (apparently without irony or objection) that 'it brings home the difficulty the clear headed English find in understanding the dreamy Celt, with his passionate loyalty to a leader, his inefficient grasp of worldly things, his lack of "saving common sense"'.[74] Dublin's *Evening Telegraph*, meanwhile, would suggest that, although 'Lawless spares the Englishman no tint in the picture of his wrongs to Ireland', there continued to be something in her work 'from which the Irishman recoils'. '[H]owever base the adventurers that are painted for us,' the *Telegraph*'s reviewer asserted, the Irish themselves 'seem to be presented by Miss Lawless as mere dirt beneath the feet of "her grace's soldiers"'.[75] As with *Hurrish*, suggestions that her Irish

---

71 Clipping of Katharine Tynan Hinkson letter printed in the *New Age* (29 November 1894), n.p. and clipping from *Boston Literary World* (1 December 1894), n.p., both Lawless Papers.
72 Yeats, *Uncollected Prose*, 386.
73 Clipping from *Irish Daily Independent* (5 November 1894), n.p., Lawless Papers.
74 *Daily News* (London) (23 November 1894), 7.
75 Clipping from *Evening Telegraph* (Dublin) (8 December 1894), n.p., Lawless Papers.

characters were stereotypically simple and servile would surface; again, she would divide her readers.

Maelcho begins, as Lawless herself indicates in its dedication, as a picaresque adventure tale, but gradually mutates into a more serious study of Ireland and the various peoples who belong to it. Three characters, each simultaneously sympathetic and flawed, act in the novel as representatives of the different factions of the Irish population: Hugh Fitzwilliam Gaynard is the young heir to an Anglo-Irish landowning family, Maelcho an Irish peasant and Sir James Fitzmaurice an Irish aristocrat. As the novel opens, the fifteen-year-old Gaynard has just survived a raid on his uncle's castle by a rival Irish clan. Although this attack has resulted in the deaths of most of Gaynard's family and friends, Lawless complicates the parcelling out of blame by detailing the extent to which the murders are the products of a relentless vendetta culture within the Irish community which has been perpetuated by pride and bigotry on all sides. Gaynard is demonstrated to be a product of this culture, and his opinions of himself, and of others in relation to himself, are subtly but consistently mocked. Through Gaynard, Lawless chastises the Anglo-Irish, comparing his blind prejudices against the Connaught 'savages' – whom he presumes to be 'possibly cannibals; at all events pagans' – to his equally blinkered opinions of himself and his antecedents.[76] Gaynard is said to be 'upborne by the sense of his own importance [as] the representative of those far-away English Gaynards about whom he knew nothing, but as to whose importance he cherished the most fervent and intimate conviction.'[77]

Gaynard's subsequent travels through Ireland serve to reinforce rather than subvert his sense of ethnic identity, an outcome which affirms his own personal obduracy more than it does any notions of his racial superiority. He may believe that his time spent in captivity among a Celtic tribe has acted to '*un*-Celtif[y] him' and harden 'the original, anti-Celtic qualities which were his by nature', but Lawless's narrative demonstrates that Gaynard is

---

76   Emily Lawless, *Maelcho: A Sixteenth-Century Narrative*, 2 vols (London: Smith, Elder, 1894), 1: 13–14.
77   Lawless, *Maelcho*, 1: 36.

able to mutate his identity in varying degrees along the stratum of Anglo-Irishness as best suits his needs.[78] His anti-Irish bias is subordinated when he becomes Sir James Fitzmaurice's aide during the Desmond rebellion, and then resurfaces as he makes his way through the ranks of the British army after the rebellion fails. In portraying this easy shift of Gaynard's loyalties from one warring side to the other, Lawless effectively destabilizes any notion that her Anglo-Irish character possesses a native or originary racial identity.

As the action in the narrative switches to Kerry, the focus moves from Gaynard to Maelcho, and through him, to Fitzmaurice and the rebellion he is planning. In line with Celticist stereotypes, Maelcho is a mystic and a dreamer, is driven by passion rather than reason, and displays a canine-like loyalty to the Fitzmaurice family: his is a 'dog-fidelity, not man-fidelity – a fidelity which would have caused him to let himself be cut into pieces, not only without any adequate cause, but probably by preference for a cause that was not in the least adequate'.[79] Images of a child-like or dog-like loyalty recur in the narrative to trouble the disruption of class and race-based notions of superiority Lawless had previously achieved through her characterizations of Gaynard, and even as she uses Maelcho as a means of undermining other prevalent stereotypes – that of the violent, degenerate Celtic Caliban most prominent among them.

Yet it is the contrasts which are shown to exist between Gaynard, Maelcho and Fitzmaurice which become the most significant aspects of their characterizations, particularly as they exalt the latter, the character who is able to extract and assimilate his most exemplary traits from the best attributes of the variety of cultures to which he has been exposed. His love of homeland is, in fact, presented as more profound because of two inter-related factors: his deeply ingrained Irishness, and his keenly felt period of exile. Thus, where Gaynard's character is driven and defined almost exclusively by a specifically Anglo-Irish form of bigotry, and he is 'ready to thank God in his prayers that he was not born a Celt', and Maelcho is the

78 Lawless, *Maelcho*, 1: 248.
79 Lawless, *Maelcho*, 1: 251.

essentialized Celt, unable to moderate his actions or his passions by any recourse to reason, the traits that define Fitzmaurice are demonstrated to have been gleaned from a long line of native Irish surrogate mothers as well as from continental ancestors.[80] As a result, he has enough Celtic imagination to dream of an altered Ireland and enough 'old Norman grip and tenacity' to make that dream a possibility.[81] Ethnically positioned between Gaynard and Maelcho, Fitzmaurice shares the logic of the former and the passion of the latter.

The collapse of his rebellion, as Lawless chooses to render it, is attributable to a catalogue of errors and misunderstandings by, among and between the Irish rather than defeat by the English. These include, most notably, the Earl of Desmond's failure to join Fitzmaurice in the rising. Desmond's reasons for withholding his support are complex, and include infighting with his stepson the Earl of Ormond, the timidity that is a legacy of years of persecution and punishment at the hands of the English, and jealousy of Fitzmaurice, who is both his cousin and a rival landowner. Desmond's brother, Sir John of Pikes, is equally but differently detrimental to Fitzmaurice's plans. An uncontrollable malefactor said to be doing his part for the rebellion by riding 'perpetually to and fro and up and down the country, harassing its inhabitants in all directions', Sir John enacts the novel's most heinous deed when he and his men ambush and kill Sir Henry Davells and Arthur Carter, representatives of the Queen sent to negotiate with the rebels.[82] The consequences are shown to be devastating:

> the murder of the two Englishmen, and the circumstances under which that murder had been committed, had precipitated matters by a leap. After this all idea of compromise, all suggestions of pity upon either side, became not so much impossible as ridiculous. Henry Davells was a man of exceptional qualities, a man liked by both sides and both creeds.[83]

80   Lawless, *Maelcho*, 1: 248.
81   Lawless, *Maelcho*, 1: 250.
82   Lawless, *Maelcho*, 1: 224.
83   Lawless, *Maelcho*, 1: 257.

Correlations between the Davells murder in *Maelcho* and the Phoenix Park murders as they are presented in Lawless's volume of Irish history are readily recognizable. In the earlier text, the Phoenix Park murders are described by Lawless as having been perpetrated by a group of 'miscreants' led by James Carey, a man who, like Sir John of Pikes, was 'of somewhat higher social standing than the rest'.[84] One of the men murdered in the Park, Lord Frederick Cavendish, had been, in common with the fictional Davells, sent to Ireland 'upon a mission of conciliation', and is described as having been widely admired in both England and Ireland.[85] In drawing these parallels, Lawless's text can be seen to comment upon both her fictional actors and their modern counterparts.

Similar correlations are drawn between Fitzmaurice's downfall and death and Parnell's political demise. Significantly, Fitzmaurice's enthusiastic and, as Lawless represents them, impetuous efforts to lead Ireland towards autonomy are brought to a standstill by an indiscretion. While Desmond's act of horse-thieving outwardly bears scant resemblance to Parnell's adultery, it is apparent that Lawless was drawing at least some of her inspiration from more recent Irish political setbacks when she portrays internal Irish rivalries exacerbated by moral recklessness as the means by which 'the only Irishman whose name carried the slightest weight outside Ireland, the only man upon the rebel side with a head to plan, a hand to execute, had gone to his account'.[86] Through her portrayal of Fitzmaurice's senseless demise, she demonstrates that it, like Parnell's, is the result of ongoing feuds and power struggles which are endemic within Ireland, rather than the result of extrinsic forces. Fitzmaurice's death leaves his rising in disarray; the death of Parnell had a similarly detrimental effect on the Irish Parliamentary Party in the 1890s.[87]

---

84 Lawless, *Maelcho*, 1: 411–412.
85 Lawless, *Ireland: The Story of the Nations*, 411.
86 Lawless, *Maelcho*, 1: 300.
87 Patrick Maume has also drawn attention to the correspondences between Fitzmaurice and Parnell and notes that 'Edith Somerville advised her friend Alice Kinkead to read *Maelcho* on the ground that the novel gave a true picture of Irish society, implying that

Maelcho's and Gaynard's paths, meanwhile, converge and diverge several times over the remainder of the narrative, the experiences of each refracting and inverting those of the other. Both are able, for instance, to forget the atrocities they witness, yet where Gaynard simply chooses to banish these unpleasant thoughts – 'with his usual practical good sense' he resolves 'to think about them as little as possible' – Maelcho's forgetfulness is prompted neither by resolve or 'good sense', but rather by the lack of them.[88] His experiences leave him directionless and with only 'the ghost of his mind', the latter an affliction Lawless portrays as a blessing: 'Heaven – merciful in this if in nothing else – had interposed a screen between him and [his past], and his own worst misfortune had become his best and his only friend'.[89] Likewise, whereas both characters witness the deaths of holy men, Gaynard comes to regard the brutal torture and execution of two priests with an equanimity that borders on indifference, while Maelcho, even in his diminished state, is profoundly affected by the (natural) death of a pious and brave monk, Michael Galbraith.

In the novel, Lawless consistently represents death as the Irish peasant's only chance of freedom. As Maelcho looks on the scene of a massacre, he is said to feel about 'all these dead creatures' that '*[t]hey* were free; *they* were out of it; *they* had got into some country where nobody could do anything more against them; *they* had even triumphed over a fashion, the only fashion in which it was open to anyone to triumph in those days in Ireland'.[90] This passage leaves little doubt that, in *Maelcho*, Lawless offers a portrait of an Irish culture which is under threat of usurpation and annihilation, and is attempting to speak to both sides of the contemporary argument over Ireland's fate. Specifically, with phrases such as 'in those days' she reminds those on the pro-Home Rule side of Irish politics of the progress that has been made since the time of the novel's setting by alluding to increased opportunities for political 'triumph', yet also warns her

---

its portrayal of sixteenth-century Ireland retained direct contemporary relevance.'
Maume, 'Emily Lawless's *Maelcho* and the Crisis of Imperial Romance', 262.

88   Lawless, *Maelcho*, 2: 168–169.
89   Lawless, *Maelcho*, 2: 200–201.
90   Lawless, *Maelcho*, 2: 309–310.

unionist compatriots, by choosing rebellion as her narrative focus, of the dangers inherent in oppressive tactics. Furthermore, the cynicism that she expresses concerning the possibility of liberation for the Irish under British rule, and more notably her inclusion of passages which portray the death of Irish characters as a preferable and expressly triumphant alternative to a life of subjection and victimization, suggest that she was able to anticipate the rhetoric of later rebel rallying cries. Irish insurgents, most notably Patrick Pearse, would argue in the years leading to the Easter Rising of 1916 that death was both a release from suffering and a rebirth to freedom: that, in the words of Pearse, the Irish people themselves might become their country's 'own Messiah, the people labouring, scourged, crowned with thorns, agonising and dying, to rise again immortal and impassable'.[91] Through her narrative themes, Lawless implies that the journey from a Maelcho-like glorification of death to the exaltation of martyrdom and Pearse's view that the shedding of blood is a 'sanctifying thing' is neither a long nor an arduous one.[92]

By the final pages of the novel, Maelcho has become a symbolic representation of Ireland, his bedraggled appearance, condition of homelessness and starvation, and pitiable resignation to his fate all suggesting the state of his native land. As he is executed by a firing squad, Lawless draws attention to the tree to which he is bound: 'like the other trees around' it, the tree is 'doomed, and would probably be cut down in the morning, for a couple of notches had been chopped in the bark, a little above the spot against which the prisoner's head rested'.[93] The image of Maelcho lashed to the tree, both he and it marked for death, suggests that their fates are intertwined – that the unnatural destruction of the indigenous flora can be linked to the unnatural demise of Ireland's indigenous people. Yet while Lawless explicitly remarks upon the British soldiers' reluctance to kill the innocent man, she also demonstrates that they are anxious to be done

91   Quoted in A. C. Hepburn, *Ireland 1905–1925: Volume 2, Documents and Analysis* (Newtownards: Colourpoint, 1998), 134.

92   Peter Costello, *The Heart Grown Brutal: The Irish Revolution in Literature, from Parnell to the Death of Yeats, 1891–1939* (Dublin: Gill and Macmillan, 1977), 76.

93   Lawless, *Maelcho*, 2: 346.

with the task in order that they can join the feast they know is waiting for them at camp. Her graphic depiction of two bullets penetrating Maelcho's heart, and of the soldiers' subsequent return to a 'rejoicing' camp and food 'enough for everybody, and to spare' – everybody except, of course, for the Irish we know to be starving around them on all sides – leaves little room to doubt that Lawless laments the fate of Maelcho, and through him, that of 'Celtic' Ireland.[94] At the same time, she conveys that his demise is the result of a complex history of errors and misjudgements on both the Irish and English sides of the conflict.

The composition of *Maelcho* proved so bleak an exercise that shortly after its publication Lawless would write to Gladstone to assert that, if she were ever to attempt another work of historical fiction, she hoped to set it during a 'period that [would] not need quite so much undiluted lamp black!'[95] On the surface this seems a strange declaration, considering that her novel *A Colonel of the Empire* (1895) was then being prepared for publication and had, in fact, already marked her first foray into a more light-hearted form of Irish historical fiction. She had referred in a previous letter to Gladstone to the imminent publication of this follow-up to *Maelcho*, notably indicating at that time her publishers' reservations concerning it: 'I have a book (laid in 1579) which I have been a little hopeful about,' she wrote in May of 1894, 'but alas! my publishers are so discouraging about its lot + feel strongly inclined, though it has begun to get into proof, to give up publishing it altogether'.[96] Considering these sentiments alongside the book's subsequent reception, her failure to mention the work in her follow-up letter to Gladstone is unsurprising. A slight, humorous work which incorporates the Wild Geese, Fenianism and marital abduction into its plot, *A Colonel of the Empire* was issued only in America, where it earned little favour with either reviewers or the reading public. Its disappointing reception would substantially alter Lawless's subsequent literary output.

94   Lawless, *Maelcho*, 2: 351.
95   Letter from Lawless to Gladstone (22 October 1894), Gladstone Papers, British Library, vol. CCCCXXXIV, add. 44519/149.
96   Letter from Lawless to Gladstone (5 May 1894), Gladstone Papers, British Library, vol. CCCCXXXIII, add. 44518/202.

In the years that followed, she issued essay and short story collections such as *Traits and Confidences* (1898) and *A Garden Diary* (1901), wrote a biography of Maria Edgeworth (1904) and produced volumes of poetry including her enduringly popular *With the Wild Geese* (1902). She would not, however, publish another novel for more than ten years.[97]

By the time she came to write her final novel, *The Race of Castlebar* (1913), the subject of Irish rebellion, with which she had dealt so prominently in *With Essex in Ireland* and *Maelcho*, had lain dormant in her fiction for nearly twenty years. It appears to be no coincidence that, while the issue of Home Rule was absent from Parliament, so too was the theme of Irish historical rebellion missing from Lawless's novels, nor is it likely that it was a mere accident that, just as a new crisis in Anglo-Irish relations loomed and the Home Rule Bill actively returned to Parliament (in 1912), so too did Lawless's fiction return to the subject of insurgence in Ireland.

The Race of Castlebar was written over an extended period due to Lawless's failing health, eventually in collaboration with Shan Bullock, a fellow Irish author and exile to England. Despite the novel's collaborative element, the study of Lawless's narrative input is simplified by her own introductory notes, which detail the points at which she took exclusive control of the tale in its opening and closing segments.[98] The novel's action revolves around an episode from the 1798 Irish rebellion in which the Irish fought alongside French troops to defeat British forces at Castlebar, County Mayo. This military victory, which was achieved in so resounding a manner that the British Army's hasty retreat from Castlebar was instantly likened to a race, reflects both the altered fortunes of the Home Rule initiative and the instability of British rule in Ireland at the time Lawless was writing. Although the Home Rule Bill would not be carried until May of 1914, six months after the novel's publication and seven months after Lawless's death, the diminished power of the Lords had rendered Home Rule for Ireland a foregone conclusion months prior to the bill's passing, and it is certain

---

97 Her return to novel-writing came with *The Book of Gilly* (1906), a children's tale.
98 Emily Lawless and Shan F. Bullock, *The Race of Castlebar* (London: John Murray, 1913), vii–viii.

that the author realized, as she put the finishing touches to the novel, that a measure of self-government would indeed be granted to her homeland. Meanwhile, the rise of the Catholic middle class and organizations such as the Gaelic League, Sinn Féin and the Irish Republican Brotherhood signalled an emergent insular Irish nationalism and an increasing tendency towards religious and racial separatism. This sense of class and religious volatility and political instability is reflected in Lawless's narrative preoccupations, which include Orangeist activity, militant volunteerism and political and religious disenfranchisement.

The central character and narrator of the novel, John Bunbury, is a young English man who, in the midst of the threat of rebellion, travels to the west of Ireland to ensure the safety of his sister, who lives in Mayo with her Protestant Irish husband. Structured as a series of letters written by Bunbury to his brother, the epistolary form of the novel allows Lawless to again represent the views of an unreliable first person English narrator as he journeys through Ireland. Set at a point when the Imperial supremacy of established European monarchies was consistently being assailed, most notably by successful rebellions in France and America, the novel capably portrays the degree to which the threat of Irish rebellion results in a sense of paranoia and partisanship in Bunbury's English neighbours prior to his departure: 'The most curious effect of the excitement', Bunbury suggests, 'was [that] the ordinary all-consuming terror of footpads and highwaymen appeared for the moment to have entirely disappeared. People who a few months ago would hardly venture to cross Fleet Street alone, now affected the courage of Spartans, offering themselves heroically to serve in the ranks and to brave death as members of the City Volunteers.'[99] By drawing attention to the rise in volunteerism at the close of the eighteenth century, Lawless again highlights the correlations between historical and contemporary circumstances. Not only are these parallels exemplified by the existence of the Ulster Volunteer Force, recently formed (in January of 1913) at the time of Lawless's writing, but also by the conspicuously analogous motives for such militancy during the two periods. In 1912–1913

---

99   Lawless and Bullock, *The Race of Castlebar*, 32.

political tensions between Britain and Germany, in particular a marked acceleration in the arms race, mimicked the threat presented by the escalation in hostile relations between Britain and France in the late eighteenth century. During both periods, the British had become concerned about the dangers presented to their own shores should a foreign power gain access to Ireland's coastline and port cities. The persistent fluctuation in the fortunes of the Home Rule initiative during the early twentieth century would also recall a similar rise and fall in the fortunes of Irish self-government at the close of the 1790s, when the Prime Minister William Pitt the Younger, who had initially supported Irish Parliamentary reforms, retracted his advocacy to sanction the Act of Union, resulting in the dissolution of the Irish Parliament. The outcome in each period was increased militancy and protectionism on both sides of the political divide in Ireland. In the midst of a period in which history was, in effect, repeating itself, Lawless would use her narrative to highlight the similarities between her historical subject matter and the contemporary moment.

While his English compatriots display a tendency to demonize the Irish and French, exaggerating the threats posed by them, Bunbury remains both unconcerned by tales of Irish unrest and unconvinced by the anti-French and anti-Irish rhetoric of his companions. Lawless quickly demonstrates, however, that both those who hyperbolize and those who minimize the extent of the dangers are mistaken in their estimation of the Irish situation. Viewed from a geographical and psychological distance, the state of affairs in Ireland is consistently distorted. Bunbury's opinions are first challenged when, upon his arrival in Dublin, he is assailed by evidence of rampant sectarianism in Ireland, manifested most notably, and in Lawless's text repeatedly, by a proliferation of Orangeist activity. Descriptions of the boatman who rows Bunbury ashore – 'a huge, uncouth fellow in a pair of patched breeches and with a filthy orange cockade stuck like a mustard poultice upon his ragged shirt' – set the precedent of anti-Orangeism which continues to inhere throughout the novel.[100]

100   Lawless and Bullock, *The Race of Castlebar*, 34.

The consistent visibility of 'orange cockades' exposes the emergence of an insular Protestantism, and more specifically the rise in prominence of the Orange order, which at the time of the novel's setting was being encouraged in its development by members of the British government.[101] In 1796, Thomas Knox, the British military commander in Ulster, suggested that Britain would find it necessary to side with the Orangemen: 'We must to a certain degree uphold them', Knox wrote to his Parliamentary colleagues, 'for with all their licentiousness, on them we must rely for the preservation of our lives and properties should critical times occur'.[102] Encouragement of sectarian separatism would be deployed regularly by the British government in their Irish policies from Knox's time onwards, Lord Randolph Churchill providing what is perhaps the most famous example of the tactic when in 1866 he suggested 'that if [Gladstone] went for Home Rule, the Orange card would be the one to play'.[103]

More surprising perhaps than these manifest anti-Orangeist sentiments are the Catholic sympathies which surface alongside them, first evidenced in Lawless's portrayal of Bunbury's fellow traveller, Vansittart Nugent. Nugent, an Irish Catholic, is subjected to various forms of bigoted bullying on his route through Ireland, while Bunbury, forced to play his own 'Orange card' by declaring his Protestantism openly, travels undisturbed and unharmed through the country.[104] Protestant proselytism likewise (and even more unexpectedly, considering her own family history) arouses Lawless's narrative censure through her depiction of the Byrne family, into which Bunbury's sister, Kate, has married. Owen Byrne, Kate's Protestant husband, is a man whose family has gained its status and lands through an act of religious conversion, and in the novel Lawless displays a distinct sense of scepticism about the legitimacy of the Byrne family's accession

101   Lawless and Bullock, *The Race of Castlebar*, 52.
102   Quoted in Thomas Bartlett et al., *The 1798 Rebellion: An Illustrated History* (Boulder, Colorado: Roberts Rinehart, 1998), 44.
103   Letter from Lord Randolph Churchill to Lord Justice Fitzgibbon dated 16 February 1866. Quoted in Sean McMahon, *A Short History of Ireland* (Dublin: Mercier Press, 1996), 153.
104   Lawless and Bullock, *The Race of Castlebar*, 59.

to the Castle Byrne estate. The narrative bias is, in fact, repeatedly placed on the side of the ancient, Catholic 'O'Byrnes', who have been usurped by the Protestant strain of the family. For Kate Byrne, the Englishwoman transplanted to Ireland who sees the matter from a perspective that is at once foreign and familiar, the situation is clear: it is the disinherited Henri O'Byrne who is the 'legitimate owner' of the castle. 'He knows by right he ought to be master here,' she tells her brother, 'So does everyone.'[105] By allowing her most admirable characters to voice these types of sentiments, Lawless implicitly acknowledges the validity of Catholic claims to Irish land.

The scenes of Bunbury's imprisonment at the home of the Bishop of Killala, which follows on from his accidental participation in the race out of Castlebar, constitutes Bullock's contribution to the narrative, the purpose of which is threefold: to demonstrate that the Catholic locals had been peaceable before Protestant and French agitators interfered with them; to portray the process by which Bunbury learns that people of all nationalities and ethnicities are capable of good and evil behaviour; and to reiterate a sense of the increasing tensions between Catholics and Protestants. In Bullock's portrayals these latter concerns are more readily attributable to the Catholic population than had been the case in the earlier, Lawless-authored passages, an alteration in narrative sentiment which is particularly in evidence during episodes in which Bunbury and his fellow Protestants find themselves isolated and endangered when Catholic violence erupts over the granting of arms to the town's Protestant citizens.

In the final chapters of the novel, which belong again to Lawless, Bunbury's own impressions of the Irish situation are increasingly sidelined as he acts as witness to the actions of the novel's central female characters, who take active control of the fates of their male counterparts by rescuing Bunbury and transporting Henri O'Byrne to safety. More important, however, are the points slightly later in the narrative at which Bunbury's perspectives are wholly eclipsed by the words and opinions of O'Byrne, for whom he acts merely as observer and reporter. As an Irish Catholic exiled to England and disinherited of an estate that is 'rightfully' his, O'Byrne's

---

105   Lawless and Bullock, *The Race of Castlebar*, 113.

position is both reminiscent of, and contrapuntal to, Lawless's own. It is his extended closing monologue, which serves no narrative purpose other than to lend insight into the state of affairs in Ireland, with which the final pages of the narrative are saturated. In it, he expresses both his concerns for the future of his country and his disappointment in the failures of British rule in his homeland:

> If I could see a few hopeful signs for this country in [the] coming years, I should die a very much happier man. Inveterate foe of British rule as I am, I could accept even that if I could see any promise for the future under it. But I cannot! [...] On the contrary, every succeeding decade seems to me to foreshadow a state of affairs ever worse and worse; greater and greater folly, grosser and grosser mismanagement.[106]

This passage, specifically concerned with Ireland's future under British rule, transposes the discourse of 1913, in which the concerns were over Britain's future after Irish Home Rule. Simultaneously, it draws attention to Britain's wasted opportunity to govern Lawless's homeland with impunity. This sense of regret endures in subsequent references to Ireland's economic and geographical isolation, both of which have, O'Byrne asserts, acted as detriments to its progress. Suggesting that exile and emigration result in privileged viewpoints and altered perspectives, he asserts about those who would leave Ireland that:

> when they returned they would at least know the world as it really is; not as fools, visionaries, and priests have pictured it to them. For them and their sons it would be impossible ever again to sink down into the old ruts. Their eyes would be open. They would no longer be dumb driven cattle, but *men* – men with all a man's heritage; his liberty, his knowledge, his magnificent and illimitable chances.[107]

Through O'Byrne's commentary, Lawless advocates the exile's viewpoint: gazing back on a time before the exodus from Ireland reached its apex in the nineteenth century, she simultaneously looks forward to a point at

---

106   Lawless and Bullock, *The Race of Castlebar*, 339–340.
107   Lawless and Bullock, *The Race of Castlebar*, 341.

which those mass migrations, and the new knowledge gained through them, might aid and abet a new spirit of industry in Ireland.

O'Byrne's monologue can also be seen to raise questions concerning the viability and legitimacy of colonial rule. Although his ideas are conveyed in comments specifically aimed at the French Empire in the eighteenth century, his sentiments are equally applicable to the British Imperial enterprise of a century later. Acknowledging that there is an existing and widespread 'belief in the permanent supremacy' of Empire, O'Byrne uses history as a means to comment on the transience and volubility of power:

> Looking along the course of history, so far as I have been able to do so, I seem to see that other countries, other races, have had the same conviction, yet that after a time circumstances have forced them to relinquish it, and to fall back within their old limits. Apparently Destiny, Fate – whatever we may agree to call it – does not intend that any such supreme dominion should be the lot – at all events permanently – of any one race or nation rather than another.[108]

O'Byrne's comments act as much as a forewarning of the inevitable decline of the British Empire as they do a reflection on the fortunes of France, and it is with these words that the disenfranchised Catholic O'Byrne is sent 'on the road to Galway', the first leg of the journey into a permanent exile from the homeland which 'clutches, grips and draws [him], as a child is drawn to its mother'.[109]

It is both poignant and pertinent that the sentiments she attributes to the dying O'Byrne are the final thoughts Lawless would convey in her fiction, and that, in them, she concentrates on the feelings and opinions of an exile forced out of Ireland by political circumstances. Yet, if Henri O'Byrne expresses one set of Irish concerns about history and its legacies, Lawless attaches other ideas to his rival and antithesis, Owen Byrne, which linger as both counterpoint to and complement of O'Byrne's thoughts and feelings at the novel's close. Byrne's hard-won victory over the rebels and their French allies costs him his hubris and leads to a new and more

---

108 Lawless and Bullock, *The Race of Castlebar*, 343.
109 Lawless and Bullock, *The Race of Castlebar*, 344.

complete understanding of the precariousness of his position as an Anglo-
Irish Protestant within Irish society: 'To have to realize that to draw one's
sword does not necessarily mean being victorious, even against a poor rabble
of "foreigners" and "rebels", Lawless remarks about the altered Byrne, 'is an
instructive, if somewhat startling little piece of experience, worth perhaps,
in the long run, a good many cheap and easily-come-by victories'.[110] Both
O'Byrne, the dispossessed exile, and Byrne, the Anglo-Irish landowner
whose family's act of religious conversion remains contentious decades
after the fact, refract the author's own position in relation to her homeland.
O'Byrne's words anticipate the fall of an Empire. *The Race of Castlebar*
itself also indicates that historical trends may hold true in microcosm: that
the dominance of Byrne's Anglo-Irish race will be transitory and that the
tide of power and influence in Ireland may already be beginning to turn.
The relationship between history and modernity is never more emphatically
suggested than when, remarking on her family's perpetually assailed claims
to Castle Byrne, Owen's wife Kate emphasizes the degree to which the past
continues to haunt the Irish present: '[t]hey never forget; no one here ever
forgets anything', she asserts.[111] The fates of Byrne and O'Byrne – one the
legitimate heir to Irish land according to the tenets of British law, the other
in the eyes of the Irish people – may be intertwined with one another, but
the land, we come to understand, cannot belong simultaneously to both.

Writing a review of *The Inalienable Heritage* (1914) – Lawless's final,
posthumously issued volume of poetry – a commentator in the *Irish
Homestead*, the organ of Horace Plunkett's Irish Agricultural Organisation
Society whose editor was the poet and artist A. E. (George William Russell),
would write:

> I cannot separate Emily Lawless in any of her work from that Ireland to which she
> was so loyal a daughter. I had read only her prose when I first stood on the Clare
> coast and looked across to Galway, but what I had read vitalised the traditions that
> came lap-lapping to my feet on the ample western tide. There was a surge in what

---

110 Lawless and Bullock, *The Race of Castlebar*, 316–317.
111 Lawless and Bullock, *The Race of Castlebar*, 116–117.

she wrote about Ireland that recalls the big Atlantic wave; and when all is said and done, whatever the title [...], she wrote nothing that was not of Ireland.[112]

A view such as this, expressed in a publication that boasted one of Ireland's most prominent Revivalists at its helm, suggests that a space of time had allowed at least some of her Irish readers to forget the elements of Lawless's own inalienable heritage that had resulted in the censure of novels such as *Hurrish* and *With Essex*. If Ireland had gradually become more accepting of her, however, her relationship to it throughout her period of expatriation had remained as uncomfortable as it was affectionate. A sense of the uneasiness of Lawless's associations to, and her feelings of displacement from, her Irish homeland is reflected in the exiled or diasporic characters which recur in her novels – including Essex, Fitzmaurice and O'Byrne – who consistently struggle to make a space for themselves in Ireland, and just as consistently fail to find one. As her novels make clear, Emily Lawless was able to see both sides of the Irish question, and by the end of her life had recognized which side would prevail. She may have found abundant room in her fiction for Ireland. She could not, however, find abundant room in Ireland for those such as herself.

112 Clipping, 'The Inalienable Heritage', *Irish Homestead* (25 July 1914), n.p., Lawless Papers.

CHAPTER 2

'You Can't Have a Big World If You Only Just Know This Part': The Critique of Cultural Insularity in the Novels of L. T. Meade

> You are very exclusive in this fair land of Erin [...] You can't have a big
> world if you only just know this part.
> — L. T. MEADE, *The Stormy Petrel* (1909)[1]

Despite producing novels and stories in a variety of genres for adult readers and children of both sexes, in popular conception L. T. Meade has always been a chronicler of and for English schoolgirls. This notion of Meade's work, limiting though it may be, was not forged without adequate reason. In a career that spanned the nearly fifty-year period between the appearance of her first novel in 1866 and her death in 1914, Meade produced at least 270 full-length volumes of fiction, of which approximately a third were written for girls. She is consistently credited with having introduced the girls' school tale to the British reading public with her novel *A World of Girls* in 1886, and during her lifetime regularly appeared on lists of schoolgirls' favourite authors. She received, for instance, the greatest number of votes in a competition sponsored by the *Girls' Realm* magazine in 1899 to find their readers' most popular living novelist, and two years later was the only extant writer to be named among the top five authors in another,

---

1   L. T. Meade, *The Stormy Petrel* (London: Hurst and Blackett, 1909), 39–40.

more academic, survey of girls' reading preferences.[2] On the latter list, only Louisa May Alcott, Shakespeare, Dickens and Tennyson outranked Meade in popularity. So resolutely was she linked to the literary subgenre she pioneered that the London periodical the *Saturday Review of Politics, Literature, Science and Art* in 1906 deemed her 'The Queen of Girls' Book Makers'.[3] More than half a century later, *The Times* (London), by referring to 'the child as conceived by L. T. Meade and E. Nesbit', was still crediting her with being the co-inventor of an implicitly feminized form of Victorian English childhood.[4]

It is, as such, unsurprising that it is primarily as a writer for girls that Meade remains of interest to literary commentators. Since the 1970s, when feminist critics began to embark upon the project of reassessing neglected texts by women, her work has received an increasing amount of critical attention, much of it focused on her children's stories. Mary Cadogan and Patricia Craig were among the vanguard of academics to explore her texts when, in 1976, they discussed three of her novels in their analysis of feminist themes in girls' fiction of the nineteenth and twentieth centuries.[5] Two decades later Sally Mitchell devoted much of the opening chapter of her study of 'the creation of girlhood – and the values, attitudes, and understandings this creation encoded' to Meade's fiction, using her texts as an 'instructive [...] first step' in chronicling and comprehending the redefinition of female adolescence at the turn of the twentieth century.[6]

Yet the relationship between Meade's personal history and the type of fiction on which her literary reputation was founded remains little

---

2   'Results of Prize Competitions: The Six Most Popular Living Writers for Girls', *Girl's Realm* 1/4 (1899), 431 and Alice Zimmern, 'Girls' Book Lists', *Leisure Hour: An Illustrated Magazine for Home Reading* (February 1901), 336.

3   'The Queen of Girls'-Book Makers', *Saturday Review of Politics, Literature, Science and Art* 102/2668 (1906), 741–742.

4   George Cloyne, 'Thursday's Child', *The Times* (London) (19 November 1959), 15.

5   See Mary Cadogan and Patricia Craig, *You're a Brick, Angela: A New Look at Girls' Fiction from 1839 to 1975* (London: Victor Gollancz, 1976), 50–51.

6   Sally Mitchell, *The New Girl: Girls' Culture in England 1880–1915* (New York: Columbia University Press, 1995), 10.

interrogated.[7] It has rarely been remarked upon, for instance, that not only had Meade never attended an English school of the type she consistently portrayed in her fiction, she had never attended a school of any kind and was not English. She was born Elizabeth Thomasina Meade on 5 June 1844 in Ireland, at Bandon in County Cork, the eldest of seven children of a Church of Ireland minister, Richard Thomas Meade, rector of Killowen, and his wife Sarah (*née* Lane). As the daughter of a Protestant clergyman raised in the south of Ireland, she embodied a form of Anglo-Irishness as archetypal as was that of many of her more renowned literary compatriots, yet the distance she was perceived to have traveled from her Irish roots by the time of her greatest publishing success is evidenced by the fact that the Irish press and public appear to have viewed her work largely with an admixture of distrust and indifference. Despite her fame, neither she nor any of her numerous novels were ever mentioned in the *Irish Monthly*, Ireland's most important literary journal throughout the period of her publishing career, and the *Freeman's Journal*, normally comprehensive in its reviews of Irish fiction, referred to her only once during her lifetime. When it did, however, it was appreciative, asserting that her novel *The Fountain of Beauty* (1909) was a 'thrilling romance' and remarking positively on her portrayal of its half-Irish heroine.[8]

One of the most popular newspapers in her native county of Cork, the *Southern Star*, mentioned her work just twice: first in 1898, when it detailed the manner in which she was satirized at a council meeting in Bandon; secondly in 1905 when it noted that Meade's popularity in England had never translated itself to her native country:

> Standish O'Grady is our greatest romanticist and Father Sheehan is another notable writer of fiction – perhaps the most popular of all living novelists with the Irish

---

7   Two noteworthy recent studies of Meade's work in this context have been written by Tina O'Toole and Beth Rodgers. See O'Toole's *The Irish New Woman* (London: Palgrave Macmillan, 2013) and Rodgers' article 'Irishness, Professional Authorship and the "Wild Irish Girls" of L. T. Meade', *English Literature in Transition* 56/2 (2013), 146–166.

8   'The Fountain of Beauty. By L. T. Meade', *Freeman's Journal* (29 May 1909), 5.

people. I do not say the most popular of all novelists. Mrs L. T. Meade is, to judge by her amazing productiveness, in this happy position.[9]

On only one occasion did she receive a prominent recognition in Ireland for the literary success she had achieved, when in 1910 she was invited alongside Rosa Mulholland, Lady Gregory, Eva Gore Booth, Violet Martin, Edith Somerville and Katherine Cecil Thurston to a gathering at the Gresham Hotel organized by the Corinthian Club to honour Irish female authors of note.[10]

For ill or good, she was viewed by her Irish contemporaries as a chronicler of English life, and regarded as a writer who had been wholly subsumed by the culture of the city, London, in which she had come to reside in the thirty-second year of her life. Yet Meade produced a substantial body of Irish work and was seldom guilty of the practice, often ascribed to Irish writers of the period, of what Rosa Mulholland once referred to as 'hiding [her] shamrock in a field of common clover'.[11] In interviews and autobiographical essays she invariably referred to her Irishness, and, as her career progressed, began to feature Irish characters and settings in her fiction more regularly.[12] In 1891, the Irish newspaper the *Nation* went so far as to suggest that the disregard in Ireland of her work was regrettable:

> Mrs Meade has done excellent Irish work, which does not seem, however, to be well known in Ireland. One of her novels, 'The O'Donnells of Inchfawn,' met with warm

---

9   *Southern Star* (Cork) (15 January 1898), 2; 'In Fiction', *Southern Star* (Cork) (8 April 1905), 1. The popularity of Sheehan's novels is presumably due to what James H. Murphy refers to as his 'assertive Catholicism' and anti-English themes, which would have found favour with the predominantly Catholic reading public in Ireland. Meade's novels, meanwhile, occasionally featured depictions of stage Irish girlhood which would have met with distinct disapproval among the same group of readers. See Murphy, *Irish Novelists and the Victorian Age*, 162.

10 See the *Irish Independent* (18 April 1910), 4.

11 R. M. [Rosa Mulholland], 'Wanted An Irish Novelist', *Irish Monthly* 19/217 (1891), 369.

12 See, for instance, 'Mrs L. T. Meade at Home', *Sunday Magazine* (September 1894), 616; L. T. Meade, 'Red Letter Days', *Sunday Magazine* (June 1899), 406–410; and L T. Meade, 'Children Past and Present', *Parents' Review* 6/12 (1896), 881–887.

approval for the insight it displayed into Irish country life, and for the fashion after which the knowledge was presented.[13]

With hindsight, it appears incongruous that Meade's work should have been championed, however briefly, by the *Nation*, a publication known for its radically anti-British politics, at the same time that the only Irish newspaper to make consistent and overwhelmingly positive reference to her writing was the *Irish Independent*, a paper whose anti-Parnellite stance was increasingly viewed as pro-British by its predominantly nationalist readership during the rise of Sinn Féin and Irish Irelandism in the first and second decades of the twentieth century. The backing of such disparate publications is revealing, however, in that it is symptomatic of the degree to which the politics of her work remained largely inscrutable to Irish commentators and readers.

The themes of many of Meade's Irish works are readily traceable to the widely variant homes with which she was familiar – the rural south of Ireland in which she was raised and the crowded English cities (London and Oxford) in which she came to reside as an adult – and the disparate values and viewpoints she was exposed to in, and able to assimilate through, her experience of these locations. The details she provided in published essays and interviews about her early life in Ireland lends context to her decision not only to actively pursue a writing career, but also to leave her homeland to do so. When she was twelve years of age, her family relocated from Bandon to 'a rather desolate part' of County Cork after her father took over the Templetrine parish at Nohoval, near Kinsale.[14] It was in this isolated district that Meade was to live the next twenty years of her life.[15] Although afterwards she referred to her parents as 'kind and conscientious', she also indicated that her upbringing had been strict and largely devoid of small pleasures.[16] She was educated by a series of governesses, at least one of whom inflicted regular beatings on her, and her favourite pastime,

13   'Through Irish London', the *Nation* (2 May 1891), 4.
14   L. T. Meade, 'How I Began', *Girl's Realm* 3 (November 1900), 57.
15   L. T. Meade, 'Children Past and Present', *Parents' Review* 6/12 (February 1896), 883.
16   Meade, 'Children Past and Present', 883.

reading, was almost wholly forbidden in the household.[17] Meade's own affection for all things literary was, she asserted, borne out of her childhood loneliness. Although her early attempts at composing stories proved so distasteful to her parents that she was forbidden any paper on which to write – undaunted, she continued to scribble them in the margins of old newspapers – by the time she was fifteen, she was declaring her intention to make writing her career, and subsequently dealing with the fallout of a pronouncement which was at first so unpalatable to her father that he refused to countenance it. 'I hope you will never say that sort of thing again', she recalled her father replying when the subject was first broached. 'There never yet has been a woman of our family who earned money'.[18]

The Reverend Meade appears to have been assuaged about, or overridden in, his objections to at least some of his daughter's literary pursuits, for her first novel, *Ashton-Morton, or Memories of My Life* (1866) was published when Meade was just twenty-two years of age and still living at home. It was issued by subscription by Thomas Cautley Newby, the London house which had first published the work of two of the three Brontë sisters, to whom Meade's Yorkshire stately home setting in the novel owes a discernible debt. Typical of Meade's earliest works, *Ashton-Morton* betrays little of its author's Irish roots in its narrative preoccupations, and, in deference to her father's wishes, the novel was published anonymously. Almost certainly for the same reason, Meade's first foray into publishing was not succeeded by a second novel for nearly a decade.

Meade later suggested that the morally and socially restrictive nature of her upbringing acted as the impetus for the feminism and suffragism which materialized later in her life, and asserted that she had become a nascent 'revolting daughter' while still living in her homeland:

> A little pocket money was well enough, but the old-fashioned gentleman [her father] still held to his firm ideas that the women of the family should be kept by the men, and should not have to work for themselves [...] The movement for the emancipation of women, it is true, was little more than in its infancy in those days, but even to

17   Meade, 'Children Past and Present', 883.
18   Meade, 'How I Began', 58.

the remote shores of the Atlantic-bound coast of Ireland, it penetrated by murmurs and whispers. Anyhow it disturbed the air, and there was one girl in an old rectory who was all too ready to take up what was in those days thought the spirit of revolt.[19]

Her drive towards economic independence intensified when, shortly after the death of her mother in 1874, she first visited London. That Meade viewed London as the de facto hub of the literary world is abundantly evident from her autobiographical writings, in which nearly all of her literary aspirations and activities are centered on it. It would only have validated such a view of the English capital that, in the midst of her earliest visit there, she received notice that her second novel, *Lettie's Last Home* (1875), had been accepted by the publishers John F. Shaw on condition that she expand it by 4,000 words. By her own admission, she did so by using much of her time in London to research the lurid and melodramatic exposés of the conditions in London's slums and workhouses that the journalist James Greenwood had published in the *Pall Mall Gazette* in the mid-1860s, employing elements of his reportage in her plot enhancements. An 1869 collection of Greenwood's work, *The Seven Curses of London*, prominently features among its litany of case histories several concerning baby farmers in the East End, one of whom is said by Greenwood to have 'got drunk, and left [a child under her care] exposed to the cold, so that it died'.[20] The plot of *Lettie's Last Home* revolves around this same type of baby farmer, a woman who starves the children with whom she is entrusted and uses the money intended to pay for their upkeep to fuel her drinking habit. As the novel opens, one of these children has recently died of neglect. When a second child falls gravely ill, the woman's young daughter, Lettie, ventures into the streets of London to find the baby's mother and warn her of his miserable condition. Subsequently discovered in this act and accused of betrayal, Lettie is severely beaten by her drunken mother. The baby survives; Lettie does not.

That London had enlarged Meade's scope of reference and exposed her to societal injustices from which she had to that point remained distanced

19   Meade, 'How I Began', 61.
20   James Greenwood, *The Seven Curses of London* (Boston: Fields, Osgood, 1869), 26.

is evident in the themes of *Lettie's Last Home*, and Meade makes no attempt to disguise the book's status as a political tract. Directly reminding her readers of the narrative's accuracy and propinquity, she posits those same readers as potential agents for change in the novel's closing pages: 'These things happen every day,' she writes, 'and still, though loud the momentary indignation, no efficient steps have been taken to crush this great existing evil'.[21] Like much of Meade's work which immediately followed it, *Lettie's Last Home* is readily identifiable as a social problem novel in which her narrative ire is directed at the inequities that existed in a mid-Victorian London with which she had only very recently become familiar. Her sudden advent into the realm of commentator on London social issues is recognizably derivative: her subjects and images perceptibly influenced by Greenwood's depictions of London's slums; her descriptive and discursive passages discernibly inflected by the same sort of reformist rhetoric he employed. Yet in her variations on Greenwood's themes can be glimpsed the true nature of Meade's literary astuteness: namely, her savvy ability to delineate popular preoccupations and mindsets. Realizing from her own family's attitudes that the reading of novels was often viewed as 'likely to lead to moral laxity', Meade was to take Greenwood's true-to-life tales and lend to his actors personalities, motivations and voices.[22] By so doing, she engaged not only the sympathies but the empathy of a readership that desired information and moral-edification as well as entertainment from their reading material. The byproduct was often socially corrective in intent, even more often broadly Christian in message – and as such acceptable to a wide variety of readers across the social spectrum.

Shortly after Meade's return from London, her father remarried a much younger woman – the sister of his daughter-in-law – and, believing that her 'father's house was no longer essentially a home' to her thereafter, she decided to pursue her literary career full-time in London.[23] Once there,

21   L. T. Meade, *Lettie's Last Home* (London: John F. Shaw, 1875), 110.

22   Mary Hammond, 'Readers and Readerships', in Joanne Shattock, ed., *The Cambridge Companion to English Literature 1830–1914* (Cambridge: Cambridge University Press, 2010), 32.

23   L. T. Meade, 'How I Began', 61.

she continued to write social problem novels which gained her increasing popularity: *Great St. Benedict's* (1876), her follow-up to *Lettie's Last Home*, concerns a London hospital (modeled on St. Bartholomew's) which serves patients unable to meet the costs of treatment at conventional medical facilities, and earned Meade her first substantial degree of publishing success. *Scamp and I* (1877) did much more: it imbued her with what was for decades an indelible popularity with the reading public. Having sold the copyright to Shaw for £30, Meade was unable to capitalize financially on the novel's success. She nonetheless reaped its benefits in other ways, as she was to recall two decades later:

> That was the book that really made my name [...] from that hour to the present day I may truly affirm that I have always had slightly more work than I knew how to get through. From that day till now I have never been obliged to ask for orders – orders have come to me.[24]

As the journalist Helen C. Black noted in 1896 – when, on her way to interview Meade, she purchased *Scamp and I* on a train platform – the novel was widely available even twenty years after its publication.[25] It remained in print for more than sixty years.

The central characters of *Scamp and I* are the London street urchin Flo and her mongrel dog Scamp – mutually figured as the lovable, innocent and unselfish victims of a London society which cannot recognize their suffering because it refuses to acknowledge their existence. Published in the year in which Queen Victoria, backed by the newly elected and avowedly Imperialist Prime Minister Benjamin Disraeli, solidified her colonial authority by proclaiming herself Empress of India, Meade's novel reveals its temporal position at the height of Imperialism through its narrative preoccupation with both Queen and country. Victoria herself is depicted twice in the novel, in the first instance when Flo glimpses her in the grounds of Buckingham Palace and realizes her own lowly status in comparison to the

---

24 Meade, 'How I Began', 64.
25 Helen C. Black, *Pen, Pencil, Baton and Mask: Biographical Sketches* (London: Spotiswoode, 1896), 225.

'great Queen of England', and again when the girl lays dying in a hospital at the novel's close.[26] In depicting Flo's ingenuous near-deification of the monarch in the latter sequence – 'I shall see the Queen,' she states, 'and I shall get well' – Meade indicates that the story is not only loyalist but royalist in the prevailing anti-republican sense of the term.[27] Yet it is notable that, in the novel, Flo is neither acknowledged nor saved by the Queen. By portraying a monarch who fails to notice the suffering of this particular underclass victim, Meade briefly touches upon themes of English and upper class indifference which would later resonate through her Irish-set works.

Meade's earliest works are concerned with English and urban social problems incongruous not only with her own personal history, but with the interests and preoccupations of the majority of her fellow Irish people. It must be noted, however, that to write about Ireland in the late 1870s, when her career began in earnest, was to write in the midst of increasing agrarian agitation and eventually the Land War (1879–1882). To construct Irish novels in the social reformist style she had so quickly adopted would thus necessarily have meant entering deep and disturbing political waters. Most importantly for Meade, it would also have entailed risking unpopularity on either or both sides of the Irish Question. Above all else, she needed her early novels to sell so that she could earn a living: 'if I could not add to my income,' she commented, 'I could not stay in London, and to come home a failure was impossible!'[28] In focusing the attention of her early novels on poor and downtrodden children in London, Meade chose an undeniably lucrative route which tapped into a prevailing, communal social conscience in England. Throughout the 1870s and early 1880s, she continued to construct narratives – including *Outcast Robin; Or, Your Brother and Mine* (1878), *A London Baby: The Story of King Roy* (1882) and *The Children's Pilgrimage* (1883) – which exploited the collective guilt of the most populous and profitable market available to her: that of middle and upper class Londoners.

26   L. T. Meade, *Scamp and I* (London: John F. Shaw, 1877), 29.
27   Meade, *Scamp and I*, 201.
28   Meade, 'How I Began', 62.

In 1879, Meade married Alfred Toulmin Smith, a barrister five years her junior, at Christ Church, Cork, in a ceremony performed by her elder brother, Gerald de Courcy Meade, then Rector of Killarney.[29] Toulmin Smith was the younger son of Joshua Toulmin Smith, a respected researcher and author of texts on topics ranging from phrenology to geology, and was also brother of the literary historian Lucy Toulmin Smith, who in 1894 became the first librarian of Manchester College, Oxford, and remained until her death in 1911 among Meade's closest personal friends. Four children were born to Meade and her husband during the 1880s: their son Alfred in 1880, and daughters Faith, Hope and Lucy Lilian Joy in 1882, 1883 and 1886 respectively. Three of the children survived to adulthood; Hope would live only fourteen hours.[30] With the advent of a family to Meade's life, her literary preoccupations discernibly altered. By the mid–1880s, she was turning to her own home rather than to the streets of London for the inspiration for her writing, and began during that same period to issue lighthearted children's stories such as *The Autocrat of the Nursery* (1884) and *Daddy's Boy* (1887), the latter based on the model of her own son. These types of tales would appear thereafter with increasing regularity.

It was not until 1890, however, that Meade began to devote the greatest portion of her time to writing children's books. In that year, she wrote six novels, of which four were intended for young readers. In the year that followed, all of her published novels were written for children. Simultaneous with this modification to Meade's literary focus came a change to the manner in which girls' education was being carried out in England. While in the first half of the century the emphasis in the formal schooling of females was on pursuits such as music, art and embroidery which were designed to transform girls into more marriageable women, in the latter half of the century girls' schools had adopted, almost wholesale, academic curricula to rival those of boys' educational establishments. By the 1870s 'the real proliferation of secondary schools for girls, mainly due to the efforts and example of the Girls' Public Day School Company',

---

29   See 'Births, Marriages and Deaths', *Freeman's Journal* (25 September 1879), 1.
30   See 'Births, Deaths, Marriages and Obituaries', *Standard* (London) (28 April 1882), 1.

an organization founded for the purpose of establishing schools designed
to train girls for the public examinations, had begun.[31] Already an advocate
of women's educational reform, Meade struck upon the idea of adapting
for a readership of girls the type of story popular with boy readers since
Thomas Hughes's *Tom Brown's Schooldays*, the first schoolboy novel, was
published in 1857. The result, *A World of Girls*, would alter the course of
Meade's publishing career. From that point forward, for better or worse,
she would be known primarily as a writer for schoolgirls.

Like her social problem novels before it, *A World of Girls* was the
product of Meade's uncanny knack for jumping early onto a bandwagon
and appearing for all intents and purposes to be both its initiating and its
motivating force, and this act of 'inventing' the schoolgirl novel was not to
mark the end of her literary experiments and innovations. Beginning in the
1880s, she would write across an ever-increasing number of literary genres,
which eventually included romance, thriller, detective fiction, schoolboy
fiction, children's literature, war stories and adventure stories in addition to
her social problem and schoolgirl novels, which she continued to generate
with regularity to the end of her life. In the early 1890s, she again used an
existing literary model – this time, Arthur Conan Doyle's stories about
Sherlock Holmes – to pioneer the subgenre of medical detective fiction.
By collaborating with a medical practitioner, Dr Edgar Beaumont (who
wrote under the pseudonym 'Clifford Halifax'), Meade ensured the scientific accuracy of her 'Stories from the Diary of a Doctor', which ran side
by side with Conan Doyle's tales in the *Strand Magazine* from 1893.[32] By
this point, she was employing two secretaries to keep pace with her copious output, which by 1894 was in excess of 5,000 words per day.[33] In 1898,
the number of her annual published works, which until then had averaged

31   Ellen Jordan, '"Making Good Wives and Mothers"? The Transformation of Middle-
     Class Girls' Education in Nineteenth-Century Britain', *History of Education Quarterly*
     1/4 (1991), 441.
32   See L. T. Meade and Clifford Halifax, 'Stories from the Diary of a Doctor', *Strand
     Magazine* 6 (1893) 91–102.
33   'Mrs L. T. Meade at Home', *Sunday Magazine* (September 1894), 616.

four full-length volumes per year, increased appreciably.[34] Between 1898 and 1912, Meade wrote at least 168 full-length volumes of work, or an average of twelve volumes per year. In her most productive year, 1904, at least seventeen titles were published under her name.

Meade's publishing history substantiates the notion that, not only was she a popular writer, she was also a populist one. She was unquestionably a meticulous delineator of trends and an ambitious self-promoter, yet to assert this fact is not to suggest that the social conscience revealed in her novels is insincere. Evidence in fact suggests otherwise. In her daily life, she was an indefatigable proponent of various political and social causes. She was active from the point of its foundation in the National Society for the Prevention of Cruelty to Children, acting as president of its Dulwich branch, and was groundbreaking in her advocacy of further education for girls, a task she undertook in the pages of *Atalanta*, the magazine she edited from 1887 to 1892.[35] Aimed at girls in their pre-teen and teenage years, *Atalanta* remains remarkable for the degree to which it promotes alternatives to the Victorian model of housebound domesticity. From the point at which Meade began to edit it, the magazine featured monthly columns on 'Employment for Girls', which included career options as diverse as 'Medicine', 'Chromo-Lithography' and 'The Civil Service'.[36] Her outspoken

34   At least one commentator has conjectured that the reasons for this sudden upswing in production were financial and may have been caused by her husband's lack of professional success and penchant for business and stock market speculation, an idea lent credence by extant evidence of Toulmin Smith's dubious business exploits and the recurring plot device of stock market-induced poverty in Meade's fiction. See Jean Barbara Garriock, 'Late Victorian and Edwardian Images of Women and their Education in the Popular Press with Particular Reference to the Work of L. T. Meade' (University of Liverpool: PhD Thesis, 1997), 148, and 'To Investors – Wanted', *Morning Post* (London) (19 July 1884), 8.

35   L. T. Meade, 'Appreciation of the late Rev. Benjamin Waugh', *The Times* (London) (14 March 1908), 7.

36   See Miss Edith Huntley, M. D., 'Employment for Girls: Medicine', *Atalanta* 1/11 (1888), 655; Clo Graves, 'Employment for Girls: Chromo-Lithography', *Atalanta*, 1/8 (1888), 474; and Millicent Garrett Fawcett, 'Employment for Girls: The Civil Service', *Atalanta* 1/3 (1887), 174–176.

work on the topic is also in evidence in copious other publications. In an 1895 article on girls' education Meade contributed to the *Strand*, for instance, she wrote:

> In these days when the 'Woman's Question' is discussed on all sides, and when even the most prejudiced of the opposite sex are forced to admit that women are their competitors in almost every walk of life, it is interesting to trace the fact to its primary source. In this last decade of the century, women are being thoroughly educated in the broadest and fullest sense of the term. Their brains are being developed, their bodies stimulated to grow to their full dimensions – in consequence, weakness, timidity, nerves, mental cowardice, are gradually, but surely, creeping into the background, and the girls of the present day are able to hold their own with their brothers.[37]

She was also among those publicly recognized for upholding the 'Steadfast Blue Line' in support of women's suffrage in *Shafts* magazine, and was active in the Pioneer Club, the controversial organization founded by Emily Massingberd whose members were denounced by their detractors as 'of all the new women and shrieking sisters, the newest and the loudest; man-hating, but mannish in their dress; and woman's-righters, without a single right notion in their heads'.[38]

For all her activism on women's and children's issues, and despite the apparent ease with which she was to deal with political topics from the outset of her career, it was only gradually that her native country, its inhabitants and upheavals were to be introduced into Meade's fiction, and then only at a point when these diversions into Irish literary territory were likely to be indulged by a readership already well acquainted with her work. Her first novel to deal centrally with Irish themes, *The O'Donnell's of Inchfawn*, would not appear until more than two decades into her publishing career, and the delayed genesis of the 'Wild Irish Girl' in her schoolgirl novels is likewise indicative of this prevailing reluctance on Meade's part to deal with

---

37   L. T. Meade, 'Girls' Schools of To-day: I.-Cheltenham College', *Strand Magazine* 9 (1895), 457.
38   See Mavis Barkman Reimer, *Tales Out of School* (University of Calgary: PhD Thesis, 1993), 34 and Hulda Friedrichs, 'A Peep at the Pioneer Club', *Young Woman* 4 (1896), 302.

Irish subjects. The student set apart from her fellows due to her unruliness and outspokenness had been a feature of Meade's schoolgirl novels from the first, when the English Annie Forest in *A World of Girls* was shown speaking and behaving in a manner shocking to her more refined and inhibited schoolmates. By the early 1890s, Meade had begun to experiment with variations on this theme by introducing characters from other countries into her fictional schools – American, Spanish, Tasmanian and especially Irish girls among them. The advent of a foreign element to her English settings allowed more scope for her characters' rebellions – their national differences went far in explaining the reasons they exhibited, and were to a degree permitted to enact, behaviours outside of English norms – and her 'Wild Irish Girl' in particular became a recurring motif from the point at which she was first introduced in *Bashful Fifteen* in 1892. Not only in her school stories, but in her other girls' tales as well, the introduction of an Irish girl to an English locale – and the clash of cultures, rules, attitudes and behaviours which results – often acts as a catalyst for the action of Meade's novels.

The device of a first-time visitor to Ireland who learns from direct experience how to understand and value its people had been employed in Irish fiction since Lady Morgan introduced readers to the concept in her novel *The Wild Irish Girl* (1806). In Morgan's text, the term 'wild' is used ironically. Her title character is an artistically gifted, refined Irish princess who acts to dispel her English visitor's preconceived prejudices that the Irish are a barbarous, primitive people. By uniting her Irish and English characters in a mutually beneficial marriage at the end of *The Wild Irish Girl*, Morgan also inaugurated the 'national tale' – a motif which thereafter recurred regularly in Irish fiction. Meade's variations on Morgan's themes invert the terms on which the Irish and English characters meet: in Meade's works, it is the wild Irish girl who travels to England to be transformed. Once there, she frequently exhibits an inability to understand prevailing codes of behaviour, often due to the fact that, like Meade herself, she arrives in England with little or no cultural knowledge beyond that which inheres in the remote region of her native country in which she has been raised. She is regularly, though not unfailingly, a rich girl whose home is a castle on or near the Irish south or west coast. Often willful and undisciplined, she is also invariably freer, more physically capable and more ingenuous than her English counterparts. As such, she chafes under the restrictions that her initiation to England places upon her and finds herself easily duped by her more unprincipled and malicious English fellow students. Yet she can also act as the means by which the artificiality of English social codes and hierarchies is exposed. These novels occasionally also offer glimpses of this cultural exchange in reverse, as English schoolgirls are introduced to Ireland and/or Irish ideas by their new fellow student only to find their own ideologies challenged by the foreign values and behaviours with which they are confronted. Throughout, the importance of cultural exchange and conciliation is emphasized: it is only through extended firsthand experience of each other that Meade's English and Irish schoolgirls can learn to negotiate with and comprehend one another. Where understanding is not achieved, cooperation and cultural assimilation are impossible.

The potential for her Irish characters to integrate into an English lifestyle is viewed pessimistically in Meade's earliest novels to feature 'wild' Irish schoolgirls. Bridget ('Biddy') O'Hara in *Bashful Fifteen* is the first of these girls to emerge in Meade's fiction. The daughter of the well-to-do landlord of Castle Mahun, Cork, Biddy has, during her Irish upbringing, become expert at secreting valuables away from the marauding Land League, firing a gun and landing a salmon – skills which are shown to be imperative in Ireland – and, once in England, she fails to understand the need for an education which she believes will be useless in her native country. Her existence at the school is compared to that of 'a wild bird who had just been caught and put into a cage'.[39] It is nonetheless apparent that a schooling in English values would prove both punishing and of benefit to her: 'the poor bird would be taught to develop his notes into something richer and rarer than Nature had made them, but the process would be painful'.[40] Because she is unwilling to learn the rules by which the society she has come to inhabit is governed, Biddy also leaves herself vulnerable to exploitation by Janet, one of the school's less scrupulous students.

39   L. T. Meade, *Bashful Fifteen* (London: Cassell, 1892), 55.
40   Meade, *Bashful Fifteen*, 55.

Within the course of the narrative, she repents for the mistakes she has made while in England, but due to the school's failure to understand and therefore to reach her, her education has had little impact on her by the time she returns, permanently, to her homeland. Once back on her native soil, she deftly manages the situations around her and is exemplary in her handling of a crisis, indicating that the type of knowledge that is valued in England is of little or no import in Ireland.

Kitty Malone, the newly arrived student at the Middleton day school in *Wild Kitty* (1897), is depicted as a curiosity to the other schoolgirls – a 'real aborigine' who hails from 'an old castle on the coast of Donegal'.[41] More headstrong than Biddy O'Hara before her, she falls into many of the same errors as her precursor when she comes under the influence of Elma, one of the school's morally lax students. Elma convinces Kitty to lend her money – an act expressly forbidden by the authorities at Middleton School in their attempts to avoid any class or wealth-based hierarchies among the students – and this act leads to a series of problematic situations for both girls. Though demonstrated throughout to be debilitated by her own lack of proper training and the poverty of her household, Elma is eventually expelled from the school for her contravention of its rules. Kitty is deemed at the end of the novel to be 'too wild for England', and willingly leaves the school forever to return to Ireland unchanged and unrepentant.[42] In both *Bashful Fifteen* and *Wild Kitty*, an upper class English standard of behaviour is challenged by the eccentricities and anomalies presented by Irish characters, whose conduct and attitudes are misinterpreted and mishandled by school authorities and therefore remain uncontrolled.

Two years after the publication of *Wild Kitty*, however, Meade was moved to create an altogether more capable and self-disciplined fictional Irish girl. In *Light o' the Morning: The Story of An Irish Girl* (1899), Nora O'Shanaghan lives in a crumbling castle in the southwest of Ireland with her Irish father, English mother and older brother. As the novel opens, the family estate is on the brink of collapse due to issues largely beyond its

---

41   L. T. Meade, *Wild Kitty* (London: Chambers, 1897), 9–10.
42   Meade, *Wild Kitty*, 364.

owner's control: a mortgage Squire O'Shanaghan has taken years before
has been sold out of financial necessity and without the Squire's knowledge to malicious English interests. Unable to meet the latest demands
for repayment and facing foreclosure, O'Shanaghan is forced to become
more stringent in the collection of his tenants' rents. This has a subsidiary
effect on the estate's tenantry, one of whom, confronted with eviction for
non-payment of his own debts, goes on to seriously wound Nora's father
in an act of agrarian outrage.

The mother and brother of the O'Shanaghan family represent its
English element. Their inherent selfishness, coldness and superficiality
are contrasted sharply with the kindliness of the Squire, the most resolutely Irish member of the family. Yet Nora's father is not without his own
Irish and class-based faults. He is constrained by notions of tradition and
pride, and therefore remains unable to countenance what are presented as
the valid complaints of his tenants – all of whom, including the man who
injures the Squire, are sympathetically drawn. Nora, hereditarily a mixture
of both English shrewdness and Irish sentiment, exists somewhere between
her brother's and parents' respective and more clearly defined national identities, and is as a result better able both to empathize with the peasantry
and to seek new solutions to the estate's problems.

During her sojourn at an English school, Nora's restraint is contrasted
favourably with the undisciplined actions of two subsidiary characters:
her English cousin Molly Hartrick, whose frustrations with the enforced
cultural propriety of her household are enacted in a series of rebellions
against her mother, and the American Stephanotie Miller, whose unbridled
appetite for sweets and freedom with money evidences a similar lack of
self-control. Combined with Meade's meticulous detailing of the sources
of current Irish afflictions – which she traces to the Famine, absenteeism
and English moneylenders – such inversions of her previous portrayals of
Irish girl characters identify this as a text more reformist in tone than its
predecessors. The notion of Britain's cultural supremacy is, in fact, repeatedly undermined, first through Molly's incompetence in the face of a series
of Irish challenges when she returns to Ireland with Nora, and most effectively at the point at which the English 'rescue' of Castle O'Shanaghan is
achieved. Though Nora's uncle is able to save the estate from financial ruin,

his 'improvements' amount to a culturally enfeebling Anglicization of the family home which alienates the Squire.[43] It is ultimately Nora who negotiates a compromise between the English and Irish factions of the family and strengthens the union between them. In advocating a girl of mixed parentage as the person most capable of envisioning the types of alliances which hold the potential to transform the Irish land, Meade indicates that the solution to Irish problems rests not with traditional resources, but rather with new modes of thinking and multicultural perspectives. Through Nora's influence, the Squire agrees to accept guidance from his wife's English family, and eventually admits that his limited Irish vision had, until that point, hindered his ability to properly manage his estate: 'I will own to it now, I'm a happy man,' Squire O'Shanaghan states in the novel's closing lines, 'there are more things in the world than we Irish people know of'.[44] The degree to which this new knowledge has involved cultural compromises with which Nora's father is unable to live is, however, embedded in Meade's depiction of his (albeit willing) ostracization from the newly modernized family home when he retreats to live in the estate's rustic barn.

From the turn of the century onwards, Meade's Irish characters evidence an increasing inclination to assimilate English ideas and ideologies, though this process always involves both struggles and concessions. This tendency is first exemplified in her 1902 novel, *The Rebel of the School*. In an attempt by her father to render her 'civilised', Kathleen O'Hara is transferred from her family's remote castle in the extreme southwest of Ireland to the town of Merrifield in England to attend the Great Shirley School.[45] Once in England, she finds both at the school and in the home in which she boards a more rigid and discriminatory social structure than she has experienced in her native country: fee-paying girls shun the 'foundation' students who are attending the school on scholarship and servants in Merrifield's homes are segregated and silenced. Though financially privileged herself, Kathleen

43   L. T. Meade, *Light o' the Morning: The Story of An Irish Girl* (London: Chambers, 1899), 191.
44   Meade, *Light o' the Morning*, 252.
45   L. T. Meade, *The Rebel of the School* (London: Chambers, 1902), 22.

recognizes the inequity of such societal formations and soon establishes a society to combat them. She and the foundation students who make up 'The Wild Irish Girls' hold secret late-night meetings to plot various non-violent schemes for disrupting the established order at the school. As such, the fictional society acts as a form of juvenile counterpart to *Inghinidhe na hÉireann*, which two years prior to the publication of Meade's novel had been founded by Maud Gonne. Like Gonne, who was English and upper class by birth, Kathleen's national and class-based identities are at variance with the majority of the members of the society for which she acts as both founder and president. Said by one of her followers to be 'graceful, and with such a power of eloquence [...] that I could die for [her]', Kathleen evokes the type of idolatry often bestowed on Gonne by her devotees, and likewise echoes the rhetoric of victimization Gonne favoured in her suggestion that 'the heritage of every Irish girl, handed down to her from a long line of ancestors, is to help the oppressed'.[46]

It was in the year that *The Rebel of the School* was published that Gonne took on the title role in Yeats's and Gregory's *Cathleen Ní Houlihan*, a play in which the main character, an old woman, acts as a personification of all Ireland and promotes blood sacrifice on her behalf. Eventually enticing a young man away from his home and into active rebellion, Cathleen is transformed at the close of the play into a 'young girl' with 'the walk of a queen'.[47] Meade's text can be seen to challenge the type of glorification of rebellion portrayed in the play by demonstrating that, while Kathleen O'Hara's motives are admirable, she is very mistaken in her methods. Her insistence on members' total isolation from the fee-paying students, for instance, has the detrimental effect of enforcing segregation rather than encouraging cooperation. While the society at first fosters a level of confidence among the foundation students, it eventually leads to suspicions and animosities on both sides and emphasizes inequalities rather than alleviates them.

---

46   Meade, *The Rebel of the School*, 138 and 131–132.
47   Quoted in Peter Costello, *The Heart Grown Brutal: The Irish Revolution in Literature, from Parnell to the Death of Yeats, 1891–1939* (Dublin: Gill and Macmillan, 1977), 27.

Instead of endorsing Kathleen's rebellious and separatist stance, the foundation student Ruth Craven, the novel's most admirable character and its consistent voice of reason, suggests instead that Kathleen use her intercultural knowledge to benefit the school by introducing 'what is good of Ireland into England'.[48] Ruth recognizes that Kathleen, by very different methods than her namesake *Cathleen Ní Houlihan*, might become an effective 'queen' of the school if only she can learn to lead by example and to work within the existing system rather than fighting against it.[49] The equivalences between the position of Meade's heroine within the school and Gonne's in relation to Ireland render it relevant to interpret Kathleen's admonishment by the school's headmistress as Meade's reproach to a wider contingent of Irish and upper-class rebel leaders:

> The girls who have joined your society and are putting themselves under your influence are the sort of girls who in a school like this get most injured by such proceedings. They have never been accustomed to self-restraint; they have not been guided to control themselves [...] They look up to you as above them by birth; your very way, your words, can influence them. Wrong from your lips will appear right, and right will appear wrong.[50]

That the novel also enacts a critique of the treatment of Irish rebels and secret societies more generally is similarly conveyed through Meade's discussion of actions taken by the school against the 'Wild Irish Girls': she notes that the only effect of the authorities' attempts to sanction the society is to publicize and arouse sympathy for it, making 'more and more of the girls want to join'.[51] That the governors of the school are not only blind to the inflammatory consequences of their own actions but are also both unwilling to countenance, and incapable of establishing, a useful dialogue with Kathleen and her followers which might lead to comprehension of their grievances is evident in their exaggerated response to the threat the schoolgirls represent. The society is described by the governors as an

---

48   Meade, *The Rebel of the School*, 130.
49   Meade, *The Rebel of the School*, 217.
50   Meade, *The Rebel of the School*, 237.
51   Meade, *The Rebel of the School*, 262.

'insurrection in our midst – a sort of civil war in our camp' and its members referred to as girls 'who preach rebellion each to the other, who dare
publicly to break the laws'.[52]

Meanwhile, by showing her fictional headmistress arguing that 'there
would be a sense of martyrdom' if Ruth were expelled by the board for her
refusal to reveal the secrets of the society, Meade's text accurately reflects
and anticipates responses to the treatment of Gonne and a long line of
Irish rebels and victims who both preceded and followed her, including
the Dublin martyrs, Fitzgerald and Tone, the Easter Rising's leaders and
the Hunger Strikers of the Troubles.[53] It is, however, Kathleen who must
ultimately step forward to curtail Ruth's expulsion by the school's board,
who remain intent on 'crush[ing] this disgraceful rebellion' despite the
headmistress's protestations.[54] Witnessing Ruth's predicament, Kathleen
realizes the errors she has made in promoting secrecy and separatism, and
encourages her fellow 'Wild Irish Girls' to renounce the society before
the board of governors. In Meade's coda to the volume, she notes that, in
subsequent years, Kathleen learns an English form of self-control which
mediates her rebelliousness and allows her to recruit admirers on both sides
of the class divide to her mission of achieving social equality.[55]

In a handful of her later novels, Meade constructs plots around impoverished Irish heroines rather than those from the landowning class. Patricia
Redgold in *A Wild Irish Girl* (1910), for example, hails from Carrigraun in
the southwest of Ireland, and is the orphaned daughter of a soldier killed in
the Boer War.[56] Raised by her grandfather, Patricia is a 'wild young savage'
whose father's dying wish is that she be sent to England to be tamed.[57] At
first enacting small rebellions against the staid London household she

52   Meade, *The Rebel of the School*, 363.
53   Meade, *The Rebel of the School*, 279. For a discussion of Gonne as a 'martyr', see, for
     instance, Karl Blind, 'An Irish Martyr', *National Observer* 7/166 (1892), 246–247.
54   Meade, *The Rebel of the School*, 280.
55   For a complementary interpretation of this novel as a 'new girl' text that enacts a
     commentary on imperialism, see Tina O'Toole, *The Irish New Woman*, 58–62.
56   See also *Peggy from Kerry* (1912) and *The Daughter of a Soldier* (1915).
57   L. T. Meade, *A Wild Irish Girl* (London: Chambers, 1910), 68.

comes to inhabit, Patricia grows increasingly unhappy when she is repeat-edly misunderstood by the English family with whom she lives. By con-sistently failing to recognize her need for freedom, the Lovel family drives Pat to a more serious form of revolt, enacted in clandestine and dangerous adventures on the streets of London. Symbolic of wider national issues, and metaphorically constructing the relationship between Ireland and England as mutually beneficial, these rebellions are all ill-fated, leading Pat to a fuller appreciation of the safety and comfort provided by her English benefactors, whose kindnesses extend to rescuing her beloved Irish home from penury. The Lovels, in their turn, learn from the Irish girl to be both more empathetic and less bound by notions of tradition and orthodoxy, with significant benefits.

Studied together, Meade's early texts evidence that, although her wild Irish schoolgirls come from similar geographical locations, their actions and attitudes can vary widely. In a particularly notable example of just how divergent these portrayals could be, two such characters at opposing ends of the behavioural spectrum emerged in a single year: *Peggy from Kerry* (1912) is almost certainly the worst behaved and least sympathetic of all Meade's Irish schoolgirl protagonists; *Kitty O'Donovan* (1912) is among her most admirable. It is also of note that, despite the fact that Meade's plots which feature Irish schoolgirl characters often allude to the factional nature of wider society through small-scale renditions of large-scale problems, her works to this point avoid any explicit reference to the religious affiliations of her various Irish characters. This trend is, however, broken in the last of her Irish girls' tales, *The Daughter of a Soldier*, in which the main character is the niece of a Church of Ireland rector. Published posthumously in 1915, the book features a heroine, Maureen O'Brien, who bears marked simi-larities to Meade herself, and simultaneously acts as the repository for the author's most positive images of Irishness. Left an orphan at the age of six after her soldier father is killed in battle, Maureen is sent to live with her uncle, the Reverend Patrick O'Brien, in County Cork. Like Meade's own childhood home of 'Templetrine', Maureen's new residence, 'Templemore', is located in an isolated position near the sea: 'five miles away from the charming, little town of Kingsala' – readily identifiable as Kinsale not only through similarities in name and location but also in detailed descriptions

of World's End.[58] Maureen also and notably has in common with her crea-
tor the gift of being 'a born storyteller' whose 'undoubted talent might be
turned to account for her benefit later on'.[59]

Maureen's is said to be 'a specially fine character' attributed to her dual
ancestry: 'for she belongs to mixed races, being French on her mother's side
and Irish on her father's'.[60] This blending of Irish Protestant with French
(and therefore traditionally Catholic) heritages, combined with overt
references to the Celtic and Catholic origins of her given name, indicate
that Maureen is not only an ethnic, but also a religious, hybrid. She increasingly acts as the embodiment of a spiritualism which transcends conventional sectarian divides, and is aligned repeatedly with her namesake, the
Virgin Mary. In the most notable instances in which such parallels are
drawn, Maureen becomes the means by which her step-cousins, Daisy and
Henrietta, achieve their respective spiritual salvations, and ultimately is
equated, through imagery and italicization, with the notion of deity: she
is the 'white angel' Daisy glimpses on her deathbed, at which point the
dying girl is described as passing 'into *His* arms, breathing out her great
and exceeding love for *Maureen O'Brien*' (emphasis Meade's).[61]

Created in the last year of Meade's life, Maureen is the most intensely
and affectionately Irish of all her girl characters. She consistently refers to
her homeland and its emotional grip on her, and is repeatedly depicted
singing songs – 'The Dark Rosaleen', 'The Wearing o' the Green', 'When
Malachy Wore His Collar of Gold', 'The Vale of Avoca', 'Rich and Rare Were
the Gems She Wore' and 'The Harp that Once Through Tara's Halls' are
all referenced – which mark her out as a national patriot. Although by the
novel's close she has relocated permanently to England, Maureen's emigration is demonstrated to be an act of self-sacrifice to which she has agreed
only reluctantly for the sake of her uncle's health. The novel is notable for
its portrayal of an Irish girl devoid of the type of stereotypical savagery and

58   L. T. Meade, *The Daughter of a Soldier* (London: Chambers, 1915), 1.
59   Meade, *The Daughter of a Soldier*, 25.
60   Meade, *The Daughter of a Soldier*, 253.
61   Meade, *The Daughter of a Soldier*, 260 and 296.

rebelliousness that often inflected Meade's earlier depictions, and for the intense degree of affection her heroine demonstrates for her homeland: Meade is careful to note at the end of the narrative that the only one of her Irish girls to be recognizably self-derived 'loved her country people beyond words'.[62] The 'country' and 'people' to which Meade refers in this passage are undoubtedly Ireland and the Irish rather than Britain and the British, yet in locating a space of comfort and companionship for the uncle in England, and in reinforcing the positive effects Maureen has on the English people she meets, Meade conspicuously shuns any sense of separatism in the novel to instead portray the relationship between her English and Irish characters as reciprocally advantageous.

Her novels written for an adult readership are similarly but more explicitly outspoken in their critique of factionalism and cultural insularity. The first of these in which the action is wholly located in Ireland, *The O'Donnells of Inchfawn*, appeared in 1887. Set in Donegal a decade earlier, the novel is steeped in the images and concerns of the pre-Land War era, its portrayals of two very different secret societies – one committed to agrarian agitation, the other formed to combat it – indicating two alternative approaches to Irish land reform. The 'Red Glen Men' who are headed by Geoffrey O'Donnell are set up to enforce changes to the agrarian system through a type of violence which is represented by Geoffrey himself as both gratuitous and innately Irish: 'there is no necessity for all this', he admits, 'but then the Irish must be melodramatic'.[63] The 'Good-will society', in contrast, is founded and run by Geoffrey's sister, Ellen, on the premise that nothing good can be gained from evil. Ellen's is an organization devoted to relieving the suffering of the poor and sponsoring emigration. The contrast between the two organizations evidences the differences in attitudes and actions not only within Irish society, but also within the same Irish family.

That the need for land reform exists remains unquestioned in the narrative. In Meade's evocation of Ireland, lands are consistently being mismanaged and tenants habitually mistreated. The Catholic O'Donnells

62   Meade, *The Daughter of a Soldier*, 328.
63   L. T. Meade, *The O'Donnells of Inchfawn* (London: Hatchard, 1887), 56.

may be 'good' landlords, but they have lost ownership of Inchfawn due to financial difficulties caused by what Meade represents as their inherent indulgence of the tenantry. The Brownlow family, who subsequently take over the estate, manage it with more pecuniary efficiency yet their miserliness and mistreatment of the peasantry fuel a revolt that threatens, yet again, to bring Inchfawn to the brink of ruin. Only Ellen, the product of a culturally mixed and inter-religious marriage, manages to escape the legacies of the past by inheriting both the generosity of her Catholic father and the business acumen of her Protestant and English-blooded mother. If in Ellen the best of both Irish Catholic and English Protestant commingle, however, the outcome of her attempts at improvements and restructuring nonetheless indicates Meade's doubts concerning the prospects for Ireland's future. Although the feudalistic system of land management in Ireland is represented as defective, it is also, in Meade's version of it, intractable. Due to local resistance to her ideas for reforming the Irish land, Ellen and her tenants are shown at the end of the narrative making plans for a new life in the Americas.

In *The Home of Silence* (1890) Meade directly addresses issues of racial prejudice among both the English and Irish. At the centre of the narrative's action is a failed national tale: Nigel Dering, the novel's central character, is the product of a mixed marriage between a violent and profligate Irish father who has died of alcoholism, and an English mother who in consequence of her marital experience 'hate[s] the Irish as a nation'.[64] Despite the flaws evident in both his parents' characters, and as with Ellen O'Donnell before him, Nigel's combined Irish and English heritage has yielded beneficial results because, Meade explains, 'he possessed at once his father's charm and his mother's common-sense'.[65] Knowing little of his father's personal or family history, Nigel travels to Cork to make the acquaintance of his Irish relatives, and promptly falls in love with his first cousin, Molly Dering, a devout Irish patriot.

64   L. T. Meade, *The Home of Silence* (London: Sisley's, 1890), 6.
65   Meade, *The Home of Silence*, 7.

Although in the novel Meade employs a hackneyed stereotype, the dissipated Irishman, as the impetus for her narrative tension, she also utilizes her text to reinforce the notion that Nigel's father was not only an anomaly among his Irish peers, but that the unhappiness of his marriage to a 'proud English wife' – 'a cold-blooded creature' – may in fact have been a prime motivating force in his subsequent acts of debauchery.[66] Mrs Dering's own prejudices are mirrored by the anti-English bigotry of her husband's brother, Meade thereby demonstrating that such attitudes run simultaneously and counter to one another. If the narrative is not entirely devoid of its own prejudices against both the Irish and English, Meade makes discernable attempts throughout to confront racial stereotypes, and takes aim in particular at prevailing notions of hereditary character defects. She challenges, for example, the existing belief in the inherent slovenliness of the Irish by describing the cleanliness of the Dering family's ancestral home with a regularity that borders on tedium. More importantly to the machinations of her plot, she also makes clear that the personal history of Nigel's father, which includes a heinous murder, is immaterial to the character of his son. By the close of the novel, the secret of the murder has been drowned in an Irish bog – 'The Home of Silence' of the title – along with the murder victim's brother, whose drive towards vengeance has by then already ruined both his health and his mind. Transcending the legacies of the past is shown to be a prerequisite for the family's survival, and becomes over the course of the narrative the means by which the unification of its Irish and English elements is accomplished through the marriage of Nigel and Molly, who are shown to achieve both an ideological and romantic national marriage in the novel's closing pages.

The Stormy Petrel (1909), the most complex and successful of Meade's Irish creations, is also among her most self-consciously political novels, constructed as it is against the backdrop of the Great Famine. Set in 1846, the novel opens in a space of relative contentment, yet proceeds to locate the sources of contemporary Irish privation in its Famine moment. 'Such was the state of things just before the terrible famine which reached its

66   Meade, *The Home of Silence*, 40.

culmination in 1847,' Meade explains in its opening chapter, 'Until then, the country was fairly prosperous'.[67] The novel is largely concerned with the tale of two siblings, Kathleen and Patrick O'Hara, who are products, yet again, of a mixed marriage between an English mother and an Anglo-Irish father. Left motherless at an early age, the brother and sister experience a more liberal upbringing than many of their Irish neighbors which manifests itself in anti-English sentiments and tendencies towards rebelliousness. Also central to the novel's action is a family story concerning an American ship wrecked decades before off the coast of the O'Hara's native village, Courtnamara, in Cork. The lone survivor of the accident is a man known only as 'The Stormy Petrel' who, having lost all his worldly possessions in the wreck, was nursed to health and given generous financial assistance by the O'Haras and their fellow villagers. The O'Hara family have learned nothing of him in the intervening years. The mystery of his identity looms large over the narrative, and is recalled in the form of the enigmatic foreigner, Fergus O'Flynn, who arrives in town as the novel opens.

As in *The Home of Silence* before it, *The Stormy Petrel* repeatedly reveals the prejudices which run concurrently and conversely to one another throughout the local Irish community. Meade lends more than a hint of Irish-Irelandism to the town's attitudes towards O'Flynn, whose accent is untraceable. Regarded with suspicion by the natives, O'Flynn is a rich man whose fortune might be used to revive the local economy, yet Kathleen in particular is unable to countenance the idea of financial assistance from any source which is not demonstrably Irish in origin. O'Flynn, in his turn, takes voluble exception to Kathleen's prejudices, pointing out the deficiencies inherent in her isolated Irish upbringing. In a passage which encapsulates Meade's narrative censure of cultural insularity and segregationist policies, evident throughout her writings but especially prominent in this novel, O'Flynn asserts that she and her fellow Irish people would benefit unequivocally from wider cultural awareness. People are 'very exclusive in this fair land of Erin', he tells her. 'You can't have a big world if you only just

---

67   Meade, *The Stormy Petrel*, 6.

know this part'.[68] Kathleen's father, meanwhile, believes that the priesthood is responsible for 'the ignorance and superstition and rebellion' which stagnates the local peasantry, while the neighboring landowner General Seeley asserts that it is in fact O'Hara's own and specifically Protestant prejudices, and his resultant self-enforced isolation from the peasantry, which have resulted in this paralysis.[69] While upper-class Catholic neighbours like Seeley himself know of the spreading potato blight and threat of rebellion in the area, O'Hara remains oblivious to these imminent dangers. 'Your eyes need opening, O'Hara,' Seeley tells him. 'If you were a Catholic, you'd have found out the truth by now'.[70] Throughout, international and interreligious alliances are advocated as an antidote to the factionalism which renders the Irish unable to recognize and resolve the issues which afflict them.

Kathleen's brother Patrick, who founds a secret society intent on violently opposing the English elements in Ireland, regards himself as the true patriot and revolutionary of the family. Yet Meade demonstrates that it is in fact Kathleen who enacts the more useful insurrections against local atrocities. As the famine escalates around them, Patrick and his 'Ribbon Men' are involved in the murder of a local land agent, Conway – a senseless act that does nothing to alleviate the country's suffering. Kathleen, meanwhile, travels to England to object in person to the policies of the absentee landlord, Lord Kirkdale, for whom Conway worked. Meade's indictment of absenteeism is evident in her denunciation of Kirkdale, whose extensive and mismanaged lands are shown to be largely responsible for the rapid spread of the blight. Kathleen conveys to Kirkdale that it is his own limited English existence which has exacerbated the problems in her homeland, and asserts that it is only through firsthand experience of Ireland, and the personal affection for and from the Irish which will result, that he will be able to manage his lands and tenants properly. 'You and your children should spend the next winter and spring and the beginning of summer until the harvest, at Ardnacarrick,' she argues. 'Ah, sir! then you would certainly

---

68   Meade, *The Stormy Petrel*, 39–40.
69   Meade, *The Stormy Petrel*, 50.
70   Meade, *The Stormy Petrel*, 52.

know what love means, what it is to have gained the hearts of the warmest, the bravest, the noblest people in the world'.[71]

Among the novel's most effective passages are those which detail the futile but strenuous attempts to thwart the spread of the blight, the pervasive deprivation and death which follows in its wake, and the attendant and unnecessary delays in receiving assistance – both physical and financial – from England. In the end, Meade gives sole credit for the cessation of the Famine to Irish-American benefactors, foremost among them O'Flynn and his father, who is revealed in the novel's closing pages to be the Stormy Petrel of O'Hara family legend. The most anti-English of all her novels, *The Stormy Petrel* repeatedly asserts that intractable English attitudes and behaviour during the Famine were the antithesis of those of 'willing and active and healthy Americans' whose multicultural perspectives meant that they 'knew what they were about'.[72]

Meade's final novel about Ireland to be written for an adult readership, *The Passion of Kathleen Duveen* (1913), rewrites the tale of true-life murder which acted as inspiration for both Gerald Griffin's novel *The Collegians* (1828) and Dion Boucicault's play *The Colleen Bawn, or The Brides of Garryowen* (1859). All three works are based on the story of a fifteen-year-old Limerick girl named Ellen Hanley who, in late June of 1819, secretly married John Scanlan, a member of the landed gentry. Scanlan was said to have quickly tired of his new bride and engaged one of his servants, Stephen Sullivan, to murder her on 14 July 1819. Two months later, her badly decayed body washed up on the banks of the Shannon near Moneypoint in County Clare. Gerald Griffin happened to be the court reporter at the Limerick Assizes when Scanlan was brought to trial there in 1820, and the Liberator himself, Daniel O'Connell, acted as attorney for the defence. O'Connell afterwards admitted that he did 'not feel the most slight regret at [Scanlan's] conviction', and referred to his client as 'a horrid villain'.[73] Scanlan

71   Meade, *The Stormy Petrel*, 223.
72   Meade, *The Stormy Petrel*, 388.
73   Daniel Griffin, *The life of Gerald Griffin, by his brother* (Dublin, 1872), 206. Quoted in Dominick Tracy, 'Squatting the Deserted Village: Idyllic Resistance in Griffin's

was hanged at Gallows Green in March of 1820, proclaiming his innocence
to the end. Later in that same year, Sullivan was also apprehended, tried,
found guilty and executed. He admitted immediately prior to his death
that he had killed Ellen Hanley on Scanlan's command.

Griffin's fictional rendition of this story centres around the parallel
tales of two college friends, Hardress Cregan and Kyrle Daly. As the novel
opens, Cregan is married in secret to the beautiful fifteen-year-old peasant girl Eily O'Connor. Like his real-life counterpart, he soon realizes his
error in binding himself to a girl of a lower social standing than his own –
Eily's brogue, in particular, becomes a marker of her difference and fuels
his increasing aversion to her – and, gradually turning his attentions to
Daly's love interest, Anne Chute, contrives to remove his new bride from
the local area and pretend the marriage never occurred. To achieve his
purposes he employs his faithful servant, the hunchbacked Danny Mann,
who, misconstruing Cregan's intentions, murders Eily and disposes of the
body in much the same manner as did the real-life Stephen Sullivan. In
Griffin's text, Cregan is realistically portrayed as a man conflicted by his
simultaneous attraction and revulsion to the peasant to whom he finds
himself unalterably allied. As a member of the landed gentry, he is also
endowed with a moral rectitude which the peasant Mann lacks. Therefore,
and despite the fact that he did not sanction it, Cregan ultimately confesses
to Eily's murder, and this act, along with his subsequent death in the midst
of his transportation for the crime, effectively restores Cregan to the realms
of the morally righteous. Griffin does not permit the long-suffering Danny
Mann, however, any such redemption.

Boucicault, whose play utilizes the same characters that populate
Griffin's tale, strays from real-life events more widely – contriving, in the
process, a happy ending for most of the actors in his drama. In *The Colleen
Bawn*, Danny Mann is killed in the midst of his attempts to drown Eily,
who is rescued from the water by an Irish peasant character, Myles Na

---

The Collegians', in Jacqueline Belanger, ed., *The Irish Novel in the Nineteenth Century:
Facts and Fictions* (Dublin: Four Courts Press, 2005), 94.

Coppaleen.[74] Boucicault adds the new dimension of financial motiva-
tion, rather than personal affection, to Cregan's pursuit of Anne Chute,
who for her part has been separated from her true love, Kyrle Daly, by an
act of misrecognition. In preparation for her marriage to Cregan, Anne
rescues the family estate from bankruptcy, so that by the time Eily reap-
pears in the play's final scene, all impediments have been removed and
both couples – Anne and Kyrle, Eily and Cregan – can be reunited. In
both Griffin's and Boucicault's renditions of the tale, the upper class is
exonerated of any criminal intent and the full burden of guilt placed on a
member of the peasantry.

Although Meade borrows some of the financial motivations which
appear in Boucicault's play and retains the tragic ending of Griffin's novel,
her narrative notably diverges from both precursors by restoring to her
peasant characters a measure of dignity and self-discipline. Like the real-
life Ellen Hanley – who was described in contemporary accounts as poor
but 'genteel' – Meade endows her peasant character Kathleen Duveen with
a demeanour and mode of speaking which are above reproach.[75] Rather
than becoming a passive murder victim, Kathleen is permitted to choose
her own fate, willingly sacrificing herself so that the social and financial
status of her aristocratic husband, Dominic O'Ferrel, might be saved. Ellen
Hanley's murderer, Stephen Sullivan, becomes in Meade's novel the similarly named Terence Sullivan, whose actions are repeatedly imbued with
an affection and intelligence denied to Danny Mann in both Griffin's and
Boucicault's versions of the tale. Sullivan's attachment to Kathleen, the
woman he recognizes as both his moral superior and true mistress, is shown
to be even more intense than that he has forged with his long-term master,
and this new fidelity leads him to question and rebuff the commands he is
subsequently given by O'Ferrel. Once having deduced his master's treach-
ery, he renounces his former servitude to him, and these added emotional

---

74   Flann O'Brien (Brian O'Nolan) used a variation of this name (generally 'Myles na
      gCopaleen', but also 'Myles na Gopaleen') as his pseudonym when he wrote columns
      for the *Irish Times*.
75   'Ireland, Limerick City Assizes, July 25: Horrible Murder', *The Times* (London)
      (4 August 1820), 3.

dimensions and informed responses render Sullivan judicious rather than merely ignorantly servile. Important, too, is the fact that he is never connected with Kathleen's death, and not only actively opposes the murderous plans that O'Ferrel has made, but also and ultimately becomes the agent by which his former master is apprehended by the law. Endowed with an agency denied to their forerunners, Meade's peasant characters are no longer the passive victims of, or minions to, the whims of their social superiors.

The contrasts Meade creates between her rivals for Dominic's affections, Kathleen and the Englishwoman Mary Lindsay, meanwhile, resonate in terms of the women's respective national identities. The *nouveau riche* Englishwoman has the monetary resources to realize his financial rescue; the Irish peasant holds the key to his moral salvation. It is only through a union with both of them that the Anglo-Irishman can be saved. Yet, having bound himself exclusively to one, he cannot avail himself of the advantages offered by the other. The allegorical implications of O'Ferrel's resultant dilemma are clear: he finds himself at a point where he must either destroy Kathleen (the peasantry) or relinquish his opportunity to retain (Anglo-Irish) ownership of the land. In failing to save Kathleen's life when he has the opportunity to do so, he becomes guilty not only of forsaking his legally and religiously binding union with her, but also of privileging financial security over moral responsibility. Equally importantly in terms of Meade's vision, O'Ferrel's deeds are shown to be largely the result of his debilitating inaction. More conflicted than equivalent characters in the works of Griffin and Boucicault, he displays an inertia unique among the characters in the novel – one which harks back to the behaviour of the English in *The Stormy Petrel*. By also and repeatedly detailing the O'Ferrel family's financial carelessness, and stealthily criticizing the tradition of absenteeism through repeated references to the supernatural curse that has befallen the estate due to their extended absences from it, Meade's text indicates that the faults of the O'Ferrel family are emblematic of wider Anglo-Irish Ascendancy failures. In the final pages of the novel it is shown to be because he recognizes that these types of failures will endure that Terence Sullivan, while remaining true to his memories of Kathleen Duveen, decides to leave Ireland with Mary, the highly capable woman not only with new money, but new outlooks.

In all of these novels which feature Irish protagonists, Meade's vision of the relationship between Ireland and England can be seen to be informed by her status as an Irish expatriate in England and therefore as a person who existed between cultural identities. Having herself assimilated the ideas of a 'foreign' culture, Meade repeatedly critiques isolationism and privileges multicultural alliances and perspectives. Throughout the course of her career, she nonetheless remained reticent to declare publicly her own political allegiances with regard to Ireland. An action she was to take in the early months of 1914, however, gives some clue as to where her sympathies were placed at the point at which Irish Home Rule appeared to be imminent, and casts doubt that the conciliatory policies advocated in her novels are accurate reflections of her own political stance at this juncture. In the spring of that year, women living in Britain were invited for the first time to sign the English equivalent of the 'Solemn League and Covenant for Ulster', an anti-Home Rule tract which had been drafted by Sir Edward Carson and his Unionist followers in 1912. Among the first female signatories of the 'British Covenant for Ulster' to be publicly acknowledged, in March of 1914, was 'Mrs L. T. Meade'.[76] Meade's act of signing the Covenant in the post-1913 political climate indicates her approval not only of Carson's radical Unionist policies, but also of the strategies he initiated for resistance to Home Rule, most prominent among them the paramilitary Ulster Volunteer Force.

Given the evidence provided by Meade's published work, however, this outcome is not altogether surprising. Although novels with Irish settings and/or characters constitute only a small percentage of her total output (less than 10 per cent), she nonetheless manages to convey through them a range of ideas which hint at her political unionism. Her Irish and English characters are often constructed as either the products of, or demonstrated to be transformed positively by, the union of the two countries: many have both Irish and English parentage, enter into inter-cultural marriages, or are rewarded for their ability to cooperate with those from the

76   See 'The British Covenant for Ulster: Women's Signatures', *The Times* (London) (10 March 1914), 8.

'other' British isle. Irish characters who promote separatist values receive her consistent narrative censure, while the national marriage, though not without its difficulties, is more often than not figured as a force for good. Despite her repeated narrative advocacy of the Irish, the underprivileged and the oppressed, it is in the promotion of such conciliatory values that the clue to the most viable reasons for Meade's lack of popularity among her Irish contemporaries also lies. To a majority of the members of a Catholic country on the brink of securing its freedom from a historically oppressive Protestant one, such messages would have been anathema.

CHAPTER 3

'No Country' for Old Maids: Escaping Ireland in the Novels of George Egerton and Katherine Cecil Thurston

> In no country in the world does the feminine mind shrink more sensitively
> from the stigma of old maid than in Ireland, where the woman-worker –
> the woman of broad interests – exists only as a rare type.
> — KATHERINE CECIL THURSTON, *The Fly on the Wheel* (1908)[1]

George Egerton's literary work is remembered today primarily as part of a brief but significant *fin de siècle* moment when the women's movement was nascent, promising, energetic, and therefore considered threatening. The controversial nature of her writing was evidenced most notably over the period of her career by the number and vehemence of attacks it instigated. *Punch*, for instance, satirized her first book of short stories, *Keynotes* (1893), in two articles which wittily but scathingly lampooned some of her literary affectations.[2] A more serious assault on her literary integrity came from Hugh E. M. Stutfield, who, in an article written for *Blackwood's Magazine* in 1895, asserted that Egerton's fiction was the 'offspring of hysteria and foreign "degenerate" influence' and 'a fairtype of English neurotic fiction, which some critics are trying to make us believe is very high-class literature'.[3]

---

1   Katherine Cecil Thurston, *The Fly on the Wheel* (London: Virago, 1987 [1908]), 224.
2   'She-Notes by Borgia Smudgiton', *Punch* (10 March 1894), 109 and *Punch* (17 March 1894), 130.
3   Hugh E. M. Stutfield, 'Tommyrotics', *Blackwood's Edinburgh Magazine* 157/956 (June 1895).

Although Stutfield was correct in relating Egerton's work to foreign influences – she readily admitted to being inspired by Henrik Ibsen, Friedrich Nietzsche, August Strindberg, Knut Hamsun and Ola Hansson – she was not, in fact, creating any type of English fiction. As her second cousin Terence De Vere White pointed out, the vernacular in which she wrote was unmistakably linked to her homeland: 'Anyone alive to the niceties of syntax,' he asserted, 'might have recognised that the author [of *Keynotes*] was Irish'.[4]

Although the censure of Egerton's work was particularly vehement, the themes of sexual and personal freedoms with which her fiction was occupied were not uncommon among women writers at and around the turn of the twentieth century, even (or, some might argue, especially) if those writers happened to be Irish: May Laffan had written forthrightly opinionated feminist novels decades prior to Egerton; the works of 'Iota' and Sarah Grand would query different, but equally contentious, aspects of the 'Woman Question' alongside her; all were Irish or had connections to Ireland. Yet it is her literary compatriot Katherine Cecil Thurston, who emerged onto the publishing scene in the first years of the twentieth century at almost the point that Egerton faded from it, with whom the most notable parallels to both her personal background and fictional themes can be drawn. In the cases of both writers, their literary fixations on women's issues and the subject of personal and professional autonomy can be traced to their Irish Catholic and nationalist upbringings, romantic alliances which were marked by scandal, and their geographical and psychological distancing of themselves from Ireland. In tracing the course of their personal histories, it is possible to identify the reasons that leaving Ireland is portrayed in their works with the same 'sense of escape' that Tony Murray has located in the fiction of much later Irish women writers who, he asserts, have often represented women's migration out of Ireland as 'the consequence of feeling

---

4   Terence De Vere White, *A Leaf from the Yellow Book: The Correspondence of George Egerton* (London: The Richards Press, 1958), 9.

trapped in a country where social and moral attitudes continue to regulate and restrict the lives of women'.[5]

From the outset of her career, Egerton's texts consistently confronted restrictive social and moral attitudes towards women. Even among the notorious New Woman and Decadent cohort with which she was aligned, her work was considered particularly degenerate and sexually licentious. The reasons for this are relatively straightforward to fathom. 'A Cross Line', the opening story of *Keynotes*, features among its episodes a number which proved shocking to many of her contemporaries. These include, most notably, one orgasmic scene in which Egerton's heroine envisions herself dancing before an audience of men, over whom she exerts a mesmerizing form of sexual control. In the passage, the woman lies on a hillside, eyes closed, and pictures herself performing on a stage 'with parted lips and panting, rounded breasts'. Gradually moving 'swifter and swifter', she experiences 'quivers' and 'shivers of feeling' as the dance gains pace, before her visions finally culminate (or, more aptly, climax) in a 'supreme note to finish her dream of motion'.[6] Although the remainder of the volume's stories deal less explicitly with sexual acts and more openly with sexual inequalities, the topics of divorce, abusive marriages and women who want to have children without the 'disgrace' of having sex with 'disgusting men' with which Egerton deals in the volume still had a tendency to shock and disturb readers accustomed to strict Victorian codes of conduct.[7] The degree to which her fiction was viewed as subversive and dangerous was evidenced not only in the indignation it aroused in the press, but also in a letter Egerton received from T. P. Gill, the editor of the *Weekly Sun*, before any of her work had been published. Believing Egerton to be a man upon first reading the manuscript of *Keynotes*, Gill strongly advised her to edit its more explicit content, arguing that it might prove corrupting to male readers: 'take the effect on a young fellow in his student period [...] of a

---

5   Tony Murray, *London Irish Fictions: Narrative, Diaspora and Identity* (Liverpool: Liverpool University Press, 2012), 6; 115.

6   George Egerton, 'A Cross Line', *Keynotes and Discords* (London: Virago, 1993 [1893/1894]), 20.

7   Egerton, 'The Spell of the White Elf', *Keynotes and Discords*, 80.

particularly warm description of rounded limbs and the rest,' Gill wrote, 'It puts him in a state that he either goes off and has a woman or it is bad for his health (and possibly worse for his morals) if he doesn't.'[8]

Darker in tone than its predecessor, her second volume of stories, *Discords* (1894), would continue Egerton's project of confronting prevailing moral and social codes which limited women's choices and therefore their lives. *Discords* featured candid depictions of extramarital affairs, free love and, while neither condemning her characters nor condoning their actions, also addressed the subjects of prostitution and infanticide. By titling one of her stories in the volume 'Virgin Soil', she indicated that she was taking at least some of her narrative cues from Ivan Turgenev's 1877 novel of the same name. Her aim in doing so may have been not only to offer a poignant pun on the familiar phrase – her protagonist is a young woman who enters into marriage without fully realizing the sexual role she will be required to fulfil and is irreparably sullied by the experience – but also to hint at the correlations between the class-based struggles that pre-occupied Turgenev and the gender-based ones on which her own work is focused. She refers in the story to the way in which young women are 'sold' into marriage 'for a home, for clothes, for food', and so that their mothers might divorce themselves from financial and personal responsibility by seeing their daughters 'comfortably settled'.[9] In Egerton's text, however, no woman is comfortable. Consisting primarily of the daughter's remonstrance of her mother for her complicity in her marital enslavement, the story overtly represents marriage as 'for many women a legal prostitution, a nightly degradation, a hateful yoke under which they age, mere bearers of children', and the degree to which these circumstances derive from a culture of secrecy and collusion which leads women to enact and enforce this type of victimization on other women is the story's pervasive message.[10]

Capitalizing on her early success, she followed *Keynotes* and *Discords* with two additional volumes of short stories, *Symphonies* (1897) and

8   Quoted in De Vere White, *A Leaf from the Yellow Book*, 24.
9   Egerton, 'Virgin Soil', *Keynotes and Discords*, 157 and 158.
10   Egerton, 'Virgin Soil', 155.

Fantasias (1898), and her sole novel, *The Wheel of God* (1898). The appeal of her work quickly faded, however, in large part due to a renewed moral stringency, both in the publishing industry and among the general public, in the wake of the conviction of Oscar Wilde on charges of gross indecency in 1895. Closely associated by both the press and the public with Wilde – with whom she shared a publisher (The Bodley Head), an illustrator (Aubrey Beardsley) and an affiliation with the *Yellow Book* magazine – Egerton would as a result of diminishing sales publish only two additional volumes of work after the turn of the century: a sequence of Ola Hansson-esque philosophical ruminations entitled *Rosa Amorosa* (1901) and a final volume of short stories, *Flies in Amber* (1905). Neither of these would prove popular and, after just a dozen years as an author, her publishing career ended.

It remains distinctly curious, however, that in drawing attention to Egerton's relation to Wilde, few if any press reports would refer to what was perhaps the most noteworthy link between them: the fact that both were Irish. This is almost certainly due to the fact that, throughout Egerton's literary career, her personal history remained a subject of public conjecture. An interviewer in the English periodical *Hearth and Home*, for example, in attempting to identify her ethnicity, was forced to speculate that she was 'of rather a Jewish type'.[11] Dismissing prevailing rumours that the author of *Keynotes* might be 'a young Irish barrister', a report in the *Glasgow Herald* meanwhile asserted that, although Egerton was both young and Irish, she was not in fact a barrister but a married woman named 'Mrs Courtmaine'.[12] Another article correctly if superficially identified her as 'Mrs Clairmonte', but noted that she had failed to turn up to a recent and prominent reception held by her publishers, and wondered why she continued to remain 'invisible' despite her ever-increasing fame.[13] Combined with the suggestion that she was a 'detester of the interviewer and all his works', the degree of speculation and misinformation about her identity evident even in reports by

11 'People, Places and Things', *Hearth and Home* 150 (1894), 649.
12 'Our London Correspondence', *Glasgow Herald* (17 January 1894), 7.
13 'People, Places and Things', *Hearth and Home* 154 (1894), 814.

journalists who had met her in person indicates that Egerton was willingly
and purposely shrouding the details of her personal life from the public.[14]

While there is no firm indication that Egerton actively sought
to disguise her Irish identity, there remain compelling reasons why
she may have wanted to distance herself from her Irish past.[15] One of
these is the fact that she was the eldest child of Captain John J. Dunne,
a man who – although he was descended from a long line of distinguished Dunnes, Perrys, Powers and Kellys who had made their homes
near Mountmellick in current County Laois – had managed to achieve a
notable degree of infamy during the period of his daughter's upbringing.
Dunne's relative financial privilege in his youth is evidenced by the fact
that he was educated at the prestigious Clongowes Wood College and,
after leaving school, gained a commission in the British Army. By the time
Egerton was born in Australia in 1859, however, he had already been cash-
iered from the military and was reduced to serving as a volunteer in the
Maori War.[16] He would later spend several months in Dublin's Marshalsea
Prison for debt, and by the end of the 1880s had been dismissed from the
prison service, for which he had worked as governor of both Nenagh and
Castlebar prisons, for misconduct.[17] Perennially unemployed and perpetually in debt throughout his life, Dunne was said to exist primarily 'on air
and other people'.[18]

The most notable scandal of Egerton's early life was, however, entirely
of her own making: her elopement in the autumn of 1887, at the age of
twenty-eight, with the Reverend Henry Peter Higginson Whyte-Melville.
Whyte-Melville was, at the time of the elopement, fifty-one years old and

---

14   'People, Places and Things', *Hearth and Home* 150 (1894), 649.
15   Privately she asserted her Irishness vehemently. See, for instance, letter from Egerton
      to her aunt, Ethel De Vere White (27 March 1926), in which she refers to herself as
      'intensely Irish'. Quoted in De Vere White, *A Leaf from the Yellow Book*, 14.
16   William J. Linn, 'George Egerton', in Robert Hogan, ed., *Dictionary of Irish Literature*
      (London: Aldwych Press, 1996), 404.
17   Letter from G. O. Trevelyan to John J. Dunne (2 June 1884), John Dunne/George
      Egerton Papers, National Library of Ireland, P9022, MS 10946.
18   Terence De Vere White, 'A Strange Lady', *Irish Times* (26 February 1983), 12.

married to his second wife, Charlotte Whyte-Melville, the woman for whom Egerton had been acting as a paid companion. Through her act of running away with this particular married man, Egerton (then known simply as 'Mary Dunne') became embroiled in what *The Times* (London) termed 'as choice a sensation as has agitated London and Dublin Church and Court circles in a good while'.[19] Whyte-Melville, who had been known prior to his second marriage as 'Henry Peter Higginson', had inherited not only his second wife's surname but also a large sum of her money when the pair married in 1866. His marriage to Charlotte Whyte-Melville was to generate its own form of retrospective notoriety in the wake of his elopement with Egerton – for, although Whyte-Melville had divorced his first wife in the United States prior to his second marriage, the British authorities had taken decades to recognize the legality of the American divorce decree and, when in the autumn of 1887 her husband absconded with both her young companion and £20,000 of her money, Charlotte sought retribution by publicly contending that her second marriage had been bigamous.[20] To render the situation even more scandalous, in December of 1887 Egerton's father fired a pistol at Whyte-Melville as 'they were being driven through the streets [of Dublin] in a hansom', an altercation that was reported at length in leading newspapers.[21] Dunne was arrested and released, while Whyte-Melville and Egerton escaped Ireland (although not the scrutiny of the press, who sporadically reported their movements), travelled widely in Europe, married in Detroit in the summer of 1888 (after the groom's second marriage had been formally dissolved), and eventually settled in Norway at a farm in Langesund near Christiania (now Oslo), where they lived until Whyte-Melville's death in June of 1889.[22]

19   'Ireland', *The Times* (London) (28 August 1888), 6.
20   See 'Ireland', *The Times* (London) (24 January 1888), 10. See also Divorce Certificate dated 6 March 1886 declaring Whyte-Melville's first marriage legally dissolved, Dunne/Egerton Papers, NLI, P9022/MS10946.
21   'Ireland', *The Times* (London) (28 August 1888), 6.
22   'Ireland', *The Times* (London) (28 August 1888), 6.

In 1890, Egerton had an intense, almost wholly epistolary, romance with the Norwegian author and future Nobel Prize winner Knut Hamsun.[23] Although she claimed to have been left devastated by Hamsun's rejection of her in early 1891, in November of that same year she nonetheless married Egerton Tertius Clairmonte, a Canadian of well-to-do family who had recently attempted, and failed, to earn his own fortunes in South Africa.[24] She returned with Clairmonte to Ireland in 1892, and appears only then to have realized the degree to which the controversy that surrounded her first marriage had alienated her from her Irish Catholic friends and relations.[25] In effect, her return to Ireland resulted in her recognition that, during her absence, she had distanced herself not only geographically but morally and psychologically from her homeland. These altered perceptions of her relationship within and to Ireland almost certainly account for the fact that, when she began her attempts to forge a writing career in a rented cottage in Millstreet, County Cork shortly after her homecoming, she assumed the pseudonym by which she is now known, a name which was unlikely to be traced to her former existence as Mary Dunne. It may also be the reason that, when her true identity as 'Mrs Clairmonte' was uncovered in the year after her first work of short stories was issued, published reports consistently queried her identity without fully resolving it.

23   Ingar Sletten Kolloen, *Knut Hamsun: Dreamer and Dissenter*, trans. Deborah Dawkin and Erik Skuggerik (New Haven, Yale UP, 2009), 69.

24   See letter from Egerton to John J. Dunne (26 February 1891) in which Egerton refers to the 'Hamsun affair' as having 'a miserable effect on me', Department of Rare Books and Special Collections, Princeton University, Selected Papers of Mary Chavelita Bright 2/17. See also E. Clairmonte, *The Africander: A Plain Tale of Colonial Life* (London: T. Fisher Unwin, 1896).

25   Margaret Stetz suggests that through her marriage to Clairmonte, Egerton believed 'her claim to respectability [in Ireland] had been restored. There seems to have been an element of social one-upmanship in the decision to show herself as Mrs Egerton Clairmonte, wife of a gentleman, so quickly after the wedding'. Margaret Diane Stetz, '"George Egerton": Woman and Writer of the Eighteen Nineties' (Harvard University: PhD Thesis, 1982). Stetz's unpublished biography of Egerton is exhaustive and invaluable.

She followed her writing career to England in 1893 and gave birth to a son, George Egerton Clairmonte, in 1895. Her marriage to the child's father, however, did not last. Egerton and Clairmonte were divorced in 1900 following his dalliance with an underage girl who gave birth to his daughter.[26] Remaining in London after the divorce, Egerton married her third husband, Reginald Golding Bright, a theatrical agent fifteen years her junior, in 1901.[27] Although this third union would last until Bright's death in 1941 and appears to have been, at least on his side, a love match – he referred to her, during their courtship, as 'my inspiration, my life' – marriage to a Protestant Englishman did nothing to close the divide between Egerton and Ireland.[28] Irish Catholic opinion more generally concerning her fiction was also to remain far from favourable. The *Irish Monthly* would suggest about her works that they dealt 'too much with the bold, bad world which conscientious people ought to shun, even in books'.[29] Almost certainly as a result of the disfavour she encountered in her homeland, Egerton's was to be a near-complete break with Ireland: she would return to her native country only once after she retreated from Millstreet in 1893.[30]

Thurston, younger by almost a generation than Egerton, would enter onto the publishing scene in 1903 already able to envision, in embryonic form at least, a fresh type of 'New Woman' more palatable to a post-*fin de siècle* readership. She was also more forthcoming about certain aspects of

26   See Stetz, '"George Egerton": Woman and Writer of the Eighteen Nineties', 82.
27   Bright is perhaps most famous for being the lone theatre-goer who jeered George Bernard Shaw when Shaw went onstage to acknowledge the rousing applause after the premiere of his *Arms and the Man* in 1894. Bright continued to 'boo' so loudly that the audience eventually fell silent, at which point Shaw offered one of his most famous ripostes: 'My dear fellow, I quite agree with you, but what are we two against so many?' Shaw and Bright afterwards became lifelong friends. See L. W. Connolly, *George Bernard Shaw and Barry Jackson* (Toronto: University of Toronto Press, 2002).
28   Letter from Reginald Golding Bright to Egerton (10 March 1901), Bright Papers, Princeton 1/12.
29   'Notes on New Books', *Irish Monthly*, 22/250 (April 1894), 221.
30   See letter from Egerton to John J. Dunne (23 September 1908), Bright Papers, Princeton 2/17.

her personal life, and biographical information about her which appeared over the period of her publishing career invariably makes specific reference to her Irish origins: 'she was born in the South of Ireland, and in the South of Ireland spent most of her life,' the *Bookman* would note about her in the year her first novel, *The Circle* (1903), was published.[31] Yet Thurston's relationship to Ireland, like Egerton's, would grow increasingly troubled over time – a fact which, although the reasons for it remained hidden from the public throughout most of her writing life, can be seen to inform her textual themes and the steadily escalating rebellions her heroines would enact as her career progressed.

The similarities between Egerton's and Thurston's respective personal histories are at times striking. Both were raised Catholic in middle class households in Ireland; both were the eldest – in Thurston's case the only – children of Irish fathers who were fervent nationalists and Home Rulers. John Dunne was described as an 'ardent Nationalist, [who] was nursed by O'Connell and lived to be intimate with Parnell'.[32] He served as secretary to Isaac Butt in the Home Government Association throughout the 1870s and there is a firm indication that the debts for which he was imprisoned were incurred due to loans made to Butt which were never repaid.[33] He went on, after Butt's death in 1879, to support Parnell. Dunne would contend that his relationship to the Irish Parliamentary Party leader was intimate to the point that, '[a]fter the publication by the *Times* of the forged letter' which implicated Parnell in the Phoenix Park murders, it was he who 'was the first to convey to Parnell the [accurate] idea that Pigott was its writer'.[34] Thurston's father, Paul J. Madden, was a director of the Munster and Leinster Bank and served as mayor of Cork on more

31   'New Writers', *Bookman* 23/138 (March 1903), 227.

32   'Obituary: Captain J. J. Dunne', *The Times* (London) (8 February 1910), 11.

33   See two letters dated 6 April 1877 and 14 May 1878 from Butt to Dunne lamenting that Butt cannot repay debts he owes to Dunne. In a letter dated 29 August 1878, Butt also expresses his regrets that he cannot help Dunne obtain a 'post of governor of one of the prisons'. Bright Papers, Princeton 1/15.

34   H-R-N [John J. Dunne], *Here and There Memories* (London: T. Fisher Unwin, 1896), 21.

than one occasion in the 1880s. Like Egerton's father, Madden was also prominent in nationalist circles and a noted ally of Parnell. A number of newspaper reports published during Thurston's early writing career give a similar account of him: 'Paul Madden, for many years Mayor of Cork, [was] a trusted friend and supporter of Charles Stewart Parnell. During the Land League days Mr Madden sacrificed much time and money to his country's cause. He was a devout Catholic, highly respected in commercial circles, and very charitable'.[35] As this report indicates, he was, like Dunne, willing to provide generous monetary support to causes in which he concerned himself, including those associated with both the Irish land reform movement and the Catholic Church.[36] From 1889, Madden also acted as Treasurer of the Tenants' Defence Fund, which would suffer a loss of subscriptions as a result of his refusal to back the deposal of Parnell after the O'Shea divorce scandal and the party split.[37] Both women were, therefore, raised in families in which Irish nationalist ideals were not only fervently but financially supported.

Egerton's and Thurston's mothers, meanwhile, are notable for their absences not only from contemporary records but also from the writing – both public and personal – of their daughters. Egerton was sixteen when her mother, Isabel George Bynon Dunne, died, and, although she remained deeply devoted to her memory, would later indicate that her mother had been an essentially ephemeral and ineffectual presence during her upbringing; 'a child amongst her children'.[38] References to Thurston's mother, Catherine Barry Madden, are wholly absent from the many newspaper and magazine articles about her – an absence made more notable by the fact

---

35   Clipping from the Buffalo (NY) *Courier* (19 November 1905), n.p., Katherine Cecil Thurston Papers, National Library of Scotland, 11378/10.

36   Among Thurston's personal papers is one of Paul J. Madden's cheque books from 1890, which includes two cheques, both marked 'PAID', which indicate the degree of his financial support. One dated 23 January 1890 in the amount of £1000 is to the Tenants' Defence Fund; another dated 16 June 1890 for £402.97 was paid to the Right Reverend Edward Gilpin Bagshawe, the Catholic Bishop of Nottingham.

37   See 'The Irish Crisis', *The Times* (London) (15 December 1890), 6.

38   George Egerton, *Rosa Amorosa* (London: Grant Richards, 1901), 35.

that nearly all make mention of her father – and the sole reference to her mother in Thurston's letters occurs in 1911, in which she briefly mentions that her mother's furniture 'was sold here in Cork when she died'.[39] If the lives of both women were, as a result, primarily shaped by their relationships to their male parents, there were mediating matrilineal factors that left them with more ambivalent views of issues on which their fathers demonstrated little or no equivocation: namely, religion and nation. Egerton was raised in the Roman Catholic faith, yet her mother was of Welsh and Protestant descent and Egerton would frequently refer to the inner conflict that the Catholic-Protestant divide she knew to exist in her heritage aroused in her. She also did not fail to assert the degree to which such conflicts were exacerbated by the religiously motivated bigotry of her Irish relatives – who, she claimed, 'confessed and communicated and were good Catholics but did not come near' her family at the time of her mother's death, when they were most needed – and indicated that this ostracization fueled her own feelings of estrangement from Ireland.[40] Thurston's parents were both Irish and Catholic, yet she confessed to having felt a similar conflict in her own nature, in part due to a Protestant grandmother, to whom, she avowed, she was 'a sort of spiritual "throw back"'.[41]

Egerton published just seven volumes of work over the course of her career, Thurston only six, and neither would use Irish characters or settings extensively in their fiction. 'A Cross Line' is set in Ireland, as is the first segment of her tripartite short story from *Discords*, 'A Psychological Moment at Three Periods', but these offer only cursory glances of, and fleeting commentaries upon, Ireland and the Irish. She began to deal at length with Irish themes only after she had gained the confidence of her audience with two successful volumes of work. Thurston's output was similar, with her Irish-themed novels *The Gambler* (1906) and *The Fly on the Wheel* (1908)

39   Letter from Thurston to Alfred Bulkeley Gavin (4 September 1911), Thurston Papers, NLS, 11378/12.
40   Letter from Egerton to Ethel De Vere White, quoted in De Vere White, *A Leaf from the Yellow Book*, 13.
41   Letter from Thurston to Gavin (30 August 1911), Thurston Papers, NLS, 11378/12.

following two successful early efforts, *The Circle* and *John Chilcote, M. P.* (1904), which had been set in England.

Because their heroines suffer under the weight of societal restraints, the spectre of suffragism seems to loom large behind these texts. Neither author, however, was willing to take a firm stance publicly on the suffrage issue. When pressed in interviews to reveal her political opinions, Egerton often affected a demure public persona that was distinctly at odds with her outspokenness in her private life. Her statement in the gentleman's magazine the *Idler* in 1894 is typical of this tactic: 'the fact of my having written a little book, for the love of writing it, not with a view to usher in revolt or preach a propaganda, merely to strike a few notes on the phases of the female character I knew to exist, hardly qualifies me to have an opinion, or present it to the average young man'.[42] Privately, however, Egerton's opinions on suffrage were clearly formed and emphatically stated by 1908, when in a letter to her father she attacked the anti-suffrage stance of Herbert Gladstone (W. E. Gladstone's son), who was then home secretary in Campbell-Bannerman's Liberal government:

> H. Gladstone that mediocre son of an overrated father is a feeble thing at the head of any department. The women won't be beaten in the long run. – In every class they have a greater average of intelligence than the men [...] It isn't a question of Rights. It is a question of *Economic change*. A Surplus population of women who must *work, outside home* life [...] means: if *I* pay the tax – *I* must get the vote.[43]

Thurston gives no opinion on the subject in her surviving correspondence. A biographical sketch of her published in 1904 indicates that she was not, at that time, sympathetic to the cause of extending the franchise to women: 'It is a truism to assert that every Irish man or woman is a born politician, and Mrs Thurston confesses that from her childhood she has been interested in politics', the writer of that article was to report, 'but at the same time she is of the opinion that a woman ought not to take the prominent place

---

42   Quoted in Sally Ledger, *The New Woman: Fiction and Feminism at the Fin de Siècle* (Manchester: Manchester University Press, 1997), 188.

43   Letter from Egerton to John J. Dunne (29 February 1908), Bright Papers, Princeton 2/17.

in party politics which some members of the gentler sex at times arrogate to themselves'.[44] Thurston's female characters, however, invariably chafe under the restrictions placed upon them due to their gender. Eve Chilcote in *John Chilcote, M. P.* is the first of a number of highly capable women Thurston creates who are eager to escape the limitations placed on them as females, and Eve is endowed with valid reasons for both her dissatisfaction and desiring the agency to act: as Thurston creates her, she is far more skilled at complex political thought than is her MP husband. To Thurston, biological sex was 'only an accident', and a recurrent motif in her fiction is the capable woman unfairly confined to a supporting role in public life.[45] Likewise, a persistent refrain of her female characters is a variation on the opinion first expressed by Anna Solny in *The Circle*: 'I wish I were a man!'[46] Woman's envy of the influence that man is able to wield, and the freedoms he is able to enjoy, is a consistent theme in each of Thurston's works, and became increasingly central to her texts as her writing career progressed. By the time she came to write her final novel, *Max*, in 1910, she was moved to base her narrative around a female character who lives independently in the guise of a man. Max/Maxine's validations for attempting to live such a life are succinctly stated: 'Mentally', she asserts to a male friend, 'I am as good a man as you are'.[47] It is a bold statement that suggests that Katharine Tynan's assessment of Thurston as 'interesting but silent' was eminently suitable.[48] Like Egerton, she was reticent to publicly reveal the degree to which she herself had been constrained by social, religious and moral codes, but used the characters in her novels as a means to explain and confront the types of values and inequities she had suffered under.

That she had indeed been restricted and censured in much the same way as was Egerton is apparent, and her gradual distancing from Ireland

44   'The Making of a Novelist', *Ladies' Realm* 17 (1904–1905), 658.
45   Katherine Cecil Thurston, *Max* (London: Hutchinson, 1910), 325.
46   Katherine Cecil Thurston, *The Circle* (Edinburgh and London: William Blackwood, 1903), 3.
47   Thurston, *Max*, 325.
48   Katharine Tynan, *Twenty-Five Years: Reminiscences* (New York: Devin Adair, 1913), 216–217.

and Irish values over the course of her career is subtly evidenced in the way in which her native country is referenced in press reports about her. While the earliest biographical sketches of Thurston invariably mention her father's involvement with Parnell and the Land League, these would progressively be overshadowed, and eventually wholly eclipsed, by reference to his business achievements. The reasons for this change of tactic on Thurston's part are readily conjectured. She had almost certainly learned from her publishing experiences that a nationalist stance on Irish political issues and a Catholic background were not necessarily beneficial to an author who enjoyed a substantial English readership. An indication of the degree of anti-Catholic bias among the British reading public can be glimpsed in the response to her submission of a short story to the *Windsor Magazine* in 1909: 'If you do not object to finding a title that is less Roman Catholic,' the *Windsor*'s representative wrote to Thurston with no attempt to disguise the magazine's prejudices, 'we shall be pleased to keep your story at present entitled "The Six Candles of the Blessed Virgin".'[49]

There are, however, additional and more significant factors which contributed to her decision to distance herself from her Irish past. Like Egerton, she entered into an interreligious marriage, eventually became one of the main actors in a marital scandal which was widely reported in the press, and, in her final romantic relationship, strayed wide of the bounds of conventional morality. She married the Anglo-Irish journalist and aspiring novelist Ernest Temple Thurston in 1901, the year of her father's death. The pair immediately left Ireland to set up home in the Kensington area of London for purposes of Temple Thurston's career and, once settled there, her husband actively encouraged his new wife to pursue a writing career alongside his own – so enthusiastically so that he took on the role of her first literary agent.[50] Her publishing success, however, quickly outstripped his and a rift in the marriage ensued. The tensions within the marriage may

---

49   Letter from Arthur Hutchinson to Thurston (1 January 1909), Thurston Papers, NLS, 11378/1.
50   See letters from William Blackwood to Ernest Temple Thurston dated 1905 and 1906, Thurston Papers, NLS, 11378/1.

also have been exacerbated by his literary preoccupations, which included anti-Catholicism, a subject which he explored in a number of his works, including his first novel, *The Apple of Eden* (1905). In dedicating the book to his wife ('As work of mine – apart from any religious differences it may raise, I dedicate this book to my wife, Katherine Cecil Thurston'), Temple Thurston indicated that the subject matter was a point of contention between them.[51] Whether or not this was the case, both Temple Thurston and his novel were highly unlikely to have met with approval from her Catholic extended family.

In 1907, the pair separated at Temple Thurston's instigation and after several extramarital affairs on his part. It was not until April of 1910 that Thurston brought a divorce action against her husband, but when she did so, the details were widely and often sensationally reported in the press:

> Mrs Katherine Cecil Thurston was granted a decree nisi yesterday on the ground of the misconduct and desertion of her husband [...] they lived happily down to 1907, [at which time he] told his wife that it was necessary for him to lead his own life, and that it was necessary, for the purpose of his literary work, that he should go down into the very depths of society [...] [He] complained that she was making more money than he was. Later, he gave another reason. He said that her personality dominated him, and he must get away from her.[52]

Although the divorce was uncontested and Temple Thurston was not present at the hearing to rebut these contentions, it is doubtful he would have done so. The 'vagaries of the man' appear by then to have become common knowledge.[53]

Unknown at the time to even the closest of her family and friends, however, was the fact that since the autumn of 1908, while she was still

---

51   Ernest Temple Thurston, *The Apple of Eden* (London: Dodd, Mead, 1905).
52   Clipping from the *Westminster Gazette* (8 April 1910), n.p., Thurston Papers, NLS, 11378/10.
53   Letter from J. T. Grein, Consul of Liberia, to Thurston (10 April 1910). See also letters to Thurston from Abie Perrin (7 April 1910), Bram and Florence Stoker (7 April 1910), Mary Bisland (9 April 1910) and Gerard Villiers Stuart (13 April 1910). All Thurston Papers, NLS, 11378/1.

legally married, Thurston had been involved in a love affair with Alfred Bulkeley Gavin, a Protestant doctor of Scottish heritage whose practice was in London.[54] When, a year after her divorce was finalized, she was making plans to wed, she also kept secret from most of her acquaintances the fact that she had converted to Anglicanism and had her first marriage annulled in Rome.[55] By August of 1911, a month prior to the date she had set for her wedding, Thurston was in the process of breaking ties with her Irish family, several of whom were then relying on her for financial support, and had begun to negotiate the sale of 'Maycroft', the home in Ardmore, County Waterford, to which she returned for a visit every summer.[56] This decision to leave Ireland more completely behind appears to have been prompted by the fact that one of her Irish cousins had leaked the news of her annulment and impending remarriage to the American press.[57] When Thurston and Gavin came to draft a marriage announcement to be printed in newspapers on the day set for their wedding, 12 September 1911, references to her religious background and any of her father's former political activities were for the first time conspicuously absent, suggesting that Thurston was by then attempting to distance herself not only from her Irish family, but also from almost all aspects of her Irish past.[58]

Effectively, both Egerton's and Thurston's relationships to Ireland were altered by their contravention of the country's social and moral codes. Both would explore, in their fiction, the shifting relationship to their homeland

---

54 The earliest extant letter from Thurston to Gavin is dated 28 September 1908, in which she writes to 'Dr Gavin' expressing her desire to become more intimate with him: 'This evening I wished you to talk to me – and could not induce myself to say so –/May I ask you now, instead, to see me – if you conveniently can – tomorrow night, when I shall be at home at ten o'clock', Thurston Papers, NLS, 11378/12.

55 Letter from Thurston to Gavin (10 August 1911), Thurston Papers, NLS, 11378/12.

56 Letter from Gavin to Thurston (16 August 1911) refers to the impending sale of Maycroft, Thurston Papers, NLS, 11378/11; letter from Thurston to Gavin (22 August 1911) refers to her break with her family, Thurston Papers, NLS, 11378/12.

57 Letters from Thurston to Gavin (10 and 19 August 1911) refer to the newspaper article which confirms that the news has been leaked and by whom, Thurston Papers, NLS, 11378/12.

58 Undated letter fragment, ca. August 1911, Thurston Papers, NLS, 11378/12.

that resulted. For Egerton, Ireland became a place in which 'censorship and cramped conduct' made her position untenable.[59] Although English people and society were alien and often unfathomable to her, London was a place where one could exist anonymously, to both good and ill effect. There, in the modern metropolis, scandals were common and less likely to attract attention, people and relationships tended to be superficial, and simple things like a 'well fitting frock, and an utter indifference' could 'carry the day' for a woman with a disreputable past.[60] Thurston found Ireland similarly limiting, and by 1908 was moved to assert that '[i]n no country in the world does the feminine mind shrink more sensitively from the stigma of old maid than in Ireland, where the woman-worker – the woman of broad interests – exists only as a rare type'.[61] For Thurston's heroines, travel abroad becomes the means by which they are irretrievably altered and therefore unable to return – psychologically – to the place from which they came. It was not, however, the act of entering England or elsewhere that proved liberating. Rather, as Thurston would contend, it was the process of escaping Ireland by which transformation was achieved: in becoming an exile, a woman simultaneously became a person who 'belonged to no country, to no sex'; she was, instead, a 'citizen of a free world'.[62]

The attempt to belong 'to no country' is one of George Egerton's own most prominent literary projects. Short stories such as 'Oony', from *Symphonies* (1897), and 'Mammy', from 1905's *Flies in Amber*, indicate that her literary preoccupation with expatriation was attributable to the fact that she viewed her homeland as a place in which those who strayed outside the bounds of conformity were consistently mistreated by those who were perceived, frequently undeservedly, to exist within the realms of respectability. In the earlier story, the Protestant Oony, an outsider in a predominantly Catholic Irish community, moves through a series

59   Letter from Egerton to Terence De Vere White (23 January 1944), quoted in
      De Vere White, *A Leaf from the Yellow Book*, 175.
60   Letter from Egerton to John J. Dunne (15 March 1891), quoted in De Vere White,
      A Leaf from the Yellow Book, 11.
61   Thurston, *The Fly on the Wheel*, 224.
62   Thurston, *Max*, 64; 68.

of abuses and rejections at the hands of her more fortunate neighbours. She is left orphaned by an act of agrarian outrage after her parents are murdered by men who see only her father's act of contravening a boycott and not the desperate financial need that has driven it. The woman who subsequently adopts her willfully misinterprets her own Catholicism as a means of excusing the abuse she inflicts on her young charge, and the man Oony loves shuns her in order to retain his social status. Ultimately, even the woman who acts as Oony's would-be saviour proves a failure when her Gaelic Revivalist pursuits distract her from noticing the girl's increasing emotional and physical distress. The critique of Revivalism implicit in this latter characterization is repeated in the manner of Oony's death, the circumstances of which metaphorically allude to the more shadowy aspects of a continued belief in, and reliance on, Celtic mythology: when the brokenhearted Oony withdraws into a 'fairy fort' with a fellow outsider to the community – a man the locals believe to be a fairy changeling – her soul is 'stolen' by the 'fairy man' as she sleeps.[63]

The events of 'Mammy', a story Austin Clarke credited with offering the first glimpse of Dublin's Night-Town in Irish fiction, revolve around the tale of a dying young prostitute.[64] The story opens shortly after a priest has been apprehended in the red light district of Dublin, an event which leaves the city's remaining Catholic clergy fearful of risking their reputations by venturing into Night-Town. On the night of a raging distillery fire, Mammy, the matriarch of a brothel, is therefore forced to carry a dying girl through the streets of Dublin so that she can be administered the last rites by the priests who refuse to come to her. Through her subject matter and imagery, Egerton reverses the traditional realms of good and evil in the story: Dublin is rendered hellish by the whiskey that runs in rivers of flames through its streets, priests are cowardly, 'respectable' Dubliners turn hypocritical, and the fallen woman is raised to near-deific status.

63   George Egerton, 'Oony', *Symphonies* (London and New York: John Lane/The Bodley Head, 1897), 159.

64   Austin Clarke, *A Penny in the Clouds* (Dublin: Moytura Press, 1990), 175.

It will take 'the Christ', Egerton writes in the story's closing line, 'to balance accounts with Mammy'.[65]

In tales such as these, Egerton takes aim at moral posturing and religious exclusionism, and in so doing addresses the key issues that had impacted on and damaged her own sense of belonging in Ireland. These ideas also permeate her only novel, *The Wheel of God*, a work which crystallizes her troubled and irretrievably fractured relationship to her homeland.[66] Like James Joyce's *A Portrait of the Artist as a Young Man* after it, it is a *Künstlerroman* in which the events closely parallel those of Egerton's early life. The opening chapter locates the young protagonist, Mary Desmond, in the nursery of her father's childhood home in Ireland, a space that highlights the tensions which exist between the girl's personal desires and the religious ethics which at once restrict and accentuate them. The room in which Mary spends her days is suffused with Irish nationalist and Catholic religious iconography, and her feelings towards nation and religion are reflected in her attitudes to the decorations that surround her. An early devotion to the political precepts of nationalism is evidenced in references to the room's 'wonderful' pictures of O'Connell, Emmet and Grattan, while the makeshift altar to the Virgin Mary, which instigates in her a sense of '*mea culpa*, for [her] daring skeptical fantasies', suggests a more troubled relationship to Catholicism.[67] Mary's rebellions against the restrictions of Catholic morality take the form of her detestation of the nursery's books, with their 'morals' which spoil her enjoyment of the tales, and in her derogatory or indifferent attitudes to the dogmatic religious beliefs which the room evokes: creation is 'enigmatical', eternity is 'dreadful', and heaven interests 'her least of all'.[68] A static and claustrophobic space with 'worm-eaten wainscotting' and iron-barred windows, the nursery is also and explicitly associated with the thwarted and concealed existences of Irish women: it is aligned not only with Mary but with the 'dead aunts' whose 'forgotten

---

65   George Egerton, 'Mammy', *Flies in Amber* (London: Hutchinson, 1905), 51.
66   See also Tina O'Toole's nuanced interpretation of the novel in terms of its unique place as an Irish female migrant narrative. O'Toole, *The Irish New Woman*, 129–148.
67   George Egerton, *The Wheel of God* (London: Grant Richards, 1898), 4; 7.
68   Egerton, *The Wheel of God*, 8.

treasures' it holds.[69] It attracts and imprisons the young girl just as Ireland will compel and repel her throughout the narrative.

Images of Catholicism as guilt-inducing, inflexible and stifling recur as Mary consistently searches for comfort in 'the faith of her childhood' and just as consistently finds only 'the granite wall of ecclesiastical authority'.[70] The daughter of an Irish Catholic father and mother of English descent, she locates her own religious doubts 'in her blood from maternal Protestant forebears'.[71] So, too, does her sense of difference from, and moral superiority to, the Irish people by whom she is surrounded have maternal origins. She takes a dim view of the intolerant attitudes of her relatives – 'her father's women-folk' are said to be 'bigoted, with shrines for little conventional gods erected in their souls (and in no place are the little gods of baser metal than in snobbish Ireland)' – and admits to disliking Ireland because her mother 'isn't of it'.[72] Her father, meanwhile, is but one exemplar of the many boyishly reckless Irish men she knows, whose actions she views with both affection and condescension, as 'a mother might [...] the vagaries of her children'.[73]

The later death of her mother accentuates her aversion to Catholicism, which by this time has become not merely a matter of 'complete indifference', but of 'sullen, rebellious resentment!'[74] Within Mary, and between her and Ireland as she perceives it, there has heretofore existed a tension of difference, and the sense that she has somehow been disinherited of a legitimate Irishness by the either-or restrictions of Protestant and Catholic, English and Irish. Yet the levelling effects of the social decline which accompanies her mother's death also serve to dispel a portion of this conflict as Mary's sense of Englishness gradually fades and her newly impoverished position instils an intensified awareness of her Irish (although never her Catholic) identity. The streets of Dublin – previously reviled, alien

69   Egerton, *The Wheel of God*, 4; 6.
70   Egerton, *The Wheel of God*, 91.
71   Egerton, *The Wheel of God*, 20–21.
72   Egerton, *The Wheel of God*, 25; 18.
73   Egerton, *The Wheel of God*, 26.
74   Egerton, *The Wheel of God*, 26.

spaces – soon become locations where she communes with the ghosts of Jonathan Swift, 'silken Thomas' and Lord Edward Fitzgerald, all of whom, like her, grew more fervently Irish over time.[75] After her mother dies, her father's friends become her own, she refers to the English as 'Sassenach' and comfort comes in the form of a brogue.[76] While she gradually becomes more attuned to her country, however, Ireland and those who hold power over her fate within it prove inhospitable to her as a female.

Mary's subsequent decision to emigrate to New York is instigated in large part by her father's failure to provide for the family. Yet the fact that Mary has no recourse to money other than to beg an advance from the North of Ireland man for whom her father has failed to complete an artistic commission, and that her days are spent idly in the library of the Royal Dublin Society, indicate that there are few or no sources of employment available to women in Ireland. In accordance with this, Egerton demonstrates that those preparing to leave for America from the docks at Queenstown are predominantly young females: 'shy-eyed, tearful colleens', 'the flower of Irish girlhood' and 'steerage girls'.[77] Extending her critique of Ireland's treatment of women, Egerton demonstrates that, once Mary arrives in New York, the convent education she has received proves wholly inadequate to the requirements of the modern world which exists beyond Ireland's borders. Useless to her in practical terms and alienating in a social context, her 'privileged' education thwarts rather than aids her attempts to achieve financial success and personal fulfillment in America.

When she does eventually find the means for return, it is to England rather than Ireland that she travels. London is, like New York, a place of greater opportunity for women; it is also just as equally a 'foreign' space where Mary feels 'the racial difference keenly' and where, ultimately, she comes to hear 'the words of the Irish clan cry' ring in her.[78] While her experiences serve to accentuate her feelings of foreignness outside of Ireland, they

75   Egerton, *The Wheel of God*, 48–49.
76   Egerton, *The Wheel of God*, 43; 62.
77   Egerton, *The Wheel of God*, 59; 60; 63.
78   Egerton, *The Wheel of God*, 111; 127; 215. The clan cry Egerton refers to, 'the hills forever', is the cry of her own Dunne family rather than that of the Desmonds.

also indicate the degree to which her opportunities have been hampered by the tendency, explicitly linked to Ireland and Irishness, to adhere to traditional patterns of behaviour. Mary's emigration leads her ever further away from notions of convention which are bound up with her ethnic identity; at the same time, her sense of belonging becomes increasingly linked to her gender. As she moves through New York and London, she finds her closest affinities not with other Irish people, but with other working women – and, more specifically, with those women whose experiences act as correlatives to Egerton's own. There are readily recognizable parallels between Egerton's experiences and those of Mary's closest friend in New York, Septima – a woman who is artistically enlightened, has a large family headed by an irresponsible father and becomes romantically involved with a married man with whom she hopes to elope to Europe. Also obvious is Egerton's kinship to a woman with whom Mary shares a boarding house in London: a character identified only as 'the bow-maker' who recognizably mimics, through her experiences and the terminology she employs to describe them, Egerton's accounts of her relationship with Knut Hamsun. In the aftermath of the Hamsun affair, Egerton decided that she 'must work, and work hard to forget all this heartache I have got', but reminded herself in her sorrow that, if one had 'to make an idiot of oneself, it [was] at least self-consoling to have done so for a genius'.[79] Likewise, the bow-maker is a woman who is recovering from the after-effects of an ill-fated relationship with an idealistic foreign 'genius' through her arduous work for his political cause. Mary later meets a self-sufficient female journalist of Celtic descent who bears a passing resemblance to Egerton as she was during her early working life in London, who bridges the gap between Mary and a pseudonymous author of feminist fiction, 'John Morton', with whom she ultimately aligns herself. The trajectory of *The Wheel of God* is, therefore, one in which Mary, a facsimile of Egerton's younger self, finds sympathies with a variety of characters who imitate the author's own progressive incarnations,

---

79   See letter from Egerton quoted in De Vere White, *A Leaf from the Yellow Book*, 19 and letter from Egerton to John J. Dunne (26 February 1891), Bright Papers, Princeton 2/17.

eventually reaching the fully formed alter-ego of Egerton at the apex of
her career: the writer John Morton, who is celebrated and controversial.

Mary's contention early in the novel, brought to mind by a glimpse of
Dublin's Golden Lane and thoughts of James Clarence Mangan, that 'all
the nicest men she had known' were tainted by moral weakness, also sites
her sympathies on the side of the ethically flawed.[80] This idea is continued
and expanded upon in descriptions of Mary's attitudes towards the numbers of morally compromised women she meets, but is most prominently
related to Ireland through references to her 'singular devotion for Parnell
that would have made her put her left hand in the fire to have served him.'[81]
It is, in fact, Parnell's fall from both moral and political favour which forms
the core of the novel and the crux on which Mary's permanent break with
her homeland turns:

> So confused are the issues of life it would have seemed almost impossible to Mary
> Desmond to realise that the fate of this great Irish leader, without whose name the
> history of England in this century can never be written, could have had any influence
> on her own life as an insignificant woman. Yet it had; for, when they forgot all he
> had done for them, and sacrificed him in obedience to bigotry and the moral fetich,
> it robbed her of the last shred of allegiance to the old religion in the old country.[82]

Proceeding to assert that, 'if the women of Ireland had been [Parnell's] followers' instead of the men, they 'would have stuck to him in the teeth of
excommunication', Egerton places the blame for Parnell's demise exclusively
and imperatively on Irish men and the Catholic religious morality 'they'
espouse.[83] At the same time, she effectively removes the question of Irish
political autonomy from its overarching British context. It becomes, in
her text, not a battle being waged between England and Ireland, nor even
between sectarian factions within Ireland. Rather, it is a struggle within
the nationalist movement itself.

80   Egerton, *The Wheel of God*, 43.
81   Egerton, *The Wheel of God*, 181.
82   Egerton, *The Wheel of God*, 181.
83   Egerton, *The Wheel of God*, 181.

Ireland as it is evoked in Egerton's text is an anti-pluralist, anti-secularist and morally intransigent space. It is also, literally, Mary's fatherland. Her decision at the close of the novel to live a communal existence with "'John Morton", the [female] journalist, and two other women' follows on directly from the morally restrictive, male-dominated Irish Catholic society Egerton creates and her related sentiments, spoken by John Morton, that it is women's responsibility to raise their sons in a way that will allow females of the future greater freedoms, opportunities and responsibilities: 'the men we women of to-day need, or who need us, are not of our time – it lies in the mothers to rear them for the women who follow us'.[84] Ireland, Egerton suggests in the novel, is no country for women, and Mary's journey beyond its borders gradually leads her to an intellectual position in which she is ready to embrace both the transformative potential of her biological sex, and to step 'into the inheritance of her self'.[85] To do so, Egerton suggests, she must move into a geographical space which is overtly envisioned as Ireland's opposite: a mother-land.

Like Egerton's, Thurston's texts would consistently privilege gendered perspectives over national (or nationalist) views and evidence her interest in issues related to what Egerton termed the 'moral fetich'. A regular preoccupation of her work is the individual struggling against both physical limitations and moral confinement to maintain a façade of respectability against the overwhelming pull of untraditional or even illicit personal desires. Gone, however, are the overt didacticism and confrontational tone of Egerton's texts, to be replaced by dissatisfied women woven into deftly suspenseful plots. Her first novel, *The Circle* (1903), sets the tone for what will follow. In it, Thurston creates two characters whose actions are misconstrued to the detriment of their reputations and personal relationships. The novel focuses on the stories of Johann, a man compelled by circumstance to lie about his personal history in order to avoid being imprisoned for a crime he did not commit, and Anna, whose attempts to aid Johann lead to her own castigation by those who know her actions but

---

84   Egerton, *The Wheel of God*, 320; 320–321.
85   Egerton, *The Wheel of God*, 321.

not their contexts. Both are eventually exonerated from blame, but before
that is allowed to happen Thurston successfully manipulates the reader
into condoning subterfuge by demonstrating that both Anna and Johann
are forced to conceal truths which should, in a just world, have been the
means of setting them free. She also manages to demonstrate that Anna,
after escaping her constrained existence working for her father in his curio
shop, achieves through her career as an actress a degree of fulfillment wholly
unimaginable in her former, and far less controversial, life.

The Circle was a prodigious debut for the 28-year-old first-time novelist,
earning her good notices from reviewers, substantial sales and a degree of
literary fame. Her second novel, John Chilcote, M. P. (1904), published in
America as The Masquerader, proved an even greater commercial triumph.
The Newark (New Jersey) Call was not alone in proclaiming it 'the success
of the season', while Harper's Bazaar reported that, during the Christmas
period of 1904, 'one bookseller, who has ordered a thousand copies every
day during December, estimates that the book is now selling at the rate of
one volume a minute'.[86] By the end of 1906, the novel had sold in excess
of a million copies and had earned for Thurston the modern equivalent of
more than £1.3 million.[87]

In John Chilcote, M. P., Thurston employs similar tactics to those she
used in The Circle, gradually manoeuvring the reader over the course of
the narrative into a position in which his or her sympathies rest on the
side of a character who is involved in the most deceitful of exploits. The
titular character is an unwilling Member of Parliament, a man who feels
he has been forced, by a sense of both duty and guilt, into the seat once
occupied by his father. Unhappy in his career and marriage, John Chilcote
has, during his tenure in Parliament, been leading an ulterior life as an adul-
terer and morphine addict. Plagued by nerves, he longs to give himself up

---

86 Clipping from the Newark (NJ) Call (5 November 1904), n.p., and clipping from
    Harper's Bazaar (8 December 1904), n.p., both Thurston Papers, NLS, 11378/2.
87 Clipping from the Liverpool Daily Post & Mercury (7 March 1906), n.p., Thurston
    Papers, NLS, 11378/10. Earnings figures are from Caroline Copeland, 'An Oasis
    in the Desert: The Transatlantic Publishing Success of Katherine Cecil Thurston',
    Edinburgh Bibliographical Society 1/2 (2007), 33.

to dissipation while allowing his reputation to remain intact: 'to keep my place in the world's eyes and yet be free', he asserts.[88] The novel opens on a scene in which he is attempting to make his way home from Westminster through a dense fog. Disoriented, he stumbles upon John Loder, a man who is revealed, as the fog lifts, to be his *doppelgänger*. Through the conversation that ensues, Loder demonstrates that he is knowledgeable on political topics, and Chilcote recognizes the means to achieve his ends.

Loder agrees to assume Chilcote's identity for an indefinite period, acting on an impulse instigated by his sense that in doing so, he is taking up the rightful place denied to him when an improvident relative squandered his inheritance. Upon entering this new life, Loder promptly demonstrates that he is, unlike Chilcote, an asset to both class and country. Ambitious and capable of empathy and sacrifice, he is also emotionally equipped to deal with the stresses of political life in a way that Chilcote is not. The question of whether he also assumes an unambiguous moral position remains more difficult to solve, despite the deception, precisely because Loder is so eminently suited to the life he adopts. Over the course of the narrative he engineers a political coup which, although the tactics he employs are ethically dubious, is the means to an end that proves beneficial not only to his party's interests and his own career, but to the country at large. He also begins to covet and in due course falls in love with Chilcote's wife, Eve. Although Thurston makes clear that Chilcote has long mistreated and often abandoned his wife, the ethical dilemmas surrounding Loder's behaviour in both his actions in Parliament and his relationship to Eve are apparent.

The nearly simultaneous ousting of the rival political party from power and Chilcote's accidental death from a morphine overdose bring Loder to a point of crisis near the end of the novel, but Thurston makes the unconventional authorial choice to leave his moral dilemmas largely unresolved, and his moral transgressions wholly unpunished, at the novel's close. Learning that Eve has known about his deception for some time, Loder expresses his wish to leave the country so that her reputation might be spared should his

---

88   Katherine Cecil Thurston, *John Chilcote, M. P.* (Edinburgh and London: William Blackwood, 1904), 54.

true identity be revealed. Eventually, however, he allows Eve – who admits to having fallen in love with him when she believed him to be an altered, better version of her husband – to convince him that his charade must be maintained. Having demonstrated not only her capabilities by acting as Loder's most trusted political advisor, but also her frustration at not being able to make full use of them by referring to how 'splendid it must be to be a man', Eve is the person to whom Loder defers all of his most important decisions.[89] His continued deception is imperative, she argues, because it will benefit not only him, but also her and the nation. He should not, she asserts, be tempted to throw away 'the substance for the shadow'.[90]

The interplay between substance and shadow is central to the novel, with Loder at one point suggesting about the underbelly of his existence that the 'the details are horrible; but there are times when we must look at the horrible sides of life – because life is incomplete without them'.[91] This and a number of additional passages suggest that a similar interchange is being enacted with regard to the novel's main characters – that, while it is overtly the story of two men, *John Chilcote* also functions as an allegory for a lone man whose inner conflicts and divided allegiances lead him to live a double life, separated between his public and private personas, one unimpeachable, the other distinctly flawed. This idea is foreshadowed when, at the opening of the novel, Chilcote and Loder happen upon one another in the fog and each man feels that he is looking, 'not at the face of another, but at his own face reflected in a flawless looking-glass'.[92] Likewise, Chilcote disbelieves that Loder is 'substantial' while concurrently not only imagining his own oblivion, but longing for it.[93] The two men's unlikely romantic attachments to the same women – Eve Chilcote and Lillian Astrupp, the former a 'wife' to both, the latter Loder's one-time and Chilcote's current mistress – support the reading of Loder and Chilcote as a single entity with dual desires, moral on one side and illicit on the other. The novel

89   Thurston, *John Chilcote, M. P.*, 203.
90   Thurston, *John Chilcote, M. P.*, 368.
91   Thurston, *John Chilcote, M. P.*, 364.
92   Thurston, *John Chilcote, M. P.*, 11.
93   Thurston, *John Chilcote, M. P.*, 11.

ultimately reads as a fantasy in which the politician's shameful private life eventually dies quietly and completely away, while the public man and the woman he loves (who happens to be another man's wife) are able to step forward into the limelight together, undetected in, and unsullied by, their transgressions. The possibility that the novel may have been intended as an elaborate Parnellite parable did not remain unremarked upon by readers or reviewers, and speculation was rife that Loder was, in fact, Parnell in fictional form.[94] Parnell may indeed be one potential real-life model for Thurston's characters; but so, too, it must be noted, might Ernest Temple Thurston. That Thurston had both a personal and political agenda in mind at the time of writing is more likely than not, but these questions aside, it is the fact that she used her narrative as a means of criticizing existing marital and political ethics, and to demonstrate the necessity of hiding private truths from a morally judgmental wider society, which is of primary interest in the text.

Thurston may culminate *John Chilcote* with Loder's assertion that his ultimate fate 'lies with – my wife' and show Eve proclaiming, 'now it's my turn [...] [t]o-day is mine', but the novel remains unique in her oeuvre for relegating its females to the sidelines of the action.[95] Concentrating her authorial attention on the masculine world was not a technique she would repeat. From the point of her next novel onwards, she consistently featured female protagonists and explored subjectivities and situations which moved gradually nearer to her own. Although the opening chapters of *The Gambler* (1906), her first Irish novel, focus on the conduct of Denis Asshlin, an Anglo-Irish aristocrat whose gambling addiction accelerates his family's decline into poverty, it is Asshlin's daughter Clodagh who acts as the text's protagonist.[96]

In its earliest passages, *The Gambler* explores Asshlin's troubled relationship to an old school ally, the Englishman James Milbanke, whose

---

94   See, for instance, clipping from the Newark (NJ) *Call* (5 November 1904), n.p., Thurston Papers, NLS, 11378/2.

95   Thurston, *John Chilcote, M. P.*, 370; 318.

96   1906 is the UK publication date. *The Gambler* was first published in the US in 1905.

well-intentioned but misguided attempts to aid his Irish friend have disastrous consequences. After Asshlin loses badly in a game of cards, Milbanke's
efforts to rectify the situation by returning his winnings evoke only anger
in his friend, the reasons for which are demonstrated to be cultural: 'You
don't understand – you never did understand', Asshlin explains to Milbanke.
'It's the cursed pride of a cursed country. The less we have to be proud of,
the more damned proud we are.'[97] Estranged as a result of this misunder-
standing, Milbanke and Asshlin are reconciled only when the latter is
on his deathbed. Possessing the riches that Asshlin has always lacked but
devoid of the compassion and diplomacy necessary to negotiate his way
safely through his Irish counterpart's ethnic sense of dignity, Milbanke
soon compounds his earlier mistakes. Believing himself, after his friend's
death, to be responsible for Asshlin's estate and two daughters, he pays
the family's debts and offers to marry the older child, eighteen-year-old
Clodagh. In the process, he fails to recognize either her unwillingness or
the means by which his actions might be misinterpreted. While this is a
love match on Milbanke's part, for Clodagh it amounts to blackmail: it is
the repayment of a 'debt of honour' incurred through Milbanke's act of
saving her family's land.[98]

The resultant marriage between Clodagh and Milbanke, a significantly older man who is consumed by his antiquarian hobbies and devoid
of any emotional intelligence, may be distinctly reminiscent of Dorothea
Brooke's to Edward Casaubon in George Eliot's *Middlemarch* (1871), but
there are cultural differences between Thurston's heroine and Eliot's which
serve to compound the marital and moral dilemmas with which the Irish
woman at the centre of *The Gambler* is faced. Having been raised without
nurturers and exemplars in a country in which her family's position has
diminished to the point that she effectively sells herself into a loveless marriage, Clodagh enters adulthood wholly incapable of romanticizing her
marital situation or her role within it. She is a different configuration of the
novelistic heroine altogether – one who, feeling increasingly ineffectual,

---

97   Katherine Cecil Thurston, *The Gambler* (London: Hutchinson, 1906), 34.
98   Thurston, *The Gambler*, 99.

isolated and ignored in her marriage, begins to assert her independence by pursuing illicit desires, including gambling and flirtations with other men. Thurston's text also offers a significant departure from the traditional national marriage plot. Rather than proving, as convention dictates, to be mutually beneficial, this marriage between an English man and an Irish woman is an abject failure.

Again in Thurston's text, conventional morality is interrogated. Her portrayal of Clodagh, who travels with Milbanke on the European Continent and in doing so moves among a group of wealthy tourists, consistently highlights the inequities of her heroine's position in relation to her hereditarily more privileged British counterparts. Throughout her own descent into gambling addiction, Clodagh is shown to struggle, however fruitlessly, against temptation and vice, and to worry about the effect of her actions on other people. In contrast, the English people with whom she associates – Lord Deerehurst, Serracauld and Lady Frances (whose characterizations also suggest the influence of Henry James's novels on Thurston's text) – goad one another into various attempts to corrupt the impressionable Irishwoman while pursuing without compunction vices from which Clodagh recoils. If their efforts at seduction are ultimately only partially successful – Clodagh falls rapidly under the spell of roulette and euchre but resists Lord Deerehurst's sexual advances – Thurston nonetheless demonstrates that, having been denied any opportunity for individual progress during her formative years, she has become easy prey to those who are positioned (socially, financially and racially) 'above' her. The lure of company, ease and plenty proves too strong for the young woman who has experienced only the isolation, powerlessness and increasing impoverishment of an Anglo-Irish upbringing.

Although each of the characters who demonstrates a propensity to gamble to excess – Asshlin, his nephew Larry and Clodagh on the Irish side; Lord Deerehurst, Lady Frances and Serracauld on the English – are driven by a lack of purposeful pursuits, the reasons for this lack are an important dividing factor in terms of cultural identity. For the English, who are freed by their riches to lead lives of leisure, gambling is just one pastime among many. Aimlessness is, for them, a choice. About the Eton-educated Serracauld, Thurston writes that his 'sufficiency of money had rendered work unnecessary'; he is, she asserts, 'a fashionable young aristocrat, whose only business in life [is] the absorbing pursuit of killing time'.[99] The Irish characters' positions are, however, the inverse. In the cases of Denis and Larry Asshlin, it is almost wholly their extant poverty that brings about their respective demises. The possibility of winning at the gaming tables is too compelling a lure for those like the Asshlins who lack any prospects for earning money by more acceptable means, leading them to grow ever more destitute as they borrow against and sell off belongings and property to meet the debts they incur.

Effectively, Thurston constructs a narrative in which her English characters remain unrepentant and unpunished for their actions, while her Irish characters, despite being endowed with far more compelling reasons to be led down ethically less-than-exemplary paths, are severely penalized. Again confronting facile moral judgments, Thurston does so for the first time within a framework that is recognizably cultural, and the idea that ethical standards are arbitrarily applied and enforced is carried through to the end of the novel. The ultimate point of crisis comes only when Clodagh, now widowed, has gambled away the last of her money and resorts to using her younger sister's trust fund to pay off her debts. In the midst of her worst troubles, and among the multitudes of dishonest people by which Clodagh finds herself surrounded, her sister Nance comes to personify a lone, conscientious and understanding voice. Though Clodagh's new fiancé, the English Walter Gore, loves her, his moral standards are ultimately shown to be too stringent: he breaks off their engagement after learning the details, but not the circumstances, of her actions. Left without options after Gore abandons her and unable to escape the legacies of her family's past, Clodagh decides to commit suicide. It is only through Nance's viewpoint that Gore is able to see his way to comprehending Clodagh's motivations rather than judging her actions according to a set of rules which cannot appropriately be applied to her situation. As a result of Nance's intervention, Gore forgives Clodagh, and her life is saved. Throughout, the exploits and attitudes of Thurston's English characters, who fail to understand their

99   Thurston, *The Gambler*, 130.

Irish counterparts, serve to debilitate and victimize Irish characters, who are shown to lead existences which are always already thwarted. Again, the woman's superior perspective is emphasized in the text; again, Thurston's morally flawed character is absolved of guilt through an explanation of the complex moral situation in which she has been enmeshed.

Forgiveness is a central theme in all Thurston's texts, including several unpublished and unperformed plays she wrote around the theme of marital adultery at the mid-point of her career. At the close of one of these dramas, *The Day After*, the play's priest-like character, Charvier, pardons an adulterous woman for her transgressions:

> You have sinned. Blot out your sin in strength and silence. Be your own judge: mete out your own punishment. Be your own pardoner, when the time comes! [...] Thousands have lived what the world calls a lie – and raised noble structures on the foundation.[100]

Although playwriting was a new pursuit for Thurston, the idea of noble structures being raised from the ruins of a dishonest past was not – *The Circle*, *John Chilcote* and *The Gambler* all share the same theme. In *The Fly on the Wheel* (1908), her penultimate and most accomplished work, her message concerning moral absolution, while it remains central, is more cynically envisioned. The first of Thurston's novels in which all of the characters share her Irish Catholic middle class background, it is also her most distinctly pessimistic work.

In dealing with an encroaching modernity that is actively being resisted in Ireland, the novel's portrayals and preoccupations balance precariously on the cusp between two centuries and two eras: the nineteenth and the twentieth; the Victorian and the Modern. This liminality can also be glimpsed in the manner in which Thurston's text draws on the themes of earlier fiction while foreshadowing the work of Irish female authors who were to follow. Like George Eliot's *The Mill on the Floss* (1860) before it

---

100 Katherine Cecil Thurston, undated typewritten manuscript of *The Day After*, Ep. III, 21, Thurston Papers, NLS, 11378/10.

and Kate O'Brien's *The Ante-Room* (1934) after, Thurston's text is an examination of an illicit love affair set against the backdrop of a claustrophobic society. Unlike Eliot's work and in common with O'Brien's, the tension of Thurston's novel is heightened by the fact that it is set at or near the *fin de siècle* and in a genteel but stifled Irish Catholic community struggling to maintain its customs and ideals against the incipient threat of change. On one side of the divide between tradition and modernity is the novel's main male character, the 38-year-old Stephen Carey. An unquestioning upholder of the tenets of the Waterford society in which he lives, which is 'tyrannical in its moral code', he is described in terms which establish him as a necessary but dehumanized part of the rigid Irish middle class machine: one of many 'men of steel' who are 'drawn from the great workshops, tempered, filed, polished to fit the appropriate place; helping to move the mighty engine of which they are the atoms, useless if cast out from its mechanism'.[101] Foreshadowing the point of crisis he will ultimately reach through this brief reference to the possibility of his becoming an outcast, Thurston affirms that Stephen is incapable of existing outside the boundaries of the culture he inhabits.

Like her characters John Loder and Clodagh Asshlin before him, Stephen is also a victim of the errors and expectations of a previous generation. His inheritance, like theirs, has been squandered by the carelessness of a male relative. Stephen's father, having been during his lifetime 'too proud to go into debt', speculated with, rather than borrowed to supplement, his remaining assets when his business began to fail, and thereby lost his fortune.[102] Left to care for his six younger brothers after his father's death and determined to see his father's dreams for the family fulfilled, Stephen has in the ensuing years deprived himself 'to the point of penury that his brothers might not turn back from their allotted paths'.[103] As his father wished, Stephen has become a lawyer, and ensures that his younger brothers in turn become a priest, an architect, a civil engineer, a banker and a sailor.

101 Thurston, *The Fly on the Wheel*, 2–3.
102 Thurston, *The Fly on the Wheel*, 7.
103 Thurston, *The Fly on the Wheel*, 7.

He is also dutifully married to Daisy, a woman 'content to shape the future on the pattern of the past'.[104] Stephen has chosen his wife in a business-like manner according to his (and his society's) patronizing views of her sex: he has considered his prospective brides, we are told, 'much as the Eastern might have studied the slave-market'.[105] As the novel opens, he has three young sons of his own to support and is on the brink of releasing himself from the responsibilities defined for him by his father. Only Frank, the youngest of his brothers, remains under his care, studying medicine in Paris.

As Stephen stands thus on the threshold of what amounts to a moment of liberation, into his life to symbolize his newfound opportunity for emancipation comes Isabel Costello. She is Frank's young fiancée, the relatively poor daughter of a deceased banker from Wexford newly returned to Ireland from a Parisian convent school to live with a maiden aunt. Isabel enters Waterford society and is openly welcomed as a curiosity, but secretly vilified as an interloper, particularly by the women of the community. Not only is she a non-native, she is also perceived to be an *arriviste* – a woman who, through her foreign education and impending marriage, is attempting to surpass what bourgeois Irish society have deigned her inherent and proper social station beneath them. As an upholder of his community's traditions, Stephen is angered that his brother has willfully controverted the business-like terms on which marriages are arranged in Ireland by choosing a wife who can bring nothing of monetary value to the family, and determines to persuade Isabel to abandon Frank. Yet in Isabel he meets a type of woman theretofore non-existent in Waterford: orphaned, only very recently repatriated and essentially rootless, with a hint of the blood of Spanish ancestors in her appearance and outlook, Isabel is not constrained by local attitudes and disbelieves in the ethics of a society which would define her by its terms, rather than her own. Provoked into anger by Stephen's demand that she terminate her relationship with Frank, she reiterates the idea that marriage in middle-class Ireland is a form of

104 Thurston, *The Fly on the Wheel*, 9.
105 Thurston, *The Fly on the Wheel*, 12.

financial transaction, but reinterprets the terms on which it is negotiated as both insular and driven by fear:

> I think it's much more to be despised to sell yourself as if you were a sheep or a horse than to marry because you care [...] You think of nothing but money – money and position. You live in a little, little world, where if people ever do feel anything, they're afraid to say so![106]

Eventually, however, Isabel ends the relationship of her own accord after realizing the extent of Frank's weaknesses, which are placed in relief by her recognition of her own, and Stephen's, strengths. The plot thereafter revolves around Isabel and Stephen's growing affections for one another, and Stephen's burgeoning awareness that he, like Isabel, is dissatisfied with a life lived within the constraints of Waterford society.

Among the novel's prominent and recurring themes is the narrowness of opportunity for women in Ireland. For Isabel and the remainder of Irish women, the convent is one of the few options available to them should they choose or be forced by circumstances into the stigmatized life of an 'old maid'.[107] Not being of the type who might find contentment in the 'placid grey monotony' of a cloistered life, however, and incapable of subduing her 'pride to the petty difficulties, the slow drudgery, that in Ireland spells self-support', Isabel is left with only two choices: 'Such women either marry or they do not marry; and in that simple statement is comprised the tragedy of existence'.[108] If the middle class is expanding, however unwillingly, to accommodate those men like Stephen's father, a builder who used ingenuity and relentless endeavour as a means to achieve a tenuous bourgeois status for his family, for women there is only one route to social mobility, and that is marriage.

In keeping with this sense of stasis, Isabel's bedroom in her aunt's home is, like Mary Desmond's in *The Wheel of God*, a shabby space filled with 'ugly Victorian furniture' and thus patterned, like much of the rest of Waterford,

---

106   Thurston, *The Fly on the Wheel*, 81.
107   Thurston, *The Fly on the Wheel*, 224.
108   Thurston, *The Fly on the Wheel*, 224.

on the past. Isabel, Daisy, and Daisy's sister's combined attempts to occupy themselves while left together in the Careys' country home on a rainy day while the men are at work amplifies the sense of women's entrapment.[109] It is, however, Isabel alone who is tempted to transgress the boundaries placed on her as a female. Venturing outside to smoke cigarettes, flirt with men or ride unchaperoned in a 'motor car', Isabel – the only one among Thurston's characters who is not native to the community and who has no immediate family – remains the lone dissenter among her female con-temporaries.[110] Through her, Thurston indicates that outsiderhood and estrangement lend a more nuanced view of behavioural mores and ethical codes than rootedness can provide.

Though the limitations placed on behaviour and opportunities are far from equal between the sexes in *The Fly on the Wheel*, they are to vary-ing degrees shared. The suggestion about Stephen that 'if only he was in England or America, what a great man he might have been', attests to the narrowness of prospects, even for men, in Ireland.[111] Stephen, realizing through Isabel the extent to which his options have indeed been limited, begins to echo her rebellious voice, but only feebly in comparison to the woman who strains and chafes at every restriction. By highlighting the discrepancies in their rebellions, Thurston consistently suggests the degree to which her male protagonist continues to remain, however reluctantly, complicit with tradition. In line with this idea, it is Stephen, a former Land Leaguer himself, who most actively denigrates the ideas propounded by his wife's brother Tom Norris, a nationalist and member of the Gaelic League. In terms which affirm both his own and his country's inability to countenance a new social or political order, Stephen asserts the futility of Tom's efforts on behalf of Irish independence: 'You'll always have young men, you know, but Ireland won't be changed by that'.[112] Isabel, however, is not among Tom's detractors. Rather, she empathizes with his position,

---

109   Thurston, *The Fly on the Wheel*, 55.
110   Thurston, *The Fly on the Wheel*, 175.
111   Thurston, *The Fly on the Wheel*, 230.
112   Thurston, *The Fly on the Wheel*, 103.

and it is to her that Tom turns when mocked by the elder members of his social circle. 'Don't listen to them, Miss Costello', he tells her, 'It's people like them that have kept Ireland where she is. We'd have been a nation long ago – a nation in the commercial and intellectual sense – only for the poisonous spirit of depreciation that's spread over every honest effort to raise the country'.[113] In subsequently comparing Ireland's inertia to Stephen's own inaction, Thurston suggests the degree to which the fates of man and nation are inextricably intertwined.

Stephen's late night drive with Isabel is his one notable act of transgression. Ultimately, however, it proves abortive. In drawing attention to the point just short of the Cork border at which he ends their journey, Thurston confirms that it is he, rather than Isabel, who is unable or unwilling to leave the space he occupies – that, as Gerardine Meaney has suggested, 'there are boundaries – psychological and geographical – which Stephen is unable to cross'.[114] When he later declares his intentions to leave Daisy for Isabel, it is with Father James Baron – and therefore with a specifically Catholic version of morality and tradition – that the true power over Stephen's fate finally rests. Father James is described in terms that leave no doubt as to his authority: he is 'a tower in the silent room' who has 'grandeur in his rugged face' and 'power in his rough voice'.[115] Drawing on his memories of the time when it looked as though Stephen and his brothers would be ruined by their father's actions, the priest dissuades him from leaving his wife by reminding him of his own earlier pledge to himself: 'I'll live it down', he recalls Stephen proclaiming after his father's death, 'but, by God, if ever I have sons of my own, they'll never have a hell of their father's making'.[116] Stephen's decision to forsake Isabel ultimately reads as an admission of defeat to the inextricable and unassailable power of religious authority

113   Thurston, *The Fly on the Wheel*, 103.
114   Gerardine Meaney, 'Decadence, Degeneration and Revolting Aesthetics: The Fiction of Emily Lawless and Katherine Cecil Thurston', *Colby Quarterly* 36/2 (2000), 171.
115   Thurston, *The Fly on the Wheel*, 287.
116   Thurston, *The Fly on the Wheel*, 288.

and social propriety, his 'broken' and 'tortured' demeanor emphasizing the degree of his sacrifice and submission.[117]

The choice Stephen makes at the end of the novel foreshadows and inverts the one that, decades later, Kate O'Brien would portray her character Agnes Mulqueen making in *The Ante-Room*. So, too, does Isabel's act of ending her own life anticipate Vincent's fate in O'Brien's novel. That in *The Fly on the Wheel* it is the man who complies with the limitations placed on him while the woman rebels against them makes Thurston's text the more radically realized of the two. Isabel's act of drinking the poisoned wine she had originally intended for Stephen comes as the result of her recognition that the position her lover occupies is inescapable and her own desires unachievable. Her suicide is, therefore, a testament of her inability to live within the moral constraints of Irish society. A comparison of the portrayals of the suicides in Thurston's and O'Brien's novels highlights important gendered and attitudinal differences between them. Vincent's suicide in the later text is notably devoid of the type of heroism with which Isabel's is infused. It is instead represented as a regression – a retreat into boyhood and the comfort of his mother, a childish deed born out of a personal despair he cannot surmount. Vincent's act is thus more akin to Stephen's in *The Fly on the Wheel* than it is to Isabel's: the decisions made by both men are registered as defeats to conventional morality. Although Agnes also thinks of killing herself in O'Brien's novel, her devotion to Catholicism, and the consequences she would suffer under it, dissuade her from it. She wishes, rather, to annihilate the feelings she has for the married Vincent and thus to destroy her sin and achieve absolution. What she reaches instead is a point of dismal realization that the act of rejecting love is a form of living death in itself: 'They are alive', Agnes says of those around her, '[b]ut I'm dying'.[118] For Isabel as Thurston constructs her, faith is a different but no less devout matter. If she has long queried the ethics of her community, she never questions those of her religion. She is said to accept '[e]very tenet of the Roman Catholic Church [...] with unquestioning belief, because to her

---

117   Thurston, *The Fly on the Wheel*, 326.
118   Kate O'Brien, *The Ante-Room* (London: Virago, 1988 [1934]), 261.

imagination those tenets were as fixed as the stars in heaven'.[119] As a believer in Catholicism, Isabel therefore is fully aware of the consequences of the deed she ultimately commits. Yet Thurston represents Isabel's death not as an act to be stigmatized or condemned, but as both the ultimate sacrifice (in killing herself, she saves Stephen) and a triumph over the confines of her existence. The final line of the novel reinforces the grandeur of her action: 'looking down into the wine,' Isabel's eyes catch 'the warmth, the redness, the glory of the sun'.[120]

In sacrificing their own desires, both Stephen and Isabel are, in common with Thurston's characters before them, able to reach a point of moral absolution. The novel's ending often disappointed English commentators, one of whom suggested that Isabel's 'convenient suicide' was 'wildly unconvincing' and that '[o]ne might have swallowed it better from the stupid wife'.[121] The verdict from Irish and Catholic publications was, however, consistently more positive. The *Waterford Herald* reviewed it at length and judged it a superlative effort, and the *Catholic Herald*, after briefly expressing its reservations about an author who believed her characters to be 'mere helpless straw[s] of the strong waters of the current of fatalism, driven in spite of all effort of will towards the maelstrom of the illicit', found far more in Thurston's work to praise than to blame: 'The presiding powers in Irish literature, such as Father Russell, of Dublin, have long sighed for an Irish story reproducing the middle-class life of the Irish provincial town. Here it is at last, fully, adequately'.[122] The advocacy of Thurston's novel from Irish and Catholic quarters is surprising given that it is a text which is openly critical of Ireland and ultimately pessimistic about the country's prospects for change: Tom Norris's nationalist arguments continue to be ridiculed, Stephen Carey's marriage remains an unsatisfactory and unhappy union, and Isabel Costello's rebellions have

---

119   Thurston, *The Fly on the Wheel*, 64.
120   Thurston, *The Fly on the Wheel*, 327.
121   Clipping from *Hearth and Home* (25 April 1908), n.p., Thurston Papers, NLS, 11378/10.
122   Clipping from the *Waterford Herald* (26 March 1908), n.p. and clipping from the *Catholic Herald* (16 May 1908), n.p., Thurston Papers, NLS, 11378/10.

achieved nothing but her own annihilation by the close of the book. In Father James's words, '[t]is easier to bridge hell than to bridge life' in a community such as the Waterford that Thurston portrays in *The Fly on the Wheel*.[123] It must be remembered, however, that it is also a novel in which tradition is (however regrettably) upheld, devotion to family is shown to be of paramount importance, and the priest is all-powerful. It is therefore a text which not only challenges, but also emphasizes the centrality of, precisely the types of values that conservative Irish Catholics embraced. It might also be persuasively argued that Thurston left herself with no other choice of an ending: for a penniless, morally compromised young woman in Waterford as Thurston depicts it, few if any viable methods of escape other than death are imaginable.

Like Thurston's evocation in *The Fly on the Wheel* of a woman more openly rebellious than the men who surround her, George Egerton's female characters are rarely the self-effacing, self-immolating heroines that so often populated the fiction of her contemporaries. She would assert in *Keynotes* that she believed women to be '[h]ermaphrodite by force of circumstances. Deformed results of a fight of centuries between physical suppression and natural impulse to fulfil our destiny'.[124] The sentiments of the same types of 'half creatures' to which Egerton refers are evoked in the words of Thurston's female characters, who consistently wish to live life in the same manner and governed by the same rules as men.[125] Thurston's resolve, in her final novel, *Max*, to create a female character able to live successfully as a man, and in the process to pursue the freedoms of a masculine existence, represents the apotheosis of the types of feminist ideas Egerton propounded. While the central device of the novel is the hero[ine]'s transcendence of his/her sexual identity, it is equally important to Thurston's fictional purposes that her character belongs to no particular nation – that Max/Maxine lives as a 'citizen of a free world'.[126]

123 Thurston, *The Fly on the Wheel*, 282.
124 Egerton, *Keynotes and Discords*, 41.
125 Egerton, *Keynotes and Discords*, 41.
126 Thurston, *Max*, 68.

In the novel, a young Russian princess escapes her homeland and impending marriage to an abusive man and travels to Paris disguised in men's clothing. On board the train taking her to France, she meets an Irishman, Ned Blake, who becomes her closest ally in her new life. Her true gender is unknown to anyone, including Blake, and she determines to live her life in Paris wholly as a man, in order that she may be permitted to pursue a career as an artist. Within days of arriving at her destination, the princess, now known as 'Max', settles in an apartment of her own to live among the bohemians of Montmartre. Blake provides her with a comprehensive introduction to Parisian life, and through him she experiences both the high and low cultures of the city.

Although Max's exploits on the seamier side of Paris are among the most skilfully evoked passages in the novel, the reservations Thurston's publisher, William Blackwood, expressed about them confirm that her subject matter was venturing into more controversial fictional territory than that of her previous novels. About one of these passages, Blackwood complained to Thurston:

> [t]he atmosphere of the whole Chapter was more or less objectionable to me. I admit the necessity for the touch of realism if your story is to have a convincing background. Unfortunately it is just this essential which raises a doubt in my mind, and obliges me to postpone a decision regarding its serial issue.[127]

Thurston consistently argued with Blackwood over the course of the novel's genesis about its scenes and characterizations, and was determined to write it according to her own principles. So resolute was she to render her portrait of belle époque Paris convincingly that, for the purpose of research, she had undertaken to visit many of the 'objectionable' establishments she depicts, including the cabaret Le Bal Tabarin and the nightclub Café du Rat Mort.[128] For his part, Blackwood would eventually inform Thurston that

---

127 Letter from William Blackwood to Thurston (20 January 1909), Thurston Papers, NLS, 11378/1.

128 See souvenirs and programmes from Le Bal Tabarin and Café du Rat Mort, Thurston Papers, NLS, 11378/1.

the book was 'evolved on lines, and is of a nature, which does not enable me to use it in my magazine.'[129] This rejection from her longstanding and principal publisher in Britain must have come as a blow, but could hardly have been surprising. *Blackwood's* was a magazine with a largely middle class and conservative readership, and an avowedly Tory political agenda.

Thurston had not only researched her settings, but had also studied her subject matter, and throughout 1909 and 1910 amassed a collection of documents about women who had lived successfully as men. Among the stories she accumulated were articles about the practice in France of licensing women to dress as men and various newspaper pieces and commemorative postcards concerned with successful tales of male impersonation.[130] The premise of the novel, therefore, was one that Thurston knew to be within the realm of possibility, and she constructs her narrative in a way that suggests that Max is consistently able to convince other characters – including Ned Blake, who remains unaware of Max's biological sex until the novel's closing pages – that he/she is male. Yet the tension between the character's masculine appearance and his/her underlying femininity is consistently and readily apparent. The degree to which the slippage in Max's performance of masculinity is made evident in the novel suggests that it was Thurston's intention, as one contemporary reviewer suggested, to portray 'the temperament of a woman showing through the raiment of a man'.[131] For some commentators, this tactic constituted a severe narrative defect. A reviewer in the *New York Post*, for example, offered a cynical but fundamentally accurate summation of Thurston's characterization:

> a girl who passes herself off as her own twin brother is a new engine of mystification [...] it is her ambition to 'possess herself', to remain independent of authority [...] Of course, there is a man in Paris who is destined to wreck this ambition: an Irishman of

129 Letter from William Blackwood to Thurston (24 July 1909), Thurston Papers, NLS, 11378/1.
130 See clipping 'Licensed to Dress as Men', unidentified newspaper, n.p., n.d., clipping from the Otago (New Zealand) *Witness* (28 April 1909), n.p., and postcards of 'Amy Bock, The Female Bridegroom', Thurston Papers, NLS, 11378/2.
131 Clipping from the *Philadelphia Inquirer* (17 October 1910), n.p., Thurston Papers, NLS, 11378/10.

the world, nearly middle-aged, who has never really loved. A quick intimacy springs up between this gentleman and the so-called 'Max.' If that young person's speech and action are correctly reported, it is hard to see how any man of ordinary intelligence could have failed to see through the disguise.[132]

As this review indicates, Thurston's Max careers wildly from assertions of independence and the espousal of unconventional philosophies about gender relations to the most stereotypically feminine of behaviours. His typical response to Blake's disapproval is to seek reassurances in language that lends a distinct homoerotic undertone to the narrative: 'Oh, *mon cher*!' Max implores Blake on one occasion, 'Forgive me! Forgive me! Say I am still your boy!'[133] When, towards the end of the novel, Blake becomes romantically obsessed with a painting of Maxine (a self-portrait of Max in feminine clothing), Max is moved to confront him in a manner which reveals an overt jealousy: 'I have given you my friendship – my heart and my mind, but I am not sufficient to you? Something more is required – something else – something different! [...] Why? Because I am a boy – she a woman!'[134] Max's transvestism becomes at this point more akin to transgenderism, and through the obvious and growing attraction between him and Blake which disturbs and queries heterosexual norms, Thurston veers conspicuously close to portraying same sex desire.

    Max is the only of Thurston's novels that she avowed (privately) to have had a very personal point of genesis. In her letters, she confirms that the book was intended as a tribute to her fiancé, Alfred Bulkeley Gavin, and that the burgeoning affections between the artistic Max and the more prosaic Blake, from friendship to romantic love, was an evocation of their own relationship. 'If ever book belonged to human being this book is yours', she wrote to Gavin in August of 1910, 'undedicated though it will be, every word, every thought in it is of you, inspired by you and yours absolutely'.[135]

---

132   See clipping from the *New York Post* (26 November 1910), n.p., Thurston Papers, NLS, 11378/10.

133   Thurston, *Max*, 226.

134   Thurston, *Max*, 223.

135   Letter from Thurston to Gavin (31 August 1910), Thurston Papers, NLS, 11378/12.

But to thus align Thurston with the character of Max/Maxine and Gavin with Ned Blake is not as straightforward a task as it may at first seem. It is in fact the case that, in 1909, she had believed so strongly that Gavin was homosexual and infatuated with one of his patients that she attempted to end their relationship. Her fiancé responded to her concerns with a nine-page letter in which he asserted his devotion in terms that are, at various points, less than reassuring: 'in defence or in explanation,' Gavin wrote, '[the patient in question] makes no pretence of being anything else than the most ardent "Homo" –, having passed through in his short life the most flagrantly "Kampy" life, and possessing a nature which he specifically states could never be faithful so that even were I the creature you fear I should find no consolation in that quarter'.[136] Although she was appeased by his subsequent protestations of love for her, she would afterwards refer to their relationship in terms that suggest it was based on a form of gendered role reversal and later hinted at her acceptance of his interest in other men. During the composition of her final novel she bestowed on Gavin the telling nickname of 'my little Max' and in the following year would suggest in a cryptic missive that she had met someone who would interest him: 'a boy from Glengarriff, who is, I am sure, of the other persuasion'.[137]

There are also among *Max*'s pages repeated and significant aphorisms, predominantly voiced by Max, which suggest that Thurston had as much of a public as a personal agenda in writing it. Throughout, the importance of liberation from the limitations of both country and sex are conveyed in references to the ways in which 'the individuality of the boy was submerged in his ambition; he belonged to no country, to no sex' and Maxine's assertions at the end of the novel, which echo those of Egerton's Mary Desmond, that she 'will belong to no one. I must possess myself'.[138] Although by the end of the novel Max – now Maxine – admits to being in love with Blake, she continues to resist his romantic overtures because she

136 Letter from Gavin to Thurston (13 September 1909), Thurston Papers, NLS, 11378/11.
137 See letters from Thurston to Gavin (April/May 1910 and 16 May 1911), Thurston Papers, 11378/12.
138 Thurston, *Max*, 64; 324.

fears that choosing a life with him will mean forsaking her life as an artist, and, more importantly, her freedom as a female to live independently and unconventionally: 'I refuse to be entrapped!' she tells him, 'I know love – I know all the specious things that love can say; the talk of independence, the talk of equality! But I know the reality, too. The reality is the absolute annihilation of the woman – the absolute merging of her identity'.[139] Most importantly, Max exposes as social constructs the restrictions placed on her because of her sex and refutes their validity: 'I made myself a man, not for a whim, but as a symbol. Sex is only an accident, but the world has made man the independent creature – and I desired independence'.[140]

Despite the litany of challenges it presented to gendered norms and regardless of William Blackwood's attendant reservations, *Max* largely avoided controversy. Few reviewers on either side of the Atlantic deemed its subject matter objectionable.[141] This is almost certainly due to the fact that, by the close of the narrative, Maxine has succumbed to the lure of the traditional fairy tale ending through her act of entreating Blake to '[t]ake me away to your castle, like the princess of old'.[142] Through Maxine's acquiescence to a feminine paradigm and reversion to her previous identity – the princess she once was – Thurston constructs a conclusion that reads as an uneasy compromise between the society she is able to imagine and the one which exists. Like its predecessor, *Max* represents the struggle to achieve personal freedom against the overwhelming disapproval of wider society. Unlike Isabel in *The Fly on the Wheel*, however, Maxine is able to countenance both a life lived within the confines of the conventionally acceptable, and a life to be lived out in Blake's native Ireland.

139   Thurston, *Max*, 326.

140   Thurston, *Max*, 325.

141   See, for example, clippings from the *Philadelphia Inquirer* (17 October 1910), n.p.; the *Boston Herald* (24 September 1910), n.p.; and the *Chicago Journal* (25 November 1910), n.p. For an overview of responses to the novel in the English press, see clipping from the *New York Herald* (22 October 1910), n.p. All Thurston Papers, NLS, 11378/10.

142   Thurston, *Max*, 338.

George Egerton and Katherine Cecil Thurston shared a vision of repressed female existence which was intensified within Ireland. Egerton clung to the subject of women, despite the detriment doing so posed to her career, because it was through altered concepts of womanhood and the power inherent in maternity that she believed society might be restructured along the lines she imagined. Her critique of the existing social order and a striving towards the 'new' in the form of altered ideas not only of women, but also of men, lingered on in her fiction after the downfall of the New Women. Her reluctance to publish any of her work after 1905 resulted from growing critical and public antipathy to her chosen themes, and she would write only a handful of short stories and plays – staged but for the most part commercially unsuccessful – after her publishing career was over.

Thurston's career was cut short by her premature death, at the age of 36, on 5 September 1911 at Moore's Hotel in Cork, a week before her scheduled wedding to Gavin. The official verdict was death due to asphyxiation caused by an epileptic seizure, yet scandal continued to plague her even posthumously. Almost immediately, the opinions of the coroner were discounted and the possibility of suicide raised, a rumour which still circulates in, among other places, the *Oxford Dictionary of National Biography*.[143] The *Irish Independent* has suggested a different scenario, reporting that stories handed down through Thurston's family indicate 'that she was poisoned, or at least medically overdosed, by the English doctor to whom she was engaged'.[144] The theory that her death was a suicide is particularly difficult to discount. Her final letter to Gavin, for instance, which was written the day before she died, is curiously anticipatory of her fate:

> I have been put to the test many times in this last month by feeling badly – and also by hearing my illness [epilepsy] discussed in others in a way – I mean with a

143 G. S. Woods, 'Thurston, Katherine Cecil (1875–1911)', rev. Sayoni Basu, *Oxford Dictionary of National Biography*, Oxford University Press, 2004 [<http://www.oxforddnb.com/view/article/36521> accessed 28 July 2014].

144 Declan McCormack, 'The Butterfly on the Wheel, *Irish Independent Online* (24 September 2000), <http://www.independent.ie/unsorted/features/the-butterfly-on-the-wheel-516190.htm> accessed 30 July 2014.

frequency – that was extraordinary [...] One case was truly dreadful, and happened
in Ardmore the day before I left – A poor wretched boy, left alone in a cottage, got
ill, fell into one of those open fires, and was found some long time afterwards with
his whole face – eyes, nose and ears – burnt beyond hope of cure – (*I beg you not
to let this conjure up fear for me*). These things give me no sense of fear. I feel that
everything in the world is meant.[145]

Others among her personal papers only add to the mystery. Deeply moved
by her first reading of Wilde's *De Profundis* (1905) in the weeks before she
died, Thurston was increasingly preoccupied by the idea of her own death.
In response to concerns she expressed at that time, Basil Wilberforce, the
Archdeacon of Westminster, forwarded to her two printed copies of the
poem 'Wishes About Death' by F. W. Faber which included the lines: 'Lord,
I have a death to die,/And not a death to choose'.[146] Her planned remarriage had resulted, meanwhile, not only in her estrangement from her Irish
family, but also from her trusted long-term housekeeper, 'Nelson', who had
recently left her employ after learning the true nature of her relationship
with Gavin.[147] Although she considered Nelson's indignant response to
learning of their affair to be a form of reverse class snobbery, and initially
convinced herself that 'the questions of scandal must be only in the servant
world', rumours that her liaison had predated her divorce quickly spread
among her Irish friends, and their reactions soon proved all too similar to
her housekeeper's.[148] On the day that she died, she was unaccompanied in
her hotel room in Cork, having for the first time declined to hire a personal
maid. Alone, divided from her family, worried about her reputation, fear-
ing the consequences of an epileptic episode and perhaps still harbouring
misgivings about Gavin's sexual orientation, Thurston may well have been
driven to suicide.

Whatever the circumstances of her death, distance from Ireland and the
risks she had felt able to take as a willing exile resulted in artistic dividends.

---

145 Letter from Thurston to Gavin (4 September 1911), Thurston Papers, NLS, 11378/12.
146 Professionally printed copies of poem on white cardstock contained in envelope
     postmarked August 1911 (day indecipherable), Thurston Papers, NLS, 11378/11.
147 Letter from Thurston to Gavin (10 August 1911), Thurston Papers, NLS, 11378/12.
148 Letter from Thurston to Gavin (10 August 1911), Thurston Papers, NLS, 11378/12.

In an article published two weeks after she died, one of the earliest proponents of her work, Nano Harris Walker, was moved to wonder whether Thurston might have gone on to become one of her country's most notable chroniclers had she lived: 'Can Ireland, in the death of Mrs Thurston,' Walker queried, 'have lost a novelist who, in process of evolution, would have devoted her talents to stories of the life and circumstances of its people? The reality, the interest, and the almost Balzacian atmosphere of "The Fly on the Wheel" makes one ask the question.'[149] Clodagh Asshlin waiting to be taken away from Ireland in the closing passages of *The Gambler* and Isabel Costello drinking the poisoned wine rather than agreeing to live by Waterford's standards reinforce the notion that, for Thurston, Ireland was a place to be transcended rather than yielded to; that, because she was a woman, her outlook was necessarily internationalist rather than nationalist. The fact that her novels dealt increasingly with Irish characters and/or Irish settings as her career progressed also suggests, however, that the more she distanced herself from Ireland, the more she imaginatively returned to it. Her final novel may be devoid of any Irish settings, yet in it she constructs a fantasy version of Ireland which belies her own reality – one in which it appears that the woman will be able to live an independent artistic existence in spite (or even because) of deciding to live out her life in Ireland.

Years after Egerton's career had ended, she would discover her closest allies among the new generation of Irish literary men, including Austin Clarke and Seumas O'Sullivan, who were to become her regular correspondents. Late in her life she would also return to writing, choosing Irish topics for a series of short stories that Clarke admired and O'Sullivan viewed with what bordered on reverence: 'I cannot pay any higher compliment to the author of "the Two Dans" than to say that I found the reading of the latter portion extremely painful,' O'Sullivan wrote to Egerton in 1938 concerning a story she had set during the Easter Rising, '[y]ou have with a skill little short of miraculous re-created the atmosphere of the places you describe and (this, I think is still more wonderful) reproduced the reactions of the

---

149   Nano Harris Walker, *T. P.'s Weekly* 18/463 (22 September 1911), 356.

crowd with a fidelity and accuracy which are beyond praise'.[150] Egerton's correspondence confirms that, to the end of her life, her reading consisted largely of Irish authors and her political interest was almost solely in Irish topics. She would nevertheless refuse O'Sullivan's requests to publish her recollections of Ireland and any of her late-life Irish stories, a type of protest she maintained against the publishing industry, De Vere White indicates, because she felt she had been judged more harshly than Ireland's male writers.[151] She died in Ifield, Sussex in 1945, having published no new work for the last four decades of her life, and having not set foot in Ireland for thirty-seven years.

By the time they came to write their Irish novels, both Egerton and Thurston had already enacted their own escapes from Ireland. Both demonstrated a tendency towards the unconventional and the controversial in their fictions; each would envision heroines who strayed outside the realms of social conformity and conventional morality. As such, the act of leaving Ireland is not portrayed in their novels as a regrettable financial imperative or a process of forcefully cleaving the woman from her rightful home, but as a necessary path to be taken in order to achieve personal fulfilment. In this, both authors appear to have been ahead of their time. Like many commentators on the changing roles of women in Irish society over the course of the twentieth century, James H. Murphy has asserted that Ireland increasingly became, after the formation of the Free State in 1922, a country 'in which for the most part women were denied independence and articulation'.[152] Gerard Leavey's research has also confirmed that, by the 1980s, many Irish women were referring to their migration from Ireland as a means to escape 'claustrophic and depressing existence[s]', and

150   See Clarke, *A Penny in the Clouds*, 178 and letter from Seumas O'Sullivan to Egerton
        (14 July 1938), Bright Papers, Princeton 1/51.
151   De Vere White, *A Leaf from the Yellow Book*, 178.
152   James H. Murphy, '"Things Which Seem to You Unfeminine": Gender and
        Nationalism in the Fiction of Some Upper Middle Class Catholic Women Novelists,
        1880–1910', in Kathryn J. Kirkpatrick, ed., *Border Crossings: Irish Women Writers
        and National Identities* (Tuscaloosa and London: The University of Alabama Press,
        2000), 77.

Tony Murray has indicated that these types of attitudes towards migration were echoed in the themes of Irish female writers whose work emerged in the latter half of the twentieth century, including Edna O'Brien and Sara Berkeley.[153] It is therefore evident that the novels of George Egerton and Katherine Cecil Thurston offer important and compelling presentiments of what lay ahead for Irish women when their country began increasingly to define itself, after independence, as a Catholic nation. It is also apparent that Egerton's and Thurston's work anticipates the literary preoccupations of later Irish women precisely because the moral censure they experienced in their own lives anticipated the restricted existences of future generations of women in Ireland.

153   Leavey quoted in Murray, *London Irish Fictions*, 7.

CHAPTER 4

'Your Dream-Ireland Does Not Exist': M. E. Francis, Catholicism, and the Irish Literary Establishment

> With all their love for Ireland, they do not seem to us to give to their readers a sufficiently bright and amiable idea of our dear country, and our dear people. They exaggerate, and, therefore, deform. As a matter of fact, we are very like other people, only nicer.
>
> — FATHER MATTHEW RUSSELL, 'Notes on New Books,' *Irish Monthly* (1890)[1]

> All these vague, poetical, romantic ideas go for nothing – your dream-Ireland does not exist.
>
> — M. E. FRANCIS, *Miss Erin* (1898)[2]

Thirty-five years into the lengthy publishing career of M. E. Francis (Mary Sweetman Blundell, 1859–1930), a commentator in the *Athenaeum* would note that the author had 'her special themes, which reappear, with more or less regularity, in each successive novel, notably dialect (of one sort or another) and the Roman Catholic religion.'[3] It is a comment resolutely in keeping with the reputation that Francis forged over the course of her writing life. She first came to prominence as a chronicler of rural Lancashire, the home she had adopted after her marriage. Her name would subsequently

---

1   Matthew Russell, 'Notes on New Books,' *Irish Monthly* 18/209 (November 1890), 614.
2   M. E. Francis, *Miss Erin* (New York, Cincinnati, Chicago: Benziger Brothers, 1898), 69–70.
3   'Novels in Brief,' *Athenaeum* 4706 (9 July 1920), 52.

become synonymous with Dorset, where she had come to live in the middle of her life and in which many of her most popular novels were set. So much so was she identified with the latter that in 1918 the Society of Dorset Men in London named her as one of only two sanctioned 'Dorset novelists'. The other was Thomas Hardy.[4] Like Hardy, whose work she greatly admired, Francis could be an exceptional chronicler of a specific place and time.[5] Unlike him, she often wrote lighthearted tales with predominantly contemporary settings in many and varied locales. Not only Lancashire and Dorset, but also Wales, Belgium, Switzerland and Hungary would figure as locations for her fiction, and she knew each of these by residence. Often and aptly compared in her day to writers such as Elizabeth Gaskell and George Eliot for her intuitive evocations of character, Francis also had a distinct capacity for inserting a moral message into her tales with little or no reversion to the overt didacticism that infected the works of many of her contemporaries in Britain. Her native land was not England, however, but Ireland, and although she would write five novels and countless short stories with Irish characters, settings and themes, she would never be linked to Irish literature as she had been to that of Dorset and Lancashire, nor would she achieve the degree of prominence with the Irish reading public that she enjoyed in her adoptive homeland.

Yet her novels – at times replete with Catholic characters, always infused with Catholic values – held particular interest for several high profile commentators, particularly in her native country, who shared her faith. Throughout her writing life, she received significant advocacy from Catholic quarters, and counted two of the period's foremost analysts of Irish literature – Father Matthew Russell and Father Stephen J. Brown, both Jesuits – among the earliest and staunchest promoters of her work. In articles they were to write in the first decades of the twentieth century,

---

4   *The Dorset Year-Book* (1919), pamphlet published by The Society of Dorset-Men in London, n.p. Held in the private collection of Mark Blundell, Crosby Hall Estate, Little Crosby.

5   Francis referred to the 'essential quality which marks out Mr Hardy's work from that of all other writers, which is unattainable, unapproachable, by any of his host of followers'. See M. E. Francis, 'Flowers in Fiction', *Academy* 1717 (1 April 1905), 362.

both Russell and Brown would lament the tendency among the Irish literary establishment to overlook her work in preference for that produced by the (predominantly Protestant) Revivalists. Whether or not, in doing so, they were suggesting that the overtly Catholic themes of her fiction accounted for this neglect, the implication was that the work of Irish Protestant writers was being favoured over the work of Irish Catholics.

It was in 1910 that Russell, the editor of the *Irish Monthly*, a literary magazine owned and run by the Society of Jesus, was moved to write an article objecting to the consistent and, in his view, lamentable exclusion of Catholic women from the Irish Literary Society's roster of notable authors. With little introduction or explanation, in 'The Literary Output of Three Irish-Women' Russell offered his readers an extensive list of works by Rosa Mulholland, Katharine Tynan and M. E. Francis, the writers he felt most ably justified his indignation, before summing up his argument thus:

> In none of these three instances have I furnished an exhaustive catalogue up to date. Is it not a splendid record of work? Yet these three Irishwomen were never named by the Rev. J. O. Hannah ('George Bermingham') in a lecture on Irish Novelists in the Irish Literary Society, 6 Stephen's Green, Dublin, and the omission provoked no protest from Mr John Dillon, M. P., and the other speakers who thanked the Lecturer.[6]

The fact that Russell felt it incumbent upon himself to include the full address of the Irish Literary Society's Dublin headquarters and to mention two of its speakers by name suggests that he himself was attempting to provoke a protest among his readers.

Two years later, Brown was inspired to pen 'The Question of Irish Nationality' for a fellow Jesuit publication, *Studies*, just as the idea of a third Home Rule Bill for Ireland was being mooted in Parliament. Brown's article was unambiguously pro-Home Rule in its mission, for in it he asserted not only that Ireland had always been its own nation, separate and distinct from England, but also that this tacit fact should be made legally and politically binding. A well-known nationalist, Brown's views would hardly have come

---

6   Matthew Russell, 'The Literary Output of Three Irish-Women', *Irish Monthly*, 38/442 (April 1910), 202.

as a surprise to *Studies'* preponderantly Irish Catholic readership, and his purpose in writing it – in preaching to the converted, so to speak – is less than transparent until he turns to the topic of literature, at which point his argument becomes an exercise in promoting novels by Irish expatriates in England as the most effective forms of pro-nationalist political propaganda: the contrast between the two nations, he argues, had 'been best drawn in the form of fiction' by 'writers [who] know both countries by long residence'.[7] Proceeding to offer a brief list of those works which best exemplified his contentions, he included books by two of the authors, Tynan and Francis, who had earned Russell's earlier advocacy. In doing so, he specifically set Catholic authors – who, he was careful to mention, share 'the religion which three-fourths of the Irish people of to-day profess' – in direct opposition to the Revivalists. While they undoubtedly had produced 'much beautiful literature', the Revivalists had not, Brown claimed, 'mirrored in their writings the actual Ireland of to-day'.[8]

In many ways the sponsorship Francis earned from these particular analysts is unsurprising, for her identity, even more so than resolutely Catholic contemporaries such as Mulholland and Tynan, was defined by her religion. The second daughter and third child of Michael James and Margaret Powell Sweetman, Francis was born into a Catholic family whose fortunes on both her paternal and maternal sides had been made in the brewing industry, and it was the case that the combination of her family's religious and financial statuses meant that her upbringing in Ireland afforded little opportunity for wider social interaction. In his research into Ireland's Catholic elite, Ciaran O'Neill has noted that, even among the relatively small numbers of Catholic families of fortune which existed in nineteenth-century Ireland, those who had made their money in the brewing and distilling industries were often derided as new money 'whiskey people'.[9] At the same time, their apparent acquiescence to a capitalist,

7   Stephen J. Brown, 'The Question of Irish Nationality', *Studies: An Irish Quarterly Review* 1/4 (December 1912), 645.
8   Brown, 'The Question of Irish Nationality', 651–652.
9   Ciaran O'Neill, *Catholics of Consequence: Transnational Education, Social Mobility, and the Irish Catholic Elite 1850–1900* (Oxford: Oxford University Press, 2014), 140.

industrialist ethos left them open to accusations of being 'West Britons'.[10] As heiress to the Powell brewing fortune, Francis's mother came into her marriage with the financial resources to purchase an estate of more than a thousand acres, Lamberton Park, in a sparsely populated district near Maryborough (Portlaoise) in current County Laois, many miles from the homes of the extended Sweetman family in Dublin, Meath and Kildare.[11] Francis's father died in 1864, and her brothers – one the oldest and the other the youngest in the family – were sent away to school at early ages. The convergence of all these factors meant that Francis's upbringing in Ireland was conspicuously insular: she freely admitted that the first twelve years of her life were spent almost solely in the company of the females of her family (and a bevy of servants) in what she presents in her 1918 memoir, *The Things of a Child*, as a form of happy seclusion.[12]

A key instigation for a change in her living circumstances occurred when, for a brief spell, she and two of her sisters attended a Dublin convent boarding school. This was to be an ill-fated educational experiment that was abruptly (and, in Francis's re-telling of it, humorously) truncated when it was discovered that the girls had developed a 'flat brogue' – 'the Irish parent's standing terror' – among the mostly middle class student population there.[13] In large part because of this experience, she and her sisters were relocated to Brussels, where their brothers were already studying, for the purposes of obtaining a more suitably elite Catholic education. From the time that she was 12, Francis's social circle therefore widened markedly, but she continued to live and move almost exclusively among upper

10 O'Neill, *Catholics of Consequence*, 17.

11 Margaret Sweetman Powell was also the owner of a 1,000-acre estate in Meath. See U. H. Hussey de Burgh, *The Landowners of Ireland* (Dublin: Hodges, Foster and Figgis, 1878), 435.

12 Her three sisters were Gertrude, Elinor and Agnes. Of the three, Elinor and Agnes (the latter under her married surname, 'Castle') would also become professional writers.

13 M. E. Francis, *The Things of a Child* (London: Collins, 1918), 289 and 'A Mid-Victorian Home in Ireland', *Saturday Review of Politics, Literature and Art* 125/3268 (15 June 1918), 535.

class Catholics. Over the course of her upbringing her family appear to have gradually aligned themselves more closely with an international, elite Catholic society than they did with a nation-based Catholic community which transcended social classes, and her own recounting of her experiences both in Brussels and in Ireland during her teenage years bears this idea out. Once in Belgium, she and her sisters were, each in their turn, presented as debutantes before the Belgian royal family at the Bal de la Cour (the Royal Court Ball), and their closest friends were prominent Catholics from a range of European countries including the pianist and composer Jan Ignacy Paderewski, later Prime Minister of Poland, and Sophie Chotek von Chotkova – 'the heroine of the tragedy of Sarajevo' – who would go on to marry the Austrian Archduke Franz Ferdinand and, in 1914, would be assassinated at his side in the most significant of the events which led to the First World War.[14] On their regular summer return to Ireland, however, the Sweetman sisters continued to find themselves in a space of social isolation. An indication of Francis's disparaging attitudes at that time towards at least some of the Irish people with whom her family associated can be glimpsed in her unpublished memoir, in which she recalls a visit to the family home of a friend of her mother's. In a failed matchmaking exercise, she found herself frequently in the company of one son of the family, who she describes as having a brogue 'so emphatic' that she 'could not help laughing' at him when he told her an anecdote. She mentions, too, that, upon her return to Lamberton, she entertained her family by impersonating him.[15]

It was in Brussels that she met Josephine Blundell, a fellow schoolgirl whose family owned an estate in what was then Lancashire (now Merseyside), and eventually made the acquaintance of Josephine's older brother, Francis 'Tansy' Blundell, who she would go on to marry on

---

14   See M. E. Francis, unpublished memoir, chapters XI and XII, held in the private collection of Mark Blundell, Crosby Hall, and Francis, unpublished memoir, 20–21, Blundell collection. Paderewski would remain a friend of the family for decades. See 'Funerals', *The Times* (London) (12 October 1912), 9, in which it is mentioned that Paderewski sent flowers to Margaret Sweetman Powell's funeral.
15   See Francis, unpublished memoir, 38–39, Blundell collection.

12 November 1879. On that same day, Francis's work first appeared in print.[16] She and her husband settled near his family's English stately home, Crosby Hall, in Little Crosby, a village which had been populated exclusively by Catholics since the Reformation, and where, the locals averred, 'there [was] not a Protestant, a public house, or a policeman.'[17] The Blundell family were recusants who had fought long and hard to retain both their religion and their property. As the daughter-in-law of the Squire of Crosby Hall, Francis found herself living once more in a position of social seclusion, in which her neighbours shared her religion but not her class status. Her marriage, meanwhile, was to be a happy but poignantly brief union. On the evening of 27 April 1884, Francis's husband died suddenly due to complications from an earlier illness.[18] In the immediate aftermath of his death, she and her three children took up residence at Crosby Hall. With family to support her but with little or no disposable income of her own, she soon found herself longing to achieve a modicum of financial independence, and this would become a prime motivating factor in her decision to pursue a literary career more vigorously from the late 1880s. It was with Father Matthew Russell's assistance that she was able to achieve the degree

---

16 Francis would claim that this first published story was titled 'Dame Grump and the Fairy Spectacles' and that it appeared in the *Irish Monthly*. R. W. Taylor's research confirms that the story published on the day of her marriage was, in fact, 'Dame Grump and the Tea Party' and appeared in the *Catholic Children's Magazine*. See R. W. Taylor, 'M. E. Francis: An Appreciation', in *In a North Country Village* (Wigan: Northwest Catholic History Society, 2008), xvi–xvii. Her second published work did, however, appear in the *Irish Monthly* just a month later. See M. B. [Mary Blundell], 'Through the Bars', *Irish Monthly*, 7 (1879), 639–649.

17 G. M. S. [Gertrude Sweetman], 'M. E. Francis', *Irish Monthly* 8/683 (May 1930), 235.

18 Francis and her husband were visiting her family at Longtown, Kildare when he died. Having left the estate to walk alone to an evening mass, Blundell collapsed after vaulting a wall. Local residents who witnessed the incident were unable to identify him, and there was therefore a delay in notifying the family of his death. Francis was heavily pregnant with their third child at the time and received no news of what had occurred until the following morning. She never remarried and wore mourning for the remaining forty-six years of her life. See Margaret Blundell, *An Irish Novelist's Own Story* (Dublin: Catholic Truth Society, n.y.), 27.

of financial independence she craved. In late 1888, Russell wrote to inform her that a serialized novel was required for the *Irish Monthly* and asked if she might be willing to take on the task. Though she had only a few weeks to produce her first installment, she agreed to Russell's proposal.

In what now reads as an affirmation of the sentiments that Virginia Woolf was to express decades later, Francis endured a series of hardships in the months that followed when she lacked both 'money and a room of her own'.[19] Crosby Hall was a vast stately home, yet despite its abundance of space she was forced to write the first segments of her novel in a room crowded with family members and pets. Due to economies necessitated by the profligacy of William Blundell, her brother-in-law and the heir to the estate, the home was largely unheated, causing the family to congregate in the few rooms in which fires were permitted. The incessant noise and frequent interruptions meant that her progress was at first slow and laboured. It was also little valued by the Blundell clan, whose own energies were most often expended in charitable and religious works. Francis would note the difficulties inherent in undertaking her task amidst both the noise engendered by, and the guilt inspired by, the constant whirring of a sewing machine employed in the making of garments for the parish poor.[20] Her recollections of the time suggest that writing was a pursuit for which she had little support or outward justification:

> I was young enough at that time to desire intensely to be taken seriously: Father Russell's cheque [a £15 advance for *Molly's Fortunes*] seemed to indicate that my 'scribblings' were really worth something, that I was doing actual *work*. [But] in spite of the hints which I dropped with a solemn face about the important nature of my new undertaking, and the inconvenience and confusion which must ensue if I did not deliver my copy in time, nobody would take me very seriously after all.[21]

There were other, more personal factors which tended to deter her from writing, as well. She admitted to Russell that 'the real true reason I do not like writing under my own name is that my dear husband did not fancy

19   Virginia Woolf, *A Room of One's Own/Three Guineas* (London: Penguin, 1993), 3.
20   M. E. Francis, 'Foreword', *Molly's Fortunes* (London: Sands, 1913), xii.
21   Francis, 'Foreword', *Molly's Fortunes*, x–xi.

it' and turned to her editor for guidance in dealing with the spiritually motivated guilt she felt concerning her literary pursuits:

> What is a constant drawback to my pleasure is the feeling that I am *too* much taken up with my work [...] I constantly remember that *no man can serve God & Mammon*, perhaps *this* is Mammon? What I want you to tell me is – and I know you will not mind some time sending me just a line one way or the other – might I make the effort to keep my *literary aspirations* for certain set times? [...] if God asks it of me I might make the sacrifice, and sometimes I feel as if He did.[22]

Out of a combination of necessity and shame, she soon began composing the monthly chapters of *Molly's Fortunes* in an unheated room in Crosby Hall which was employed as a store for mattresses. Having a private space in which to write, however inadequate it may have been, meant that she was able to submit each of her installments to Russell on time.

The novel which resulted was *Molly's Fortunes*, which ran in the *Irish Monthly* from February of 1889 to January of 1890. Its plot revolves around Molly Mackenzie, a young working class Irish woman who is a lady by nature if not by position. Molly is the only traceable descendant of Hugh O'Neill, a member of a landed family disowned for his participation in the 1798 Rebellion. Upon discovering her ancestry, Molly is thrown together with the elderly owner of Castle O'Neill, a woman who believes her to be the sole remaining heir to the estate. Miss O'Neill is at once a politically minded, reforming landlord and irremediably eccentric in some of her opinions.[23] So radical did Francis believe those opinions to be that she wrote to Russell on two occasions during the composition of the novel to divorce herself from them. 'I hope you will not object to Miss O'Neill's politics', she explained as the novel was beginning its run, 'I am only the dispassionate

22   Letters from Francis to Matthew Russell (16 November 1887 and 12 July n.y.), Papers of Father Matthew Russell, Jesuit Archive (Dublin), Folder J27/19.

23   Evidence in Francis's memoir suggests that her characterization of Miss O'Neill is closely based on a Sweetman cousin who lived at Longtown House in Kildare. See Francis, unpublished memoir, 27, Blundell collection.

chronicler, & am by no means responsible for them'.[24] Two months later she was again expressing the hope that 'my old lady's political views have not given offense in any quarter' and admitted to being 'alarmed' that some of her character's opinions had been mistaken by readers for her own.[25] Francis's apparent dismay is, however, suspect, for although many of Miss O'Neill's arguments are clearly meant to be seen as ludicrous, others are the most persuasively defended in the text. She shows the character asserting, for instance, that the current strain of Irish nationalism has been tainted by its own democratic principles – 'the scum is too likely to come to the surface – in former days the cream used to rise to the top' – and offers a litany of lucidly worded arguments to support Miss O'Neill's opinions that allowing the Irish people to govern themselves is a 'dangerous expedient'.[26] The level-headed and likeable Molly, meanwhile, is said to recognize both 'an under current of truth in much that [Miss O'Neill] said, an earnestness and sincerity', while finding some of the older woman's opinions 'palpably untenable'.[27] In failing to elucidate precisely which of Miss O'Neill's theories Molly deems accurate, which flawed, Francis constructs a literary manoeuvre of avoidance. While those (presumably very few) readers aware that the author of *Molly's Fortunes* came from a prominent brewing family would have been able to surmise that Miss O'Neill's harsh criticisms of Ireland's 'mushroom aristocracy' who had 'earned their fortunes from the beer-vat or the whiskey-still' were antagonistic to Francis's own viewpoints, elsewhere it is not a straightforward task to extract her own sentiments from the narrative evidence.[28]

In terms of its politics, it is a text which is particularly difficult to pin down precisely because it can be seen to advocate both sides of an argument at the same time: even as it seems to condone some of the anti-nationalist sentiments Francis ascribes to Miss O'Neill, the text also appears to sanction

24   Letter from M. E. Francis to Matthew Russell (30 January 1889), Russell Papers J27/19.
25   Letter from M. E. Francis to Matthew Russell (8 March 1889), Russell Papers J27/19.
26   M. E. Francis, *Molly's Fortunes* (London: Sands, 1913), 31; 30.
27   Francis, *Molly's Fortunes*, 35.
28   Francis, *Molly's Fortunes*, 32.

a form of Irish exclusivity that borders on Irish-Irelandism. England and the English are in fact mentioned only as a means of revealing prejudices against them. When, for example, Miss O'Neill learns that one of her former tenants is now working in Britain, she derides his mother for allowing him to leave Ireland in terms that defy the English civility/Irish savagery diametric stereotype. 'He will be picking up all sorts of strange customs, or marrying some low English girl,' Miss O'Neill asserts, 'and, mark my words, if he does that, you may say good-bye to him. I'll have no English settlers in *my* village'.[29] When at a later stage in the story's development an Irish-American man turns up to claim Castle O'Neill, Molly promptly rejects his offers of both marriage and financial assistance. This rejection, along with the American's subsequent ruinous management of the estate, reasserts a skepticism, evident until the novel's closing pages, about the introduction of outside influences to Ireland. Considering that conservative contemporary commentators, including both Lawless and Meade, promoted English and/or American sources as means of achieving pecuniary and political stability for Ireland, the fact that Francis ignores the former and effectively disparages the latter suggests that her text is advocating an independent, autonomous Ireland.

Francis's first novel sets the tone for all her Irish works in portraying Irish problems without envisioning their solutions. Yet of all her novels, *Molly's Fortunes* comes closest to suggesting that Ireland's woes are remediable, and that at least part of the cure may lie within its own borders. The character of Molly herself – working class by birth and aristocratic by nature – acts as a model for a space in which traditional social distinctions can be transcended. Occupying a position in which she often feels she has 'fall[en] between two stools', Molly is the instrument by which Francis exposes the eccentricities of both the class from which she is descended and the class in which she was raised, but she remains distinct from, and superior to, members of both.[30] In line with this, after the American claimant to Castle

29   Francis, *Molly's Fortunes*, 42.
30   Francis, *Molly's Fortunes*, 58.

O'Neill is discovered to be illegitimate, and entirely by her own efforts, Molly is able to return the estate to its former glory.

Considering what has gone before, Francis's decision to end the novel by marrying Molly to a penniless French nobleman descended from the elder (and therefore more legitimate) line of the O'Neill family appears to backtrack on an early revisionary promise. It is as though she either could not sustain her vision of a working class female successfully managing an Irish estate on her own, or could not foresee her reading public accepting such a vision. Molly's management of the property is also, in the end, only marginally more egalitarian than that of her predecessor, in whose image she is shown to willingly cast herself. If Castle O'Neill's hierarchy is no less feudalistic under the new order than it was under the old, however, the fact that its governance has been rendered stable by the union of aristocratic authority and democratic justice, as they are personified by the Baron de Sauvigny and Molly, strikes a minor note of subversion. Ultimately, however, what can be seen as most significant about her portrayal of adequate land management in Ireland is that, through the union of her Irish working class and French aristocratic characters, Francis may envision it as transcending class and national boundaries, but she offers no indication that it can span religious ones. The marriage that ends the novel and makes the estate's ownership unassailably legitimate is, in fact, a wholly Catholic alliance.

Francis's correspondence written between 1890 and 1892 confirms that, immediately following the run of *Molly's Fortunes*, she began writing two additional Irish novels, *The Story of Dan* (1894) and *Miss Erin* (1898). Her intent from the first therefore appears to have been to write widely on Irish topics, a tendency further evidenced by her early involvement in the Irish Literary Society in London.[31] Yet to Russell she would complain that publishers consistently objected 'to the Irish & Catholic elements in the books' and noted in March of 1893 'that just at this moment anything

---

31   William Patrick Ryan would later refer to her as one of the Literary Society's 'able Lady members who are apart from its actual sphere of work'. William Patrick Ryan, *The Irish Literary Revival* (New York: Lemma, 1970 [1894]), 117.

dealing with Ireland is rather unpopular'.[32] Her inference is that the second Home Rule Bill – which had only a month before been introduced in Parliament by Gladstone – was to blame for the reluctance by publishers to consider Irish-themed works. While her Irish stories languished, Francis instead mined the rich vein of inspiration around her at Crosby Hall and in the environs of Little Crosby. 'At present I am studying Lancashire dialect & character which I find more satisfactory [than their Irish equivalents] in every way,' she wrote to Russell in 1892. 'There is no bias for or against either, & one's literary wares have a chance of being judged on their own merits'.[33] *Whither?* (1892), the first of her full-length creations to be set in the Lancashire landscape she inhabited, was initially rejected by the publishers Griffith and Farran because they believed her fictional setting to be 'untrue to nature'. Undaunted, Francis urged a meeting and, once in their offices, was able to explain that her imaginary village, populated entirely by Roman Catholics and untouched by the Reformation, was in fact a very thinly concealed portrait of her adoptive hometown. Afterwards, she wrote excitedly to Russell to say that her interventions had resulted in the novel's acceptance: 'the Catholicity, which I thought would be so strongly objected to,' Francis confided, 'had become the chief attraction of the book'.[34]

Whither? was issued shortly thereafter and was widely and positively reviewed. Even William Patrick Ryan referred to it, in his otherwise dismissive account of Francis's contribution to the early Literary Renaissance, as a novel which had 'made a stir of no transient kind'.[35] It was closely followed by another and even more recognizable portrait of Little Crosby and its inhabitants, the short story collection *In a North Country Village* (1893), destined to become her most enduringly popular work. Like Elizabeth Gaskell's *Cranford* (1851) before it, it is a collection of tales of rural community life told with unmistakable affection and subtle humour, for which

32   Letter from M. E. Francis to Matthew Russell (13 March 1893), Russell Papers J27/19 and Letter from M. E. Francis to Matthew Russell (13 March 1893), Russell Papers J27/19.
33   Letter from Francis to Matthew Russell (26 July 1892), Russell Papers J27/19.
34   Letter from Francis to Matthew Russell (29 April 1892), Russell Papers J27/19.
35   Ryan, *The Irish Literary Revival*, 117.

Francis had a true gift. The reviews were overwhelmingly positive and among its professed admirers was Thomas Hardy.[36]

The earliest of Francis's Lancashire-set stories go far in revealing the discrepancies that would come to mark her fiction, a disparity in narrative tone and fictional preoccupation which was to be firmly demarcated along ethnic and national lines. Her Irish-set texts are, in fact, unique among her body of work for their depictions of suffering and the extent of their politicization. *Molly's Fortunes* is easily the least bleak of her Irish novels, yet in its pages she deals with issues of poverty, profligacy, illness and prejudice. *The Story of Dan* (1894) is a much more pessimistic creation altogether and, despite her longstanding friendship with Russell, it was promptly rejected when she sent the manuscript to the *Irish Monthly*.

There is no question that Russell's advocacy was an important factor in her literary success to that point in her career. It was also, however, double-edged. To his correspondents and the *Irish Monthly's* contributors, he made no secret of the fact that he believed Irish novelists should contribute only positive pictures of Ireland to the national literature and, more importantly, to their English neighbours. The majority of Irish authors, he admitted, therefore did not meet with his approval: 'With all their love for Ireland, they do not seem to us to give to their readers a sufficiently bright and amiable idea of our dear country, and our dear people. They exaggerate, and, therefore, deform. As a matter of fact, we are very like other people, only nicer.'[37] Russell objected to what he viewed as Francis's stereotypical portrait of rural Ireland in *The Story of Dan*, and was disappointed by the novel's overwhelming bleakness. Francis would in turn protest that, bar one, every character in the novel was based closely on real-life models from the Lamberton estate, and contended that the protagonist himself was

36   In a letter to Matthew Russell (24 March 1893), Francis relates that she has been told by the publishers of *The Story of Dan* (Osgood, McIlvaine) that 'Mr Thomas Hardy (whose last work is published by them) is "delighted with the North Country Village"'. The work of Hardy's that Francis refers to is *Tess of the D'Urbervilles* (1891). Russell Papers J27/19.

37   Matthew Russell, 'Notes on New Books', *Irish Monthly* 18/209 (November 1890), 614.

'in real life married to a woman years older than himself whom he adores, and little knows the tragedy he is at present marching – on paper.'[38] Yet Russell remained unconvinced. One of his severest criticisms was leveled at her representation of the Irish brogue, which he compared to that in Lawless's notorious *Hurrish* (1886). *Hurrish* had for years been vilified in Ireland for its depictions of the peasantry, and Russell's accusation evidently stung Francis deeply. 'I *am* a little horrified at being considered an imitator of *Hurrish*', she would respond, asserting in the process that Lawless's novel was her 'pet abomination!'[39]

Although she was said to be 'one of those rare beings who never had an enemy and never lost a friend', Francis could be seen to fight her corner when pressed, and did so repeatedly with Russell.[40] So strongly did she feel that her portrayals of Ireland and the Irish were defensible, and more particularly that the artistry and accuracy of her novels should not be sacrificed to sociological principles, that she would firmly voice her exceptions to his opinions concerning Irish literature: 'I do not at all agree with you in your theory that the *best* only should be put forward', she argued in 1893, 'I – in all humility – cannot see any advantage in a one-sided view, either of an individual, or a race. You must have shade as well as light in a picture, and literature will not be artistic without either.'[41] Rather than alter her creation to comply with Russell's demands, she began to market *Dan* elsewhere, eventually securing its publication with Osgood McIlvaine, a London house. It is an indication of her growing estrangement from the literary values that were being promoted in her homeland that not only did she begin to curtail her involvement with the Irish Literary Society at this juncture, but also, from the point of *The Story of Dan* forward, issued all her full-length works, Irish or otherwise, first in England.

She would admit to Russell afterwards that his criticism of her novel had marked something of a parting of the literary ways between them: 'I

38   Letter from Francis to Matthew Russell (14 August 1893), Russell Papers J27/19.
39   Letter from Francis to Matthew Russell (25 October 1893), Russell Papers J27/19.
40   Clipping, 'A Gifted Authoress, Mrs Francis Blundell (M. E. Francis): A Memory and an Appreciation', *Western Gazette* (Yeovil) (21 March 1930), n.p., Blundell collection.
41   Letter from Francis to Matthew Russell (7 November 1893), Russell Papers J27/19.

tell you the truth,' she wrote in 1894, 'I had privately resolved never to send you anything Irish again after your reception of "Dan"'. Francis had realized that, in her friend and editor's eyes, '"Paddy" apparently in any shape can do no wrong'.[42] Although she would renege on her own promise not to send Irish stories to Russell, she continued to express her chagrin when he censored their content or excised characters he deemed disagreeable, arguing that he would not have objected to these portrayals had her characters 'been English or Scotch'.[43]

If Russell's attitudes to Francis's novel can be seen to prefigure those that J. M. Synge's *The Playboy of the Western World* (1907) would later so famously instigate, *The Story of Dan*, plotted around a murder which pits the Irish peasantry against a devious and authoritarian 'law', also anticipates many of the themes in Synge's play. Like *The Playboy's* Pegeen Mike, Francis's central female character, Esther Daly, is a woman of changeable affections and dubious morality who discards Dan, her fiancé, for a less trustworthy man only recently arrived in their rural Irish village. When the other man is subsequently found murdered, the peasant inhabitants of the community are convinced of Dan's guilt, but their collective instinct is, much as in *Hurrish* before and *Playboy* after, to shelter him rather than cooperate with the investigating authorities. Dan's own 'dread of the law' reverberates through the community as a whole, the members of which are 'likely to share that clannish feeling which made them hang so closely together, and shrink with so much horror from the very notion of turning "informer"'.[44] Throughout, 'the law' looms as a menacing outsider to the community; a malevolent foreign force.

There, however, the similarities between Francis's and Synge's texts end, as she chooses to concentrate on themes of Irish ingenuousness rather than subterfuge. Dan is accused of the crime yet refuses to defend his innocence by revealing the truth not only because he mistrusts and misapprehends

---

42   Letter from Francis to Matthew Russell (4 July 1894), Russell Papers J27/19.
43   Letter from Francis to Matthew Russell (4 July 1894), Russell Papers J27/19.
44   M. E. Francis, *The Story of Dan* (Boston and New York: Houghton and Mifflin, 1894), 246; 255.

the law, but because he is protecting Esther's mentally disabled brother, who is the actual murderer. Dan's virtuousness, lack of worldly knowledge and willingness to trust those closest to him are figured as quintessentially Irish traits, and it is this 'unsophisticated, unreasoning Irish point of view' which in fact acts to exacerbate his appearance of guilt.[45] Esther, an aspiring social climber who fails to recognize that Dan is not only blameless of the murder but also actively shielding her from harm, is figured as the calculating antithesis to Francis's protagonist. The only person to break ranks and testify willingly against Dan at his trial, she is an aberration in the Irish working class community she inhabits. Her testimony, replete with exaggerations and untruths, is acceptable and even laudable in the eyes of the authorities, but becomes the novel's most heinous type of crime: one committed against a local version of morality. The novel ends with a guilty verdict and Dan's death: he collapses at the end of his trial and cannot be revived after realizing the depth of Esther's betrayal. The closing lines of the novel, spoken by the kindly priest who has known Dan all his life and is willing 'to swear that he had never lost his baptismal innocence', enact a specifically Catholic commentary on his fate: 'Hush!' the priest tells the coroner when he suggests that Dan's sudden death has been brought about by guilt and shame. 'Who are we that we should condemn him? Has he not passed beyond the reach of our faulty judgments to a higher Tribunal? Leave him to his God.'[46] The novel's ending affirms that it is a specifically Catholic form of judgment – that of 'his God' – which will ultimately prevail in Dan's case.

The Story of Dan was well reviewed by the press, but it remained less successful with the reading public than Francis's more lighthearted, English-set immediate predecessors: the Saturday Review noted, for instance, that, while it was written with 'skill and sympathy' it was also 'painful reading'.[47] Despite Dan's relatively poor reception, just a year after its publication

45   Francis, The Story of Dan, 281–282.
46   Francis, The Story of Dan, 290.
47   'Review. The Story of Dan. By M. E. Francis.' Saturday Review of Politics, Literature, Science and Art, 78/2038 (17 November 1894), 543.

Francis received what she would come to consider the most significant validation of her career when her novel *A Daughter of the Soil* was chosen as the first full-length work of fiction ever to be serialized in *The Times* (London).[48] *A Daughter of the Soil*, in its turn, was to have a reciprocally beneficial effect for the newspaper. The paper's editor, Charles Frederic Moberly Bell, noted in a letter to Francis 'that the weekly edition touched its highest circulation 35000 odd on the 15th Feb [1895]. When you began writing [the first installment of *A Daughter of the Soil*] it was under 20,000'.[49]

Popular as it seems to have been, Francis's novel was not, however, without its detractors, and Moberly Bell would also forward letters to her in which his readers expressed their indignation at 'the Times being used for the promulgation of Popery'.[50] Though these charges appeared ludicrous to Francis at the time, it is not difficult to locate the passages on which such claims were founded. Many of the conflicts in the novel are instigated by a clash of values between those embodied by its heroine – Ruth Sefton, a Lancashire farmer's daughter and Roman Catholic who has been refined by her education at a convent school – and the man she loves, Anthony Clifton, the profligate and atheistic heir to the local estate. Ruth remains steadfast in her love and innocent of any wrongdoing throughout the novel; Anthony, for his part, drinks, gambles, and womanizes his way through the plot, his moral transgressions extending as far as bigamy. Ruth's fondest wish is that Anthony become a Catholic, so that his soul might be saved: a feat achieved, at least metaphorically, when following an epiphany of self-loathing in which 'he could even believe that there *was* a God, and that he had betrayed Him', Anthony repents on Ruth's doorstep.[51] There, he is promptly forgiven and allowed to enter her house.

In reviewing the novel upon its formal publication, the *Times* praised it unequivocally as an anti-feminist, morally edifying text: Ruth Sefton is referred to in the review as 'the antitype of the New Woman' and the book

48   See 'M. E. Francis', *The Times* (London) (15 March 1930), 23.
49   Letter from C. F. Moberly Bell to Francis (27 March 1901), Blundell collection.
50   Letter from Francis to Matthew Russell (3 February 1895), Russell Papers J27/19.
51   Letter from Francis to Matthew Russell (3 February 1895), Russell Papers J27/19.

is regarded as leaving the reader 'better for the reading and more disposed to regard human nature as fundamentally good'.[52] In many respects the most Catholic of all her works, *A Daughter of the Soil* is not, however, an Irish novel. The next of these, *Miss Erin* (1898), would not appear for another three years. When she was composing it in 1897, Francis wrote Russell to express her excitement at the 'vista of infinite interests' her tale of a revolutionary Irishwoman afforded.[53] Confirming in the same letter that she intended the novel to deal 'in a dispassionate & impartial way with life, manners & policies in Ireland & England as may strike an unbiased observer', she also noted that she was planning to use the text of the speech made by Russell's brother, Sir Charles Russell, at the Parnell Commission hearings (in 1888–1889) as a template for the nationalist opinions of her heroine.[54] The most studied of all her works, *Miss Erin* has been interpreted persuasively by both James H. Murphy and Mary S. Pierse as a text in which the tenuous romantic alliance achieved between an English conservative politician and the book's Irish heroine at the novel's close reflects optimistically on the Hiberno-English political relationship: Murphy suggests that it 'offers a vision for a renewed Ireland' and Pierse that it hints at 'a new "Act of Union" with the possibility to re-write history'.[55] Heidi Hansson meanwhile has drawn important attention to the feminist elements of the text by focusing on the parallels Francis constructs between her protagonist and both Antigone and Joan of Arc.[56] Yet while there are, as these commentators suggest, elements of the novel which enact a positive commentary

52   'A Daughter of the Soil', *The Times* (London) (26 April 1895), 13.

53   Letter from Francis to Matthew Russell (5 September 1897), Russell Papers J27/19.

54   Letter from Francis to Matthew Russell (5 September 1897), Russell Papers J27/19
     She used the speech as her template because, as she explained to Matthew Russell,
     'it puts the case for Irish Nationalism in a nutshell'.

55   James H. Murphy, *Irish Novelists and the Victorian Age* (Oxford: Oxford UP, 2011),
     237 and Mary S. Pierse, *Irish Feminisms: 1810–1930*, vol. 3 (Routledge: London and
     New York, 2010), xx.

56   See Heidi Hansson, 'Patriot's Daughter, Politician's Wife: Gender and Nation
     in M. E. Francis's *Miss Erin*' in Heidi Hansson, ed., *New Contexts: Re-Framing
     Nineteenth-Century Irish Women's Prose* (Cork: Cork University Press, 2008),
     109–124.

on Ireland, it more frequently reflects pessimistically on the current state of affairs between England and Ireland, and condemns the attitudes and behaviours of both its central characters.

Like Molly Mackenzie and Ruth Sefton before her, Francis's Erin Fitzgerald is born into one class yet shaped by another. In *Miss Erin*, however, the most important movement the protagonist makes is not up the social ladder, but down it: Erin is the orphaned daughter of an 1848 patriot from a Catholic landowning family, but her opinions on Ireland are distilled through her experiences among the Irish peasantry. The action of the novel begins in Ireland, moves through Belgium, proceeds to the North of England, and eventually returns briefly to Ireland. Yet despite these diverse cultural settings, Francis's characters have in common with the author herself the fact that they live and move in almost wholly Catholic societies.

The novel begins with Erin, whose father had years before been exiled to America for his rebellious activities, being returned to Ireland as an infant after her parents' deaths. She is legally the ward of her father's brother, an anti-reformist landowner whose apathy towards her leads to her being raised by others, and her rebellious nature develops in her formative years through her close affiliations with two interrelated Irish factions: the Catholic clergy and the peasantry. Through the kindly local priest, Father Lalor, and his collection of books about Irish history, Erin learns of her people's past mistreatment by the English; about "'plantations" and "penal laws," and the sufferings of Irish Catholics in those bygone terrible times'.[57] Through her interactions with the Nolans, the family with whom she lives in the first years of her life, she witnesses at first hand the hardships currently being endured by the Irish peasantry, as well as some of that class's weaknesses and excesses. Her good-natured adoptive father, Pat Nolan, struggles with his tendency to abuse alcohol. As a result, he eventually falls behind on his rent, and he and his family are evicted from their home on the orders of Erin's uncle. Arrested for fighting with the police tasked with forcibly removing him from the estate, Nolan is only able to escape a prison sentence by migrating with his wife and children to America.

57   Francis, *Miss Erin*, 69–70.

These events lead directly to Erin's radicalization, through which she becomes determined

> to let the world hear of it some day [...] Perhaps, like Joan of Arc, she would fight for her country, and free it from landlords and Englishmen and all other tyrants and usurpers. Why should there not be an Irish Joan of Arc? The idea, at first merely an idle fancy, gradually took root in her mind. What if she, the child of an Irish patriot and an Irish peasant, were in future years called upon to deliver her country?[58]

Erin's dreams of becoming the 'Irish Joan of Arc' draw recognizably on the rhetoric employed by Maud Gonne, who a decade prior to the publication of Francis's novel had commenced a project to 'free Ireland as Joan of Arc freed France'.[59] Given that it was in 1897, the year prior to *Miss Erin*'s publication, that Gonne first achieved widespread public attention for her protests against the celebration of Queen Victoria's Diamond Jubilee in Ireland, it is tempting to read Francis's heroine as a straightforward rendition of Gonne.[60] Yet the correlations Francis draws between Erin and Gonne serve to highlight their discrepancies more so than their similarities. Unlike Erin, Gonne had spent only two years of her life in Ireland and had little understanding of the country's people or its politics when she first announced her mission to become the figurehead of its political revolution. In contrast, Erin is resolutely Irish, and Francis is at pains to demonstrate not only her heroine's substantial scholarly knowledge of her country's history, but also that she possesses a deep and longstanding affinity with Catholicism and the Irish peasantry. As such, her rebellious nature is justified to a degree that Gonne's was not, and it is relevant to speculate that Francis emphasizes her protagonist's various rationales as a means to offer her readers a closer psychological proximity to revolutionary motivations from which to interrogate them. Viewed in this context, it is an implicit yet damning indictment of Ireland's foremost female revolutionary that Erin is ultimately forced to confront the error of her ways.

---

58   Francis, *Miss Erin*, 88.
59   Maud Gonne MacBride, *A Servant of the Queen: Her Own Story* (Dublin: Golden Eagle, 1938), 61.
60   See J. J. Tighe, 'God Save the Queen', *Irish Times* (29 June 1897), 6.

While Erin can be seen to resemble Gonne, she also closely follows
the path of Francis herself. Francis's daughter, Margaret, would note that
her mother, like Erin, 'was deeply sensible of the hardships and wrongs
suffered by the peasant tenants of absentee landlords', and her son, Francis
Nicholas Blundell, would likewise assert that she 'hated the evictions'.[61] In
a correlative to Francis's own life, after the Nolans' departure from Ireland,
Erin is sent to Brussels to be schooled among the Catholic elite. Once there,
her closest friend is Joan Tweedale, who, like Francis's own companion
Josephine Blundell, is the daughter of a landed Catholic family from the
North of England who has been sent to Belgium so that she 'might enjoy
the advantages of foreign education and young companionship'.[62] The opinions of the two girls on political matters remain widely variant, however.
When, for instance, Joan suggests that the Irish should simply forget the
wrongs perpetrated on them by the English, she does so by comparing their
sufferings to those endured historically by English Catholics like herself –
who would 'never think of brooding and letting ourselves be embittered
by these things!' Erin quickly and cogently dismantles Joan's opinions:

> 'My dear Joan', cried Erin, very much nettled, 'your argument does not in the least
> apply. You English can afford to let bygones be bygones, because you are now so well
> off. We in Ireland [...] are still oppressed by an alien government, still trampled upon.'[63]

Likewise, Joan's derisive comments concerning the overt patriotism of the
Irish arouses Erin's ire: 'We in Ireland make efforts – what seem to out-
siders ridiculous efforts – to assert our nationality in every way we can.

---

61   Margaret Blundell, unpublished biography of M. E. Francis, 25, Blundell collec-
     tion and letter from Francis Nicholas Blundell to Margaret Blundell (28 June 1931),
     Blundell collection. As an MP, Francis Nicholas Blundell would become the sponsor
     of the Roman Catholic Relief Act of 1926, 'which abolished almost all the obsolete
     laws affecting Catholics' in the United Kingdom. See Brian Whitlock Blundell,
     'Blundell, Francis Nicholas Joseph (1880–1936)', *Oxford Dictionary of National
     Biography*, Oxford University Press, 2004 <http://www.oxforddnb.com/view/
     article/65565> accessed 11 August 2014.
62   Francis, *Miss Erin*, 131.
63   Francis, *Miss Erin*, 173–174.

We try to reanimate the smouldering spark of patriotism in breasts where it has been stifled by [...] Centuries of wrong'.[64]

Far more difficult to negotiate is Erin's relationship with Mark Wimbourne, Joan's cousin, an anti-Home Rule politician. When Erin asks Wimbourne what he intends to do about the 'Irish Question', he condescendingly replies,

> I should serve out Maxim guns gratis to both sides of the National party, and let the Parnellites and Anti-Parnellites mow each other down at their leisure. In course of time the Unionists would have it all to themselves, and we should have a nice, loyal, peaceable little Ireland.[65]

As in Egerton's *The Wheel of God*, published in the same year, Francis here shows her character suggesting that Ireland's most imperative political battles are being waged within the nationalist movement itself. At the same time, she also reinforces, through Erin's reflections on Wimbourne's answer to her question, that opinions such as Mark's are predicated on stereotypes of Irishness that are only tenable from a position of geographical and psychological remove:

> The man must have a horrible mind who could even suggest such a thing. Erin's vivid imagination conjured up the scene of carnage – seeing whole rows – not of mere impersonal 'Irishmen', but of the individual Pats, and Jims, and Micks of her acquaintance – slaughtered, 'mown down' by the diabolical weapons they could not see. 'The idea is not so original as you think', she cried, with scary sarcasm. 'It is very, very old – in fact, it has always been the English idea of governing Ireland – to exterminate the bulk of the people, that the wretched slavish minority, who are not Irish at all, may have everything their own way.'[66]

Here, Erin's heartfelt response to the dehumanization of her Irish neighbours acts to align the reader's sympathies with her heroine's own at the same time that Francis affirms, through references to what can only be

64   Francis, *Miss Erin*, 154.
65   Francis, *Miss Erin*, 154.
66   Francis, *Miss Erin*, 154–155.

presumed are Protestant landlords as 'not Irish at all', that Erin views authentic Irishness and Catholicism as inextricably bound to one another.

As a romantic attraction develops between Erin and Wimbourne, it becomes clear that a viable relationship between the two, should it be achievable, can only take place if their politically motivated bigotries are eliminated. Francis demonstrates, however, that errors of thought and behaviour continue to occur on both sides. Where his calm and often rational voice is juxtaposed favourably against the din of her impulsiveness and emotional excesses, her direct experiences and intimate knowledge of Ireland consistently destabilize his narrow-minded opinions about the Irish. Erin and Wimbourne are, each in their own way, ultimately and equally failures who are proved to be very wrong in their opinions about their respective countries. While their prejudices each against the other have been formed through mediated (and therefore distorted) representations of history and politics in the books and newspapers that they read, their new and more complete understanding of one another comes only through their subsequent firsthand experience of events in Ireland. As an eviction Erin is protesting against turns violent, Wimbourne sees the British authorities behaving in a manner that challenges his faith in the moral rectitude of his countrymen. Meanwhile, Erin's confidence in the integrity of her own rebellious ideologies is undermined when the violence she instigates escalates beyond her control.

That Erin Fitzgerald is intended as a personification of all (Catholic) Ireland is evidenced not only through her name but also via her upbringing, which allows her to assimilate various attitudes and occupy divergent positions in Irish society. That Wimbourne, inflexible and wrong-minded but primarily well-intentioned, is also emblematic of his nation becomes increasingly clear as the narrative unfolds. It is therefore significant to an understanding of Francis's vision that Erin's thoughts at the end of the novel are unambiguously pessimistic about the potential to achieve change in Ireland through rebellious methods: 'her past efforts', we are told, 'had resulted only in failure, and it seemed to her that, do what she might in the future, failure would still await her'.[67] That Francis's text actively

---

67   Francis, *Miss Erin*, 289.

condemns confrontational approaches to resolving the Irish Question is also apparent in her portrayal of Wimbourne, who, even when he is at his most sympathetic after his reconciliation with Erin, continues to assert that Ireland can only be changed for the better through approaches other than open rebellion: 'in some way you did not think of – a better way, Erin'.[68] Although Erin ultimately agrees to ally herself with Wimbourne through marriage, she does not, however, yield to his conservative political principles, nor does the text suggest that she should do so. In constructing his final act of meeting Erin in Ireland, and therefore on her home territory, Francis confirms that it is her English character who must travel a greater distance to reach her Irish character on common ground. As such, hers is an English-Irish relationship which is stalled at an impasse because it is flawed on both sides, but unevenly so: on the Irish side the problems are shown to be in method; but on the English, more detrimentally, in motive.

Miss Erin was the first of Francis's Irish novels to be written after she relocated to Dorset (in 1895), a move that was accompanied by a shift in literary focus to Dorset-set works such as *Fiander's Widow* (1901), *Pastorals of Dorset* (1901), *Wild Wheat: A Dorset Romance* (1905), *Dorset Dear* (1905) and *A Maid o' Dorset* (1917). So strongly did her readers come to identify her with this region of England that, even after her return to Crosby Hall in 1909, when her son succeeded to the ownership of the estate, her novels set elsewhere repeatedly met with failure. She once lamented to the actor and theatre manager Sir George Alexander 'that her public would not then *allow* her to write about any other subject than Dorset folk'.[69] It was not until 1912, and only with the persistent encouragement of both Catholic Archbishop Thomas Whiteside and Protestant Bishop Francis James Chevasse, the two most senior ranking religious officials in Liverpool, that Francis was once again persuaded to focus on Irish themes in her work. Whiteside and Chevasse were among those who organized a meeting, held in Liverpool in the autumn of that year, to publicize and garner support for the Criminal Law Amendment Act intended to curb the trade in women

68   Francis, *Miss Erin*, 290.
69   Margaret Blundell, unpublished biography of M. E. Francis, 36, Blundell collection.

for the purpose of prostitution, then commonly referred to as the 'White Slavery Bill'. Francis, who was at that time president of the Liverpool branch of the Catholic Women's League, was invited to the gathering as a special guest and appeared on the platform with dignitaries including the two bishops, the Lord Mayor of Liverpool and the MP Arthur Lee, the sponsor of the bill. Over the course of that evening, and after a joint entreaty from the bishops, Francis became convinced that she must do everything that 'lay within [...] her power to rouse the public conscience'.[70] The result is arguably her finest work, *The Story of Mary Dunne* (1913).

The novel is loosely based on the real-life tale of Susan Smith, who, 50 years prior to the time of Francis's writing had sailed from Liverpool to New York, where she and approximately a dozen other Irish women were kidnapped and forced into prostitution. Smith eventually escaped her captors and, due to the fact that her initial emigration (along with that of more than one hundred other young Irish females) had been charitably sponsored in a post-famine relief effort, her ordeal was prominently reported in the press, particularly in Ireland. These news stories led directly to the debates which eventually instigated the White Slavery Bill.[71] The story from which Francis drew the plot of *Mary Dunne* thus was not only closely related to her mission in writing the novel, but also had its roots in two locations, Ireland and Liverpool, she knew by residence. It is almost certainly due to her close personal affiliations with the setting and her deep interest in the subject matter that this book reveals more of Francis's opinions on the treatment of women than her novels which preceded it. Her project in writing it, as she herself indicated, was to make the public

70   Margaret Blundell, unpublished biography of M. E. Francis, 5, Blundell collection.
71   Details revealed by Smith at the trial of her captors confirm that she was forced into prostitution, beaten, locked in a small room and starved during her ordeal. In Francis's novel, Mary Dunne suffers precisely the same abuse. See 'A Sad Story', *Freeman's Journal* (5 September 1857), 1; 'America', *Daily News* (London) (7 October 1868), 5; Frederick Foster, 'The City of Mobile Passengers', *Freeman's Journal* (9 September 1857), 1; Vere Foster, 'Morality on Shipboard: To the Editor of the New York Tribune', *Freeman's Journal* (9 October 1857), 1; and 'Emigrants-Beware!', *Freeman's Journal* (5 December 1857), 1.

aware of the dangers with which women were faced through immigration, but the book also enacts an unfavourable commentary on attitudes towards women within Ireland. That young women, and young Catholic women in particular, are revered as moral paragons and insulated from societal and educational progress causes her protagonist to be more vulnerable to victimization not only by men in modern English cities, but also in rural Irish locations and by her Irish peers.

Like Susan Smith, Francis's fictional Mary Dunne is a young woman who chooses to emigrate from Ireland, is kidnapped aboard ship, forced into prostitution and, after escaping her captors, is found in a desperate condition on the streets of a large city: in the case of Francis's novel, Liverpool rather than New York. Featuring an extended prelude which is set in Mary's rural Irish community, Kilmachree, the novel suggests that her reasons for leaving Ireland are not dissimilar to those imagined in George Egerton's and Katherine Cecil Thurston's texts. Mary is engaged to Mat Kinsella as the novel opens, and both she and Mat are contentedly employed in the home of the parish priest. Their lack of money, however, precludes them from buying a home and thus from entering into married life. For this reason, Mat leaves Ireland to work in America. After his departure, Mary is reprimanded in the priest's home for conversing with a man other than her fiancé (he has offered her an apple and she speaks to him only to refuse it) and is asked to leave her employment solely because the attention she is receiving from other men is causing disruption in the household. Thereafter succumbing to the lure of Lancashire and its lucrative mill work, she travels to Liverpool by ship, where she is befriended by an elderly woman who, once they arrive in port, delivers her to her captors.

Avoiding any portrayal of Mary's experiences in the brothel, Francis concerns herself thereafter with depicting Mary's fate following her escape. In the aftermath of her ordeal, her mother, brother and the local priest are made fully aware of the details of her kidnapping, and welcome her back to Ireland as an innocent victim, 'unsullied in soul'.[72] But it is deemed necessary to shelter both her father and her fiancé from the knowledge of what

---

72   M. E. Francis, *The Story of Mary Dunne* (London: John Murray, 1913), 180.

is repeatedly referred to as her 'shame'. For this reason, Mary breaks off her engagement, but Mat promptly returns to Ireland to seek out a more thorough explanation. He eventually learns her full history and afterwards cannot dispel his feelings that the woman he had not only loved but idolized is lost to him forever: 'She's gone from me altogether – I can't feel it's her that's in it at all,' Mat explains to the priest, 'I could never look at her again'.[73] Francis indicates that Mat's 'revulsion of feeling' has been prompted by his idealization of her sexual purity: in his travels to and through America, he has carried the mental image of his last glimpse of a Madonna-like Mary at prayer, surrounded by her younger brothers and sisters, which he has viewed as 'not only a picture, but a promise'.[74] Mat's distress soon leads him to seek out her captor. Witnessing the man attempting to kidnap another young woman, Mat is overcome with rage and kills him.

Francis's consistent narrative censure of Mat's attitudes and their reper-cussions can be seen to enact a commentary on the inherent dangers of the idealization of the virginal female and of its correlative: the demonization of the fallen woman. This idea is reiterated and emphasized through the depiction of Mat's trial for murder, in which, in a lengthy and compellingly written trial sequence, his lawyer asserts that the issue of White Slavery has been disparaged and relegated in importance as 'a woman's question', when it is emphatically a 'man's'.[75] Francis's condemnation of this type of cultural marginalization and victimization of women is carried through to the ensuing episodes, in which trial onlookers 'titter' and 'laugh' as Mary describes her abuse on the witness stand.[76] It is primarily due to this tes-timony, which is movingly and heroically depicted, that Mat is convicted of a lesser charge of manslaughter. It is also through watching Mary testify that he ultimately recognizes that she has not only retained the virtue he imagined she had lost, but is ethically superior to everyone around her, and his love for her is restored.

73   Francis, *The Story of Mary Dunne*, 178.
74   Francis, *The Story of Mary Dunne*, 180; 29.
75   Francis, *The Story of Mary Dunne*, 282.
76   Francis, *The Story of Mary Dunne*, 284–285.

By evoking the Kilmachree priest's testimony on the witness stand in a manner reminiscent of a naïve and disillusioned boy speaking to his father – 'Sir, if I had had any notion that such things could be, I would have warned her; but how was I to warn her about a state of things which I never could have dreamt possible in a country like England?' – and in depicting Mary's restoration at the end of the novel to the type of 'shining innocence which adorns the souls of newly-christened babes', Francis posits these characters as the ingenuous Irish opposites of their morally corrupt English counterparts.[77] Her simultaneous propensity to interlace her text with tacitly critical metaphors of Empire and conquest, such as occur in the lawyer's closing arguments, meanwhile emphasize the barbarism of England's colonial policy and its unheeding complicity in the victimization of its own citizens. It is figured as a parent country which has failed to defend and protect its own:

> *here, now,* in the twentieth century, in civilised England, the uplifting of whose flag is supposed to ensure enlightenment and freedom to the most distant parts of the Empire, here and now, thousands of helpless creatures are lured to a state of slavery equal to, if not worse than, any practised in bygone ages or in savage realms.[78]

That the insular position of the priest has rendered him unable to warn Mary of the dangers that await her, and that her abuse is prompted, facilitated and extended by the oppressive sexual morality imposed on Catholic women in Ireland, is, however, also manifest in the text. The fact that Francis's novel can be seen to engage in a negative commentary not only on the moral decay of wider society, but also on the degree to which such decay might be enabled and exacerbated by Irish Catholic values concerning women, suggests that even as she continued to associate herself closely with her religion, she recognized the ways in which it might be – and in Ireland, had been – distorted and misused to the detriment of her sex.

Shortly after *The Story of Mary Dunne* was published Francis embarked upon the research for another Irish novel, *Dark Rosaleen* (1915). To achieve

---

77   Francis, *The Story of Mary Dunne*, 303; 312.
78   Francis, *The Story of Mary Dunne*, 280–281.

the degree of authenticity she desired, she traveled to the north and west of Ireland in late 1913, the year prior to the passing of the third Home Rule Bill. Published seven months before the Easter Rising, *Dark Rosaleen* demonstrates that 'the times' in her homeland were, as she maintained, 'heavy with menace'.[79] In it, she constructs characters who act as allegorical representations of the political and religious divisions within Ireland, charting the life of Hector McTavish, a young man who, in common with her Irish protagonists before him, is born into one social sphere yet spends formative years in another. His family having been transplanted from Belfast to Connemara some time before his birth, Hector lives out the early years of his life as the sole Protestant child among the Catholic peasantry in the extreme west of Ireland. There he is nursed by Honor Burke, a Catholic woman with an infant son of her own. In one of the novel's earliest images Francis portrays Honor feeding both her own child, Patsy, and the infant Hector simultaneously at her breast and, in doing so, succinctly states the novel's allegorical mission. Honor is, Francis explains, 'emblematic of Ireland herself [...] the very type of bountiful motherhood, nourishing at the same bosom the child of her own flesh and the stranger within her gates'.[80] These metaphors are carried through to Hector's biological mother, Rose – aligned with England through both her name and the inability to care for her own (displaced) child – and the two boys – one a Protestant from the north, the other a Catholic from the south – who are able to live amicably, as brothers and friends, only as long as they remain unschooled in their country's endemic sectarian prejudices. That the Protestant child from the north is figured as both foreigner and interloper sets the tone for what will follow.

The Orangeist element in the novel is introduced in the form of Alexander McTavish, Hector's father. What is at first presented as McTavish's reluctant tolerance of the friendly Connaught natives, among whom 'the Protestant' is said to be 'rather popular than otherwise', gradually gives

79   M. E. Francis, *Dark Rosaleen* (New York: P. J. Kennedy, 1917[1915]), iii.
80   Francis, *Dark Rosaleen*, 11.

way to hatred.[81] His transformation to the novel's villain culminates in an episode in which – after seeing his son riding on horseback with Honor's brother, a priest – McTavish reveals the depth of his bigotry and fear: 'Tisn't for good he'd be wantin' ye,' Alexander tells his son after pulling him violently from the saddle. 'It 'ud be to carry ye off and make a Catholic of ye [...] Doesn't the Pope o' Rome pay out money for every man that turns?'[82] His situation in the village of Cloon-na-hinch thereafter becoming untenable, McTavish forces his family to return to Belfast. In the years that follow, his anti-Catholic prejudices fester.

Hector, having retained an intense affection for his adoptive childhood family despite acquiring a level of distrust of their religion during his time in Belfast, returns as an adult to Connemara sometime after his father's death. Once there, he falls in love with Honor's daughter, Norah. Through a complex series of events which see the pair stranded on an island and forced to spend several days together away from her home, Norah's moral reputation is (unjustly) compromised, and the pair must marry. The remainder of the action is played out primarily against the backdrop of Derry, where the couple come to live. It is a space riven by suspicion, violence and prejudice on both sides of the sectarian divide. Events inside Hector and Norah's marital home increasingly mirror those exterior to it, and Francis demonstrates that this discord is prompted almost wholly by ignorance and fear. The rituals Norah enacts at her makeshift bedside altar to the Virgin Mary are shown to be edifying to her yet are seen as foreign and threatening to Hector; his portrait of William of Orange serves a similar purpose for him and evokes analogous responses in her. In portraying the couple's varying and irreconcilable renditions of the Siege of Derry, Francis also points to the ways that Irish history can be distorted and misused to amplify religious animosities. Though he is at first largely devoid of prejudice, Hector soon becomes alarmed by his wife's behaviour and beliefs, increasingly viewing her as an embarrassment in social terms and her religion as an ever greater threat to his cultural identity. As a result, he enacts a dual subterfuge. Not

---

81   Francis, *Dark Rosaleen*, 15.
82   Francis, *Dark Rosaleen*, 34.

only does he deceive the outside world about the Catholic wife he harbours within his home, he also deceives Norah about his role in the public life of Derry, concealing his radical Orangeist activity from her like the shameful secret he seems, at times, to recognize it to be.

Orangeism receives prominent condemnation in Francis's text; but to a lesser degree so, too, does Irish nationalism. Patsy Burke, having become in adulthood the priest Father Pat, laments the conflicts between Protestants and Catholics in the country, and along with several other Catholic characters expressly names the drive towards Irish self-government 'as the bone between them': 'It's a terrible thing,' he remarks about the Home Rule initiative, 'to have stirred up all this religious hatred again that was dead and buried so many years'.[83] It is also through Pat's opinions that Francis points to the levels of distrust that have rendered Ireland and England irreconcilable and reveals the depth to which her Catholic characters harbour their own longstanding prejudices and animosities. Remarking upon the measures his Irish neighbours have been required to take to stop the spread of foot-and-mouth disease, Pat wonders, for instance, whether the whole business is yet another English ploy to reduce the Irish to privation: 'it wouldn't be the first time England put a spoke in Ireland's wheel,' he claims. 'Didn't they destroy her cattle-raising industry? Didn't they pull down her woollen industries and pass laws against it?'[84]

Matters culminate when a son is born to Hector and Norah and a metaphorical battle for the baby's soul quickly becomes literal. Hector's belated fears that his marriage, solemnized in a Roman Catholic church and therefore entailing the promise that all children born to the union be raised in Norah's faith rather than his own, will result in the annihilation of his family's Protestant heritage echo prevailing fears in the north of Ireland that Home Rule would result in an obliteration of the North's religious and cultural legacy. It is these fears that drive Hector to violence, as he travels to Connemara along with a group of armed Orangemen to prevent the christening of his son. In the battle that ensues, Father Pat is chased down

83   Francis, *Dark Rosaleen*, 332.
84   Francis, *Dark Rosaleen*, 334.

at gunpoint, but just before he is dealt the injury that will prove fatal, is able to baptize the child. Hector, too, is seriously wounded in the fight. At the end of the novel he and Patsy lay together, their heads resting side by side in Honor's lap, and are reconciled in the moments immediately prior to what is certainly Patsy's death and may also be Hector's: the doctor believes he may live; Honor does not, because, she says, he and Pat 'have each other by the hand'.[85] In suggesting that the fates of her anti-nationalist and Northern Irish characters are intertwined, Francis indicates that Home Rule will result in the death (for Ireland) of its Ulster province. In making it clear that the deathbed reconciliation of the surrogate brothers can only be achieved through repentance on Hector's part and absolution on Patsy's, she also implies that it is the Protestant and northerner who shoulders most of the blame for this tragedy. So, too, in her final description of the newly baptized baby as 'typical of Ireland – a new Ireland that might achieve great things, though it was the child of blood and tears', does she declare her own bias.[86] For in her vision of the child, she also asserts the religious identity that a reborn Ireland must have, and it has indeed been christened Catholic.

In his detailed deconstruction of the novel's themes, John Wilson Foster has distilled the essence of *Dark Rosaleen* aptly: 'its implication,' Foster writes, 'is that no solution is possible that compromises the spiritual hegemony of Catholicism'.[87] Yet, even as the novel conveys the sense that a form of Catholic self-government is an inevitable conclusion to the factionalism which assails her homeland, this outcome is never represented as an easy or straightforward resolution to Ireland's problems. While its vision finally rests on the hope of a new Ireland which is embodied in the baby, its ending also asserts that the fate of her country may be more terrible than beautiful: that Ireland's future may be 'to mourn like Rachel over her slain'.[88] The idea of a Catholic nation may assert itself in the novel's

85   Francis, *Dark Rosaleen*, 372.
86   Francis, *Dark Rosaleen*, 372.
87   John Wilson Foster, *Irish Novels 1890–1940: New Bearings in Culture and Fiction* (Oxford: Oxford UP, 2008), 142.
88   Francis, *Dark Rosaleen*, 372.

final moments, but her novelistic visions for such a nation are equivocal and apprehensive.

According to her daughter, Francis 'was not convinced that Home Rule would solve Ireland's difficulties', and *Dark Rosaleen* acts as evidence that its author's pro-Catholic views did not translate to pro-nationalist sentiments.[89] It is almost certainly for these reasons that the *Irish Monthly* conspicuously neglected to review or mention it – the first time any of Francis's Irish novels would fail to be appraised in that publication, and despite the fact that a novel by her daughter, Margaret Blundell, was being serialized in the magazine at the time the book was published. Even Stephen J. Brown, in his seminal bibliography of Irish works (published in 1916), failed to remark upon *Dark Rosaleen*'s allegorical status, and the comments he included in the volume were distinctly muted:

> The story of a 'mixed marriage' between Norah, a Connemara peasant girl, and Hector, a young engineer of Belfast origin. They go to live at Derry. Bitterness and misunderstanding come to blight their love, and the end is tragedy. The two points of view, Protestant and Catholic, are put with impartiality.[90]

Although the novel fared well enough in England to be granted a second edition in 1917, and the British periodical the *Bookman* referred to it as 'emphatically a book that should be read', it was destined to be ignored by the Irish public.[91]

In return, Francis neglected Ireland. She would revisit the subject of her homeland only rarely in her works published after 1916, but these were always cursory or tangential representations. The memoir of her Irish childhood, *The Things of a Child*, appeared in 1918; her novel *Napoleon of the Looms* (1925) features an Irishwoman as a character but is set in Lancashire; and *Cousin Christopher* (1925) tells the story of two Irish characters displaced to a Lancashire estate. This tendency to avoid the subject of her

89   Margaret Blundell, unpublished biography of M. E. Francis, 25, Blundell collection.
90   Stephen J. Brown, *Ireland in Fiction: A Guide to Irish Novels, Tales, Romances, and Folk-Lore* (Dublin and London: Maunsel, 1916), 92.
91   Edwin Pugh, 'Four Novels', *Bookman* 49/289 (October 1915), 25.

homeland post-1915 may be in part attributable to the reception that *Dark Rosaleen* received, yet is also almost certainly the product of her disappointment in her Irish compatriots on another level. Her son was to recall that 'when the Easter Rebellion broke out in 1916 she said, "If there were any method of doing so open to me, I would abjure my Irish nationality"'.[92]

Although female personifications of Ireland had long existed in the figuring of the country as Erin, Dark Rosaleen, Cathleen Ní Houlihan, Hibernia and the Sean-Bhean Bhocht, the era in which Francis produced all her Irish novels (1889–1915) was also the point at which feminized and romanticized imagery intensified with the advent of movements such as the Gaelic League and the Literary Revival. Francis consistently writes against such idealized representations of her homeland by employing the rhetoric of these personifications in novels such as *Miss Erin* and *Dark Rosaleen* only to subvert the imagery traditionally associated with them. Hers is always an Ireland which is flawed and riven, rather than heroic. One of her most revealing novelistic comments, couched in the words of Mark Wimbourne in *Miss Erin*, is directed at precisely the type of idealism that her work attempts to challenge. Separated from the text, this passage can be interpreted as the author's own call to her native country to deal in authenticities rather than metaphors:

> Erin, Erin, this is folly! cruel and perverse folly! Child, open your eyes, and see things as they are. You are deluding yourself, making a kind of fetish of this imaginary personification of Ireland. All these vague, poetical, romantic ideas go for nothing – your dream-Ireland does not exist.[93]

Seeming to speak directly to the literary and political movements of the day, this extract evidences what was mistaken about Francis's texts in the estimation of much of the Irish public. In it, she emphasizes realism and pragmatism, but it was new forms of both fiction and political thought that were necessary to the conception of a new Ireland on the brink of

---

92 Letter from Francis Nicholas Blundell to Margaret Blundell (28 June 1931), Blundell collection.
93 Francis, *Miss Erin*, 285.

nationhood, and it was the Revivalists and the revolutionaries who would invent them. Francis's fiction can be accurately described as being written of and for her religion, but it was not the type of fiction that was required of and for her country at the time.

In 1892, a commentator in *United Ireland* claimed that it was 'one of the misfortunes of this country that while we complain that we have no present-day literature, we really have, but do not know it. For we do not read our own books'.[94] The reasons for this neglect are abundantly in evidence in the variety of articles and essays written by Irish Catholic commentators between the fall of Charles Stewart Parnell and the Easter Rising. For them, the Revival remained primarily a Protestant construct with aims and ideologies at odds with their own interests. The search for a representative Irish Catholic novelist therefore persisted. Rosa Mulholland, in sending out her own plea for an Irish novelist in 1891, asserted that there were only a 'few Irish writers who continued to write for Ireland', and regretted that those who did so did 'not more often [dip their pens] in the milk of human kindness when describing the faults and shortcomings of [their] worser fellow-countrymen'.[95] Likewise, the last public assessments Father Matthew Russell was to make of Francis's work – written for the *Irish Monthly* in 1912, the year of his death – were overtly critical of her Irish output. Commenting on the subject of Irish Catholic Literature, Russell was to echo Mulholland's sentiments, rebuking Francis for not 'excluding all that is hostile and offensively hostile to our country and our creed' in her novels. For that reason, he proceeds to confess, '[M. E. Francis's] Irish stories do not please me as much as the long and brilliant series of novels that deal chiefly with Lancashire and Dorset'.[96] The overriding impression that can be gleaned from the opinions of both commentators is one of exaggerated nationalist sensitivity. To them, the works of writers who

94   Clipping 'A Great Irish Novelist', *United Ireland* (June 1892), n.p., Emily Lawless Papers, Marsh's Library, Dublin Z2.1.15/27.
95   R. M. [Rosa Mulholland], 'Wanted An Irish Novelist', *Irish Monthly* 19/217 (July 1891), 370.
96   Matthew Russell, 'A Word about Irish Catholic Literature', *Irish Monthly* 40/468 (June 1912), 311.

criticized Ireland and the Irish, no matter how briefly or trivially, were unacceptable. These types of sentiments, echoed in the words of other Irish essayists throughout the country's newspapers and magazines, acted as a form of unofficial suppression – as censorship in all but name.

While Russell's support for Francis's work gradually waned, however, Stephen J. Brown's did not. In the aftermath of the Easter Rising, Brown was to recognize that those frequent, late-nineteenth and early-twentieth century appeals for an Irish Catholic novelist had not, in reality, gone unheeded. Over time, he would temper his advocacy of Mulholland's and Tynan's novels, which he came to believe did not 'embody in some sort the national idea or some phase of it'.[97] Yet he remained unfalteringly supportive of Francis's work, finding among her portrayals many 'in which the national temperaments of Celt and Saxon were ably contrasted'. 'I venture to say that the reading of the fifteen or twenty novels that "M. E. Francis" has published', Brown was to suggest in 1920, 'would impress almost any reader with the greatness of the difference in character and outlook which distinguishes [Ireland from England]'.[98]

It is also true that Brown was decades younger than Russell and would outlive him by almost fifty years. He was thus granted the benefit of both an optimism and a hindsight which his fellow Jesuit lacked. Russell had lived through the Famine and the Land Wars, and had already reached late middle age by the time of Parnell's fall and the defeat of the first two Home Rule Bills. He had ample reason to be discouraged about the prospects for Ireland's future, and would write his final opinions on Francis's work at a point immediately between the quashing of an Irish devolution 'scare' and the passing of the third Home Rule Bill in Parliament. In 1912, Ireland's future hung in the balance, and Russell knew only too well that novels could act as political instruments which might sway opinion in favour of or against the Irish cause. He therefore urged Irish authors to portray their

97   Stephen J. Brown, 'Novels of the National Idea', *Irish Monthly*, 48/563 (May 1920), 255–256.
98   Brown, 'Novels of the National Idea', 260.

country in the manner which he felt would most benefit her in the political process. He would not live to see the Home Rule initiative pass Parliament.

Francis survived her mentor by nearly two decades, dying in 1930 at the last of her many adopted homes in Wales. Over the course of her career, she had published at least sixty volumes of prose. On her deathbed she was granted an Apostolic Benediction 'in recognition of good service done [on behalf of the Roman Catholic Church] with her pen'.[99] Her final novel, *Wood Sanctuary* (1930), written in collaboration with her daughter Margaret, appeared just days after her death. In a review, the Catholic publication the *Tablet* would note the degree to which Francis's last work was suffused with her own spiritual values:

> This brings us to our crowning praise of 'M. E. Francis' – whose death last month hugely bereaved English literature [...] In these columns we have argued again and again that truly Catholic novelists are not necessarily novelists who write about Catholics. Rather are they those who write about life in a Catholic way. No priest nor nun, nor mass nor shrine, is mentioned in *Wood Sanctuary*; but all is viewed *sub specie aeternitatis*.[100]

Her daughter would echo these sentiments in a reminiscence published not long afterwards, in which she asserted that her mother's defining characteristic was that '*she saw life through her Catholic eyes*'.[101]

Father Stephen J. Brown lived until 1962 – through the passing of the Home Rule Bill, the events of the Easter Rising, the forming of the Free State, the Civil War and the creation of the Irish Republic. He would make what turned out to be his final and brief assessment of Francis's work in 1935 when he included her in his survey of exemplary Catholic novelists.[102] Five years after her death, he was able to recognize that the values she

---

99   Margaret Blundell, *An Irish Novelist's Own Story* (Dublin: Catholic Truth Society, n.y.), 27.

100   'Outstanding Novels, No. XXXVII, *Wood Sanctuary*', the *Tablet* (12 April 1930), 486.

101   Margaret Blundell, 'M. E. Francis', *Catholic World* 134/804 (March 1932), 689.

102   Stephen J. Brown, 'The Catholic Novelist and His Themes', *Irish Monthly* 63/745 (July 1935), 435.

promoted most prominently in her works had not been those of her nation, but those of her religion. But by then, of course, he was no longer burdened with the task of privileging texts he knew would help his country to nationhood. Its nationhood had been achieved.

'Affection for England and Love of Ireland': The Altering Landscapes of Katharine Tynan

> I had lived eighteen years in England, I had come to believe that affection for England and love of Ireland could quite well go hand in hand.
> — KATHARINE TYNAN, *The Years of the Shadow* (1919)[1]

From the advent of her career in 1878 to her death in 1931, Katharine Tynan regularly issued books of poetry, eventually producing more than twenty-five full-length volumes of original and collected work in the genre. Her poetic interest was focused in no small measure on her native Ireland from the first: her earliest published poem, 'A Dream', appeared in the nationalist *Young Ireland Magazine*, and she soon thereafter began using Celtic mythology as the inspiration for her work.[2] By 1881, she had written poems based on the folklore of her homeland frequently enough that she wrote to Father Matthew Russell worried that this predilection might be viewed as derivative or uninspired: 'Do you think I ought to continue writing legends?' she wondered, 'I like them, because the story is made for me, and sometimes I feel like the young man that told Hans Andersen that he wished to be a poet but that all the subjects had been written about before his time.'[3] One

---

1   Katharine Tynan, *The Years of the Shadow* (London: Constable, 1919), 204.
2   Peter van de Kamp has corrected Tynan's own assertion that her first published work was titled 'In Dreamland'. See Peter van de Kamp, 'Wrapped in a Dream: Katharine Tynan and Christina Rossetti' in Peter Liebgrits and Wimm Tigges, eds., *Beauty and the Beast: Christina Rossetti, Walter Pater, R. L. Stevenson and Their Contemporaries* (Amsterdam and Atlanta: Editions Rodolpi, 1996), 63.
3   Letter from Katharine Tynan to Matthew Russell (March 1881), Russell Papers J27/73.

of her finest poems in this vein, 'Waiting' (1884), a dramatic monologue based on the prehistoric legend of the giant Finn awaiting his chance in the caves of Donegal to fight for Ireland's redemption, anticipates the work produced from similar sources in the ensuing years by William Butler Yeats, Douglas Hyde, Lady Gregory, George William Russell ('A. E.') and John Todhunter. For this reason, A. E. later recognized that it was Tynan who had been 'the earliest singer in that awakening of our imagination which has been spoken of as the Irish Renaissance'.[4]

That she ultimately did not choose to fashion her work solely in the Revivalist mould is in no small measure a reflection of her peripatetic lifestyle: Tynan simply could not stand still, whether in her life or in her work. Over the course of her lifetime, she would not only occupy many different homes in Ireland and England, but would also experiment in a variety of poetic genres, producing much religious, domestic and pastoral poetry, in due course securing herself a place as one of the most beloved poets of the First World War. Yet despite the degree of popular acclaim she attained on both sides of the Irish Sea, Tynan's poetic achievements were destined to be eclipsed by those writers whose names subsequently became synonymous with the movements in which she worked most prominently: it was the name 'Yeats' rather than 'Tynan' which would become emblematic of the Irish Literary Revival; and it is to the work of Siegfried Sassoon, Rupert Brooke and Wilfred Owen that the sobriquet 'War Poets' is most readily applied. When Tynan has been remembered by literary scholars in the years since her death, it has often been in her capacity as a correspondent of Yeats in the formative years of his poetic development, and more frequently still as the author of six volumes of memoir which have provided a succession of researchers with valuable insights into the activities and personalities of those who were at the forefront of Revivalism in its nascence.[5] It is perhaps the case that her work was too diffuse to be

---

4   A. E., 'Foreword', *Collected Poems by Katharine Tynan* (London: Macmillan, 1930), vii.

5   Tynan's personal letters and published memoirs have proved useful to the authors of a range of seminal works on Irish literature from Richard Ellmann's *James Joyce* (Oxford: Oxford University Press, 1959) to Ulick O'Connor's *Celtic Dawn: A Portrait*

readily categorized and eventually too copious for her to fulfil the literary promise to which her earliest poetry had pointed. Despite the fact that she continued to consider herself (and was considered by others) to be primarily a poet, she would ultimately produce far more fiction than verse: of her more than 150 published works, at least ninety-four are novels and at least twenty-three collections of short stories.[6]

That Tynan's body of work eventually became weighted far more heavily on the side of novels than poetry is in many ways unsurprising, for she had more in common with other Irish women novelists who settled in England than she did with the majority of the Revivalists. She would, for example, share at least some of the perspectives of each and every one of the writers discussed so far in this study. Like Emily Lawless, she was an avid student of Irish history and politics who, through the writing of historical fiction, employed the politics of the past to illuminate the politics of the present: placing 'old wine in new bottles', was how Tynan herself described it.[7] Like L. T. Meade, who she considered a friend and mentor, she was a suffragist, unabashed career woman, and ambitious self-promoter whose novels were written with a view to popularity.[8] She was also, like Meade,

---

of the Irish Literary Renaissance (Dublin: Town House and Country House, 1999) and both volumes of R. F. Foster's *W. B. Yeats: A Life* (Oxford: Oxford University Press, 1997).

6   Some of Tynan's novels, such as *Paradise Farm* (1911), which was published in America with minor alterations as *Mrs Pratt of Paradise Farm* (1913), were issued in other countries with alternative titles. It is also the case that works such as *Molly, My Heart's Delight* (1914), a fictionalized account of the life of Mary ('Molly') Granville Delany (1700–1788), and *A Rose of the Garden* (1912), again a fictionalized version of the life of Lady Sarah Napier (1745–1826), are difficult to categorize. This is therefore a conservative estimate.

7   Katharine Tynan, *Lord Edward: A Study in Romance* (Dublin: Maunsel, 1916), 243.

8   In an undated letter to Matthew Russell, Tynan writes, 'Willie Yeats and I had tea yesterday with Mrs Meade at Atalanta. She is a delightful woman.' In a later letter (27 July 1889), she noted to Matthew Russell that she 'had tea with Mrs Meade (at Atalanta) a nice open-faced Irishwoman, who has taken me quite into her friendship'. Both Russell Papers J27/73. Tynan was a regular contributor to *Atalanta* over the course of Meade's editorship of the magazine.

a prolific producer of texts who published countless journalistic works in
addition to an array of novels which ranged in genre from Gothic murder
mysteries to domestic melodramas. She had in common with George
Egerton and Katherine Cecil Thurston an interest in women's rights and
roles, and could, like them, not only trace her lineage to both Catholic
and Protestant forebears, but also entered into an interreligious marriage
which altered her relationship to her homeland. A devout and lifelong
Catholic like M. E. Francis, Tynan also enjoyed both a close friendship and
intimate correspondence with Matthew Russell, during which he took her,
too, to task for her unflattering portrayals of her fellow countrymen. She
also shared the position of all these writers as a long-term, willing expatriate from Ireland, and would live eighteen of the twenty-six years between
1890 and 1916 in England. More than any of the other writers covered
thus far, Tynan's place in society and in relation to her homeland altered
over the course of her lifetime. The gradually varying political perspectives which accompanied her shifting geographical and social landscapes
are reflected in the portrayals in her novels, many of which deal explicitly
with the subject of Ireland.

That Tynan came to live eighteen years in England is to some extent
incongruous with her personal history, for her life until 1893 was passed
exclusively in County Dublin, and there were few indications before that
year – the thirty-fourth of her life – that she was inclined to roam. She was
born in 1859, the fifth child of Andrew Cullen Tynan and his wife Elizabeth
(*née* O'Reilly).[9] Tynan's father was a cattle farmer who was able to achieve a
newly elevated economic status in the latter half of the nineteenth century
as the result of a post-famine surge in beef prices. According to Donald
Jordan, these alterations in the market made large-scale cattle graziers 'the
dominant economic force in Ireland with an increasingly powerful voice

9   The year of Tynan's birth has been disputed, but Peter van de Kamp's thorough
     research points to 1859 as the accurate date. See Peter van de Kamp, 'Some Notes on
     the Literary Estate of Pamela Hinkson', in Warwick Gould, ed., *Yeats Annual No. 4*
     (Houndmills, Basingstoke: Macmillan, 1986), 186.

in politics' by the 1870s.[10] As was the case with many large-scale farmers, much of Tynan's father's grazing land was rented, although he did own the acreage surrounding her childhood home, 'Whitehall', a good-sized farmhouse near Dublin which once belonged to John Philpot Curran. The family's economic means were sufficient enough to send Tynan (at least briefly) to convent boarding school and, according to Tynan's sister Nora Tynan O'Mahony, the trappings of new wealth were everywhere in evidence during their upbringing:

> She [Tynan] was one of 'an old-fashioned family' originally numbering twelve as well as the father and mother! There was also a huge staff of servants [...] a cook and house-maids, laundrymaids and nurses and dairymaids, as well as coachmen and gardeners, and farm-workers well-nigh innumerable, of both sexes. For our father was a man of big enterprises and ideas, by far the largest employer of labour in our neighbour-hood; and our old home, 'Whitehall,' was ever a busy hive of life and of industry.[11]

After the 1870s, the family's financial status was less secure, threatened as it was by Andrew Tynan's passion for taking financial risks which did not always pay off, including a disastrous contract to supply cattle to the army in both Ireland and England.[12] Tynan's social status is therefore difficult to pinpoint: her father was both a landowner and a tenant farmer, yet neither the terms 'landowner' nor 'tenant', as these have conventionally been used, are applicable. It is apparent, however, that the Tynan family were located somewhere at the more privileged end of the agricultural middle class.[13]

---

10   Donald Jordan, 'Merchants, "Strong Farmers" and Fenians: The Post-Famine Political Elite and the Irish Land War', in C. H. E. Philpin, ed., *Nationalism and Popular Protest in Ireland* (Cambridge: Cambridge UP, 1987), 321.

11   Nora Tynan O'Mahony, 'Katharine Tynan's Girlhood', *Irish Monthly* 59/696 (June 1931), 358.

12   Katharine Tynan, *Twenty-Five Years: Reminiscences* (London: Smith, Elder, 1913), 67.

13   As a farmer whose land and lease-holdings exceeded 50 acres, Andrew Cullen Tynan would have been among the upper 10 per cent of what Samuel Clark refers to as Ireland's 'agricultural class' (which excludes large-scale landowners). See Samuel Clark, 'The Importance of Agrarian Classes: Agrarian Class Structure in Nineteenth-Century Ireland', *The British Journal of Sociology* 29/1 (March 1978), 30.

Tynan's father indulged and encouraged her literary aspirations with much the same enthusiasm as he approached his own flights of business fancy.[14] After the poetry that she began to produce in her late teens found a regular market in periodicals such as the *Irish Monthly* and the *Graphic*, he encouraged his daughter to begin hosting a weekly literary *soirée* at the family's farmhouse in a room set aside and redecorated exclusively for the purpose of promoting her career and enhancing her circle of literary friends. Tynan's sister would remember those gatherings as extravagant affairs:

> Katie's friends came every Sunday into the quiet green country, where they enjoyed first of all a hearty lunch of somewhat Gargantuan proportions – oh, those old lavish and carefree days! Afterwards, in the intervals between lunch and tea – usually taken on the tennis lawn – and the later heavy supper, they talked literature and poetry or politics – for my sister, indeed, held, even in those days, what was quite a 'salon' of her own, enjoyed by everyone who was *anyone* in the artistic and literary or political life of the Dublin of that day.[15]

Over the course of the years, the leading lights of Irish literature – including John and Ellen O'Leary, Douglas Hyde, A. E. and Yeats – all became regular

14   The Tynans had been before her and would remain a clan of writers and storytellers. A near relation of Tynan's, Sir William Howard Russell, was the Crimean War correspondent who coined the phrase 'the thin red line'. Her father himself was an avid teller of tales who inspired two short stories in Yeats's *The Celtic Twilight*, 'An Enduring Heart' and 'A Knight of the Sheep'. Tynan's younger son Giles Aylmer Hinkson would become a journalist and eventually the South American correspondent for *The Times* (London). Her daughter Pamela Hinkson was a journalist, author of non-fiction books and novelist whose works included the critically acclaimed *The Ladies' Road* (1932). Tynan's sister Nora Tynan O'Mahony was a poet, novelist, journalist and the woman's editor of the *Weekly Freeman's Journal* from 1918 to 1923, and was the mother of Gerard J. C. Tynan O'Mahony and grandmother of David Tynan O'Mahony, the former a journalist for and eventually manager of the *Irish Times*, the latter better known as the comedian Dave Allen.

15   Nora Tynan O'Mahony, 'Katharine Tynan's Girlhood', *Irish Monthly* 59/696 (June 1931), 361.

Sunday visitors to Whitehall, which was situated 'four Irish miles' from Dublin in what was then the countryside between Clondalkin and Tallaght.[16]

Early on, Tynan recognized that her position in and amongst the Irish literati was a social anomaly: 'The cleavage between Catholics and Protestants in Ireland', she noted in her memoirs, 'prevented their meeting, unless the circumstances were exceptional.' In her own case, she explains, 'they were exceptional'.[17] If it appears from her sister's description that Tynan was welcomed readily into Dublin literary circles, however, the degree to which she was privately considered by at least some members of those circles to be socially unacceptable is vividly evidenced in the diaries of Hyde, who noted upon his first meeting with Tynan in 1887 that she had 'a frightful brogue'.[18] His descriptions of a second encounter with her and her sister two days later at Trinity College Dublin are even more revealing in terms of his sense of superiority to her: 'I was terribly embarrassed lest anyone should see me talking to them,' Hyde wrote on that occasion, 'Katherine [sic] was all right but her sister was a sight'.[19] The discrepancies to which Hyde refers in his private writings between his situation as an Anglo-Irish Protestant and Tynan's as the daughter of a Catholic farmer confirm that he believed there to be a substantial social gulf between them.[20]

Although she does not appear to have been aware of Hyde's early objections to her family, Tynan eventually recognized that her voice not only acted as a marker of difference between her and her literary colleagues, but also as a barrier to her words carrying authority and gravitas with listeners.

---

16   Tynan O'Mahony, 'Katharine Tynan's Girlhood', 360–361. Whitehall, now a ruin, is still known locally in Clondalkin as 'Tynan Hall', and a portion of the Tynan family's land has now become Tynan Park.

17   Tynan, *Twenty-Five Years*, 111.

18   Quoted in Dominic Daly, *The Young Douglas Hyde: The Dawn of the Irish Revolution and Renaissance 1874–1893* (Totowa, NJ: Rowman and Littlefield, 1974), 87.

19   Daly, *The Young Douglas Hyde*, 87.

20   Tynan was touched when in 1889 Hyde wrote a poem, 'Fluffy Ultimatus', in honour of her recently deceased dog, but her terse descriptions of Hyde as a manipulative if clever politician and an unimaginative card player indicate that she was not among his admirers. See letter from Tynan to Matthew Russell (1 April 1889), Russell Papers J27/73 and Tynan, *Twenty-Five Years*, 206, 208, 243 and 284.

Over time she begrudgingly came to realize that it automatically made her a figure of amusement among both the Anglo-Irish and the English, and it was with a sense of what she referred to as 'desolation' that she found herself forced, when speaking publicly, to adopt a jocular tone in order to conform to the ingrained attitudes of her audiences, 'who would begin to laugh the minute I opened my mouth, because I had a brogue!'[21] Evidence that she remained sensitive to these types of responses can be found in her novels, in which she consistently defends her middle class Irish characters, discerning in their brogues something 'rich', 'musical' and 'sweet' rather than undignified or discomfiting.[22] That Tynan's accent, and by extension her class status, was so closely scrutinized suggests that notions of authority, rather than of what might be termed authenticity, were of utmost importance in deciding who was permitted to speak on behalf of Ireland, and accounts for a degree of the distance that was placed between Tynan and the majority of the Revivalists then, and continues to define her position in relationship to the movement even now.

That she did indeed find herself distanced from the literary values espoused by the Revivalists is evidenced in the fact that, even in very early assessments of the Revival, she is figured as an outlier to the movement. In his 1894 study *The Irish Literary Revival*, William Patrick Ryan suggested, for instance, that Tynan's poetry had always been at odds with the tenets of Revivalism as these had been conceptualized by the movement's insiders: 'Miss Katherine [sic] Tynan won speedy fame with poetry which showed that a welcome new personage had strayed to Irish fields,' Ryan explained, 'though neither the spirit nor the form of the work was Celtic as we had understood it.'[23] Ernest Boyd, in his later and more thorough assessment of her work in his *Ireland's Literary Renaissance* (1916), likewise

---

21   Katharine Tynan, *The Wandering Years* (London: Constable, 1922), 333–334.
22   See, for instance, Katharine Tynan, *The Dear Irish Girl* (London: Smith, Elder, 1899), 39; *That Sweet Enemy* (London: Archibald Constable, 1901), 325; *A Girl of Galway* (London: Blackie & Son, 1902), 33; *Julia* (London: Smith, Elder, 1904), 33; and *Cousins and Others* (London: T. Werner Laurie, 1909), 50.
23   William Patrick Ryan, *The Irish Literary Revival* (New York: Lemma, 1970 [1894]), 96.

indicated that she was an innately different type of writer than the main-stream Revivalists. She was, Boyd wrote, 'the only writer of any importance whose Catholicism has found literary expression' – other Irish Catholic writers, he claimed, had 'effaced their religion from their work'– but she had been 'too prolific for one whose gift is manifestly of slender propor-tions'.[24] Proceeding to locate the narrowness of Tynan's poetic vision in the anti-aesthetic qualities of her specifically Irish strain of Catholicism, Boyd asserted that 'Irish Catholics have none of the easy tolerance and freedom of religious majorities elsewhere, but have the narrowness and hardness of a small sect'.[25] In the process, Boyd tellingly failed to acknowledge the number of reasons the situation and attitudes of Catholics in Ireland were at variance with those of Catholic majorities elsewhere.

That such assessments of her literary influence not only rankled but wounded Tynan is apparent. Shortly after Boyd's book appeared, she sought solace in the form of two of her closest long-term Irish literary friends, A. E. and Susan Mitchell (both of whom worked for the *Irish Homestead*). In letters to Tynan, each would suggest that Boyd had unfairly diminished her importance to the Revival, A. E. asserting that she deserved a place alongside 'Seumas O'Sullivan, Colum, Campbell & the rest'; Mitchell arguing more vehemently that Boyd

> apparently doesn't set much value on feminine intelligence. It is ridiculous of him not to have assigned you your rightful place. A. E. is really the only person who ought to write that sort of book. He has a sense of values. These people learn the business of critic & learn it badly in a bad school, the school of depreciation.[26]

Some of the reasons that Boyd, Ryan and others came to reach such valu-ations can, however, be traced to Tynan's own appraisals of her work. In her detailed research into Tynan's non-fiction writings, Aurelia Annat has argued for instance that the sustained scholarly confusion with regard to

24   Ernest Boyd, *Ireland's Literary Renaissance* (London: Grant Richards, 1923), 107.
25   Boyd, *Ireland's Literary Renaissance*, 107.
26   Letter from A. E. to Tynan (1 June 1917), Tynan Papers, Manchester, 9/17, and Susan Mitchell to Tynan (1 December 1916), Tynan Papers, Manchester, 8/5.

Tynan's politics can be attributed to her tendency to edit and censor her memoirs according to her altering personal and professional circumstances: 'By 1913, when her first volume of autobiography was published,' Annat asserts, 'Tynan was embedded in the British establishment through her literary work', and her position 'had therefore become increasingly precarious, balancing between conflicting commitments and loyalties'.[27] It is for this reason, Annat goes on to suggest, that Tynan indicated in her memoirs that her involvement in cultural and political nationalism was more fleeting and frivolous than was in fact the case, a contention which is borne out in the many variances that can be found between Tynan's personal papers and her later memoirs in terms of her descriptions of and opinions towards events of political import to Ireland.[28] She was undoubtedly a cautious editor in this regard, and although this proclivity would become more conspicuous over time, she had in fact been performing similar balancing acts from the outset of her publishing career.

Her reasons for doing so are relatively straightforward to fathom: namely, because her identity as a Catholic woman made it necessary for her to justify her literary and political pursuits to a degree that was not required of her Anglo-Irish Protestant male colleagues. Tynan herself affirmed that she had been constantly reminded during her upbringing that 'Mary, Mother of God, is the ideal set before all Catholic women. From their childhood they are taught to weigh their actions by her modesty and humility and patience'.[29] Raised in a household in which a reverence for Irish nationalist poetry was also instilled in her (Tynan had long held the work of James Clarence Mangan in particularly high esteem), she likewise

27   Aurelia Louisa Spottiswoode Annat, *Imaginable Nations: Constructions of History and Identity and the Contribution of Selected Irish Women Writers 1891–1945* (D.Phil thesis, University of Oxford, St. Hugh's College, 2009), 131–132.

28   For a more detailed discussion of these variances, see Whitney Standlee, '"A World of Difference": London and Ireland in the Works of Katharine Tynan' in Tom Herron, ed., *Irish Writing London, Volume 1: Revival to the Second World War* (London: Bloomsbury, 2013), 70–83.

29   Katharine Tynan, *A Nun, Her Friends and Her Order: Being A Sketch of the Life of Mother Mary Xaveria Fallon* (London: Kegan Paul, Trench, Trübner, 1891), 119–120.

was brought up to believe that the writing of literature carried with it a political responsibility. The challenge which was therefore presented to Tynan through her writing was to strike a delicate balance between religious decorum and political ambition. It was almost certainly to achieve such ends that she readily admitted that her poetry was produced primarily for religious edification, referring to it as her 'divine art' and expressing her wish that it would 'turn souls to God'.[30] Presumably for analogous reasons, she would often adopt the strategy of using her literature as a means of aligning the values of her religion with the promotion of her interests on behalf of her nation and her sex. It is a tactic she can be seen to employ in her first published volume, *Louise de la Vallière* (1885), in which both the title poem and 'Joan of Arc' are concerned with the experiences of Catholic women who exercised significant political influence. Works such as 'Waiting', 'The Dead Patriot' and 'The Flight of the Wild Geese', meanwhile, refer to the Christ-like suffering and sacrifice of those (Finn, A. M. Sullivan and Patrick Sarsfield, respectively) who historically remained true to their vision of an independent Irish nation. It remains difficult to comprehend how the latter group of poems in particular could have failed to earn the respect of Ryan, but the evidence provided in assessments of her work suggests that, over time, an even wider contingent of commentators would come to be convinced that her literary focus was Catholic rather than Celtic: in 1903, Russell would emphasize to his *Irish Monthly* readers that her poetry was infused with the values instilled in her through her period at boarding school, 'all that convent atmosphere of prayer, all that affectionate familiarity with the saints, has had no small share in making her the poet that she is', while another priest, Father J. B. McLaughlin, in a laudatory review of her writings to 1913, noted that Tynan's was 'a Catholic mind in the highest sense'.[31]

---

30 Letter from Tynan to Mrs Pritchard (30 June 1885), quoted in Katharine Tynan, *Katharine Tynan: Letters 1884–1885* (n.c.: Apex One, 1973), 23, and letter from Tynan to Mary Gill (14 November 1891) Tynan Papers, Manchester, 16/3.
31 Matthew Russell, 'Poets I have Known. No. 5: Katharine Tynan', *Irish Monthly* 31/359 (May 1903), 253 and J. B. McLaughlin, 'Katharine Tynan', *Ampleforth Journal*, 18 (1913), 278.

By the time that Russell, McLaughlin and Boyd were making these
types of assessments of her work, Tynan had realized that the merging
of her religious and political loyalties was more readily achievable in her
literature than in her life. She acknowledged that the publication of her
first poem in 1878 coincided with her awakening fervour for political
nationalism – which, in her case, soon transcended the bounds of literary
expression to include active involvement in nationalist organizations.[32]
She was first motivated to join such an organization when, angered at the
arrests of the Land League's leaders, Michael Davitt and Charles Stewart
Parnell, she became a member of the Ladies' Land League upon its incep-
tion in 1881.[33] She remained an avowedly 'ardent Parnellite' ever after,
despite suffering both personal and professional attacks in the largely
Catholic-driven backlash against Parnell which resulted from the public
disclosure, in December of 1889, of his long-term affair with the married
Katharine O'Shea.[34] After the party split which followed in the wake of
these revelations, Tynan's father was highly visible in newspaper reports
for his attendance at pro-Parnell rallies and for chairing National League
committee meetings in and around Dublin. Tynan herself made a pub-
licized appearance at the Round Room of the Rotunda upon Parnell's
famous return to Dublin on 10 December 1890.[35] In that same month,
she also (almost certainly unintentionally) found that the extent of her
political involvement was being advertised in the pages of the *Freeman's
Journal* when the newspaper decided to reprint, in a prominent position,
a letter she had written to the Parnell Leadership Committee requesting
membership in the National League:

32   Tynan, *Twenty-Five Years*, 71.
33   Tynan, *Twenty-Five Years*, 72.
34   Tynan, *Twenty-Five Years*, 378.
35   See 'Mr Parnell in Ireland', *Daily News* (London) (11 December 1890), 5; and
     'Mr Parnell', *Freeman's Journal* (11 December 1890), 5.

Dear Sir,
Will you please add my father, Andrew C. Tynan, to the list of your committee. I suppose, as you have admitted Lady Florence Dixie, sex is not a disqualification. In that case I should be very glad if you would give me membership also. Very sincerely yours

— KATHARINE TYNAN[36]

Among the very few women who were subsequently granted admission to the League, Tynan thereafter found herself treated with hostility, primarily by her fellow Irish Catholics.[37] As a result, she was denounced 'on record' by a local committee (incidentally headed by a priest) as 'brazenfaced Katherine [sic] Tynan' and branded 'a disgrace to the fair fame of Irish womanhood' for having joined 'Parnell's infamous League'.[38] Readers boycotted the *Irish Monthly* when Tynan's work appeared in it, and Russell himself refused to review or publicize the book she issued during the period of the Parnell controversy, a biography of Mother Mary Xaveria Fallon, due to the part she had taken in politics.[39]

When she came to write of these experiences in her 1913 volume of memoirs, her editorial omissions were surprisingly minimal. She would glance over her negative experiences with Russell and rewrite a portion of one of her own letters to remove her references to the 'intolerance and un-Christian uncharitableness' of priests (replacing them with a sentence likening her detractors to 'the Pharisee in the Gospel in the sight of God').[40] Yet the passages she wrote remained detailed and largely in tune with accounts she provided at the time the events occurred, and reveal a lingering and palpable sense of incredulity that she, as 'a Catholic woman' was made to suffer to such an extent for 'being a staunch follower of Mr Parnell'.[41]

36 'The Country and Mr Parnell', *Freeman's Journal* (12 December 1890), 6.
37 Tynan, *Twenty-Five Years*, 376.
38 Tynan, *Twenty-Five Years*, 378.
39 See letter from Tynan to Mary Gill (14 November 1891), Tynan Papers, Manchester, 16/3.
40 See original letter from Tynan to Mary Gill (14 November 1891), Tynan Papers, Manchester, 16/3, and Tynan's altered version of it in *Twenty-Five Years*, 377.
41 Tynan, *Twenty-Five Years*, 378.

Then again, by the time she came to recall this episode of her life, Home Rule for Ireland was a foregone conclusion and Parnell's reputation had been restored. There was little for her to lose by advocating him, yet even here she can be seen to draw attention to the similarities between the precepts of her religion and those of her politics. In her memoir, Parnell's suffering and martyrdom are specifically figured as the reasons his reputation has been retrospectively resurrected: had he died in the relative placidity which existed before 1890, she notes, 'he would have left comparatively little mark behind'.[42]

Through her experiences during the Parnell split, Tynan undoubtedly recognized the public profile she had achieved and the type of political impact her literary work might hold (or be perceived to hold). It is also the case that her political involvement did not stop at membership in the Ladies' Land League and the National League. She continued to be active in a variety of organizations and in a range of capacities throughout her life. She was a member of the National Literary Society from its foundation in 1892 and served, along with Maud Gonne, as one of only two female vice presidents elected over the course of the organization's existence.[43] Senia Pašeta credits Tynan with being among the most prominent of the primarily female contingent of contributors to *Shan Van Vocht* (1896–1899), a periodical which, Pašeta contends, 'helped to fuse the link between cultural nationalism and advanced nationalism and thus to create a wider space for women's involvement in nationalist politics'.[44] Tynan would also, in time, become a member of the Irish Catholic Women's Suffrage Association (ICWSA) and act as a vice president of the Irish Federation of Suffrage Societies.[45]

Yet in both her personal letters and in her memoirs she would reveal a tendency to deride the importance of her literary output and the impact of her political voice. In the earliest days of her publishing career, she had also

42   Tynan, *Twenty-Five Years*, 368–369.
43   See Senia Pašeta, *Irish Nationalist Women, 1900–1918* (Cambridge: Cambridge UP, 2013), 27.
44   Pašeta, *Irish Nationalist Women*, 31.
45   See Pašeta, *Irish Nationalist Women*, 89 and Marie O'Neill, 'Katharine Tynan Hinkson: A Dublin Writer', *Dublin Historical Record* 40/3 (June 1987), 88.

simulated a laissez faire attitude towards her work and adopted a (seemingly more ingenuous) stance of self-deprecation, insisting to Russell that she did not spend as much 'time and trouble' on her writing as did other poets and consistently referring to hers as a 'commonplace muse' and to her work, on occasion, as 'great rubbish'.[46] Though she could, after a particularly heady success, temporarily be convinced of the literary merit of her writings, she more often expressed the belief that the praise she earned from friends and colleagues was wide of the mark. Looking back on her career from the vantage point of 1922, for instance, she noted that

> I had been adjured by friends in the 'nineties and since to let myself go, as though there was always *that* held back. It was no use telling them that I let go what I had. They used to shake their heads sorrowfully over me, and say that I had *It* right enough if I would only let myself go. I think in time they gave up thinking, or even suggesting, that I had *It*.[47]

Yeats himself almost certainly fueled Tynan's insecurities by more often expressing his disappointment in her work than his approval of it, and it is telling that, even as he referred to her in an 1887 review of her poetic volume *Shamrocks* as 'at the beginning of a long and famous career', he described her as 'an Irish Jean Ingelow [an English writer of religious verse], neither very subtle nor very thoughtful'.[48] In contrast, Tynan recognized Yeats's poetic promise from the point of their first meeting in 1885, when she described him as having 'the saddest, most poetical, face [she] ever saw'.[49] Very soon thereafter, she declared him a 'genius'.[50]

46 Letters from Tynan to Matthew Russell (22 November 1883), (12 September 1883) and (31 July 1899), all Russell Papers, Folder J27/73.

47 Tynan, *The Wandering Years*, 288.

48 Yeats, review of Tynan's *Shamrocks* (1887) from *Truth* (11 August 1887), quoted in Carolyn Holdsworth, '"Shelley Plain": Yeats and Katharine Tynan' in Richard J. Finneran, ed., *Yeats Annual No. 2* (London and Basingstoke: Macmillan, 1983), 63.

49 Letter from Tynan to Mrs Pritchard (30 June 1885), quoted in Tynan, *Katharine Tynan: Letters 1884–1885*, 23.

50 Undated letter fragment from Tynan to Matthew Russell, which can be dated to the mid- to late-1880s due to Tynan's references to A. E. as a boy 'in age about 19', Russell Papers J27/73.

Comparisons of Tynan and Yeats, who were the most intimate of friends during the 1880s, are rarely to her advantage, but here prove illuminating in terms of their respective attitudes towards the purpose and potential of their literary output. At the beginning of his publishing career Yeats wrote despondently (and poetically) to Tynan to lament that his efforts during the composition of *The Wanderings of Oisin* (1889) had resulted only in failure:

> All seems confused, incoherent, inarticulate. Yet this I know, I am no idle poetaster. My life has been in my poems. To make them I have broken my life in a mortar, as it were. I have brayed in it youth and fellowship peace and worldly hopes. I have seen others enjoying, while I stood alone with myself – commenting, commenting – a mere dead mirror on which things reflect themselves. I have buried my youth and raised over it a cairn – of clouds.[51]

Yet Yeats continued to work 'without being false to my literary notions of what is good' and with what appears to have been an unassailable confidence that his artistic promise would one day be fulfilled.[52] As A. E. suggested to Tynan about their mutual friend, 'Yeats realised at an early age that he was going to be famous & has never written anything publicly or privately which he need be ashamed of'.[53] It is evident from her own letters that Tynan resented (and perhaps envied) what she perceived as Yeats's leisure and egocentricity, and the workmanlike approach she adopted to her own pursuits stands in stark contrast to his more distrait attitudes to the creation of literature. 'I had Willie Yeats staying here since last Monday,' Tynan wrote to Russell in 1891:

51   Letter from Yeats to Tynan (6 September 1888), in Roger McHugh, *W. B. Yeats: Letters to Katharine Tynan* (Dublin: Clonmore and Reynolds, 1953), 64.
52   McHugh, *W. B. Yeats: Letters to Katharine Tynan*, 57.
53   Letter from A. E. to Tynan (n.d.), Tynan Papers, Manchester, 9/17. The letter's date is ca. 1916, due to references to his reading of her recently issued memoir *The Middle Years* (London: Constable, 1916).

> He went away last night. He is an extremely bothering visitor. He thinks all the rest of the world created specially to minister to him, and there is no rebuffing of him possible. I did nothing while he was here, nor should if he was here a twelvemonth.[54]

As the son of an Anglo-Irish artist (no matter how financially feckless his father might have been), Yeats had been raised, according to Douglas Archibald, to believe in 'the fundamental values of intellectual energy and freedom, devotion to the truth, [and] artistic independence', and, it must be said, as a male had far more reason than Tynan to trust that he might one day secure artistic patronage.[55] There is no precedent for such beliefs in a middle class Irish Catholic family, and particularly not for the daughter of such a family. For these reasons, the distance at which Tynan was placed (and placed herself), not only from Yeats but from the majority of the Revivalists who shared his Anglo-Irish and male identities, had existed long before Ernest Boyd published his assessments of her.

That Tynan did not achieve the degree of artistry and acclaim that Yeats did was inevitable. It is likewise difficult to fault her for placing herself at a remove from the members of a literary movement who consistently and often publicly emphasized the degree of her distance from them. Had the opinions of Hyde, Ryan, Boyd and Yeats been her only reasons for altering her literary focus, that change of focus would have remained understandable. Yet Tynan had other and more important instigations. Of those events that rendered Tynan's relationship to Irish cultural nationalism more equivocal than it once had been, two of the most important occurred simultaneously in 1893: her move from Ireland to England and her marriage to the Protestant Henry Albert Hinkson. The result of these changed circumstances was a conspicuous shift in her literary output: it was only after she migrated to England and married that she began to write novels. That the beginning of her career as a novelist coincided with the beginning of her marriage is no mere coincidence, for, in marrying Harry Hinkson, she left financial security behind. Thereafter, she found herself

---

54   Letter from Tynan to Matthew Russell (17 August 1891), Russell Papers J27/73.
55   Douglas Archibald, 'John Butler Yeats', in David Holdeman and Ben Levitas, eds., *W. B. Yeats in Context* (Cambridge: Cambridge UP, 2010), 113.

turning to the writing of novels as a means of 'boiling the pot'.[56] From 1898, with the advent of children to their household, the necessity for her to earn from her writing became even more pronounced: it was, she wrote, her duty to 'keep the fire on the hearth for the children and the securities and sanctities of home about them' – things that her husband apparently was unable to do.[57]

Tynan had met her future husband when, in November of 1888, she was introduced to him by an English friend who was visiting Hinkson at Trinity College.[58] After graduating from Trinity, Hinkson taught Classics at Clongowes Wood School and by the time of their marriage was working as a schoolmaster in London. Less than two years later, however, serious problems arose in Hinkson's professional life. In May of 1894 Tynan wrote anxiously to Russell to say that her husband had received a letter from the principal of the school suggesting that 'there were a great many complaints of Harry's manner to the boys, etc [...] such a letter that Harry had no option but to write and say that if desired he would leave at the month's end'.[59] Forced out of teaching, Hinkson next tried his hand at journalistic work and over the course of the period between 1898 and 1912 wrote and published more than a dozen novels, none of which appears to have been a significant source of income for the family. He studied law, was called to the bar and authored what was then the definitive tract on copyright, yet

---

56   Tynan, *The Middle Years*, 353.
57   Tynan, *The Middle Years*, 353. Tynan gave birth to five children. The first was a stillborn son; the second, a son named Godfrey, lived only a few weeks. Her three remaining children – Theobald Henry ('Toby'), Giles Aylmer ('Bunny' or 'Patrick') and Pamela – all outlived her.
58   The friend in question was Francis Fagan, the brother of Tynan's first (unrequited) love, Charles Fagan. Charles had died in India in 1885, but Tynan remained friendly with the Fagan family for a number of years afterwards. See letter from Tynan to Matthew Russell (8 September 1885), in which she tells Russell of her heartbreak over Charles Fagan's death and of his engagement to a woman other than herself, and letter from Tynan to Matthew Russell (3 November 1888), in which she notes that Francis Fagan will be staying during his upcoming visit 'with a Mr Hinkson in Trinity College', both Russell Papers J27/73.
59   Letter from Tynan to Matthew Russell (29 May 1894), Russell Papers J27/73.

his attempts at legal practice were abortive, and his only verifiable source of regular income over the course of his twenty-six-year marriage to Tynan came when his wife's long-term friendship with Lord and Lady Aberdeen resulted in his appointment as Resident Magistrate for Mayo in 1914. By that time, Yeats's sister Lily was writing to her father to describe Hinkson's longstanding problems with alcohol, in the process also referring to Tynan having worked herself 'to rags' to alleviate the 'good deal of debt' the family had incurred.[60]

Yeats's first negative appraisal of Tynan's poetry came in the series of articles he wrote on Irish literature in the *Bookman* in 1895, the year that her first novel was published. If the implication of the juxtaposition of these events is that Tynan's change of literary focus had the effect of diminishing her poetry and thereby of disappointing her old friend and colleague, it nonetheless made sound financial sense. Novels were by then the favoured format among the British reading public and their sales were continuing to grow at an exceptionally rapid pace, as an 1894 report in the *Bookman* makes clear:

> And what about the novels? 'Unprecedented' is hardly a sufficiently strong adjective to apply to the present demand for this class of publication. Perhaps 'phenomenal' is nearer the mark. Anyhow, the number now being sold is enormous.[61]

Tynan, already known to many reading households in both Ireland and England through her poetry and journalistic work, found a ready readership for her fiction and quickly settled into a pattern in which she produced on average three novels per year while still managing to generate a steady and copious volume of newspaper and magazine articles, memoirs, biographies, school textbooks, volumes of poetry and short story collections. Although she would claim about her novels that they were created

---

60   Letter from Lily Yeats to John Butler Yeats (10 October 1914), National Library of Ireland, Yeats Correspondence, Ms 31,112 (23). My sincere thanks to Janet Wallwork for drawing my attention to this letter.

61   'Monthly Report of the Wholesale Book Trade', *Bookman* 7/39 (December 1894), 74.

'not to please [her]self, but to meet demand', more than a third are set in
Ireland, and the necessity of writing them did not deter her from using
them as a means to confront the serious topics about which she had been
debarred from speaking, because of her brogue, *in propria persona*.[62] That
she believed her work to be imbued not only with the ability to aid her
family financially and to promote her religion, but that it also held the
potential to alter opinions on political and personal issues in which she
had a vested interest, is evident in her novelistic themes. It is her novels,
more so than her poetry or memoirs, which offer her most candid, detailed
and immediate perspectives on the changing relationship between Ireland
and England over the course of the period 1890–1916.

Her first novel, *The Way of a Maid*, is a case in point. Published in
1895, it is markedly concerned with the topic of inter-religious marriage in
Ireland and deals with issues with which Tynan had long been acquainted.
Some of the novel's inspiration may, in fact, have come from her father,
who was the product of an ill-fated interdenominational marriage, about
which Tynan writes in her memoirs:

> My father's mother, being a Catholic and an only child, had run away with and mar-
> ried in a Protestant Church one Tynan, a young Dublin man. The prejudice against
> mixed marriages being very strong at that time, the marriage was bitterly resented
> by her parents. Her husband dying and leaving her and her two children unprovided
> for, she returned to her parents, who brought up the children in their own name.
> My father claimed his real name when he grew to manhood, but he could learn very
> little about his father, whom his mother had not long survived.[63]

Her use of the past tense in this passage to describe Irish religious prejudices belies the reality in Ireland at the time that she was writing and more
particularly of her own situation, and *The Way of a Maid* is also undoubtedly a more personal testament to the intolerance she herself experienced
after her marriage to Hinkson. Among those who were reluctant to bestow
their blessings on the union her father figured most prominently, but the
marriage provoked a falling out between Tynan and others, including

62   Tynan, *The Middle Years*, 353.
63   Tynan, *The Wandering Years*, 249.

Rosa Mulholland, one of her literary heroes, who had written to her in the first week of her marriage to say that it 'would always be a painful subject between' them.[64] In early 1895, the year *The Way of a Maid* was published, Tynan learned that her former neighbours in Clondalkin were circulating rumours that she had renounced both her faith and her country, and Russell also accused her of 'praising bad books' in her journalistic work and of conveying anti-Catholic and anti-Irish sentiments in her fiction.[65] More recent scholars on the subject of mixed marriage indicate that reactions in Ireland to such unions tended to be profoundly negative, ranging from resentful tolerance to blatant persecution, and such appears to have been Tynan's own experience.[66]

In *The Way of a Maid*, she argues that cross-religious alliances are of benefit to Ireland and its people. Many of the almost exclusively Catholic inhabitants of her fictional town of Coolevara are, she explains, descended from the Protestant Cromwellian soldiers who long ago came to vanquish and remained to be subjugated and converted:

> Those inconquerable warriors settled down in various parts of the fertile Irish country, and, in days of peace, had to ground arms before the violet-eyed daughters of the mere Irish. In course of time they or their sons renegaded to the Scarlet Woman, and became as sturdy on her side as they had been on the other in their psalm-singing days. Admirable results these marriages have had.[67]

While she notes that 'the cleavage between Protestants and Catholics in Coolevara, as elsewhere in Ireland, is incredibly great', and that there 'is no common ground for these adherents of the different religions to meet', one of the novel's projects is to show the extent to which mutuality of

---

64 Letters from Tynan to Matthew Russell (25 February 1895) and (23 March 1895), Russell Papers J27/73.

65 Letter from Tynan to Matthew Russell (5 March 1895), Russell Papers J27/73.

66 See, for instance, Eoin de Bhaldraithe, 'Mixed Marriages and Irish Politics: The Effect of "Ne Temere"', *Studies: An Irish Quarterly Review* (Autumn 1988) 77/307, 284–299, and Donald Harman Akenson, *Small Differences: Irish Catholics and Irish Protestants: 1815–1922* (Dublin: Gill and MacMillan, 1988), 111–116.

67 Katharine Tynan, *The Way of a Maid* (London: Lawrence and Bullen, 1895), 6–7.

thought and experience exists between the denominations.[68] She also offers a warning to her English readers of what might be achieved if the disparate Irish factions were ever to recognize that many of their political goals are shared. Regarding the Protestant gentry, for instance, the local land agent, Mr Oliver, explains to his wife's English nephew, St. Edmund Hilliard, that

> Their idea is equality with England, not subservience to her, and, by Jove! some of your clever English fellows would be amazed at the haughty mental attitude toward you of the Irish class whom you regard as the best friends of your domination. So they are, but it's from distrust of their Roman Catholic fellow-countrymen. If they could get over that you'd have something to do to hold your own in this island [...] [Parnell], now, is an example of an Irish Protestant who has broken free from the fear of the Catholics.[69]

The novel also features two interreligious romantic entanglements – one between the Irish Catholic Nora O'Halloran and the Protestant Hilliard; the other between the Irish Catholic Jim Hurley and the Irish Protestant Jessie Oliver – and demonstrates that the gulf which separates the religions is vast, though not unbridgeable. In Tynan's text, the difficulties in securing these cross-religious alliances all reside in the ingrained prejudices of the older generation. For Jessie and Jim, it is their parents' objections that must be confronted before their union can be achieved. Mrs Oliver must overcome 'her slight consternation at having yet another Papist received on friendly terms by her family', and Mrs Hurley her worries concerning her son marrying 'one alien to him in creed and traditions'.[70] The novel's most poignant confrontation comes, however, when Jessie broaches the subject of her marriage to her father, whose opinions might very well echo Andrew Cullen Tynan's own: 'I am a broad-minded man,' her father tells her, 'but I don't like a mixed marriage for a daughter of mine [...] But for the religion I should say "yes" willingly [...] How will it be when your dearest faiths are not shared by the human heart you have to lean upon all your life?'[71]

---

68   Tynan, *The Way of a Maid*, 7–8.
69   Tynan, *The Way of Maid*, 63.
70   Tynan, *The Way of a Maid*, 270; 275–276.
71   Tynan, *The Way of a Maid*, 282.

Jessie's answer is to convert wholeheartedly to Jim's Catholic faith, as the town's Cromwellian forebears had done: 'Your people shall be my people,' she tells her fiancé at the end of the novel, 'your God my God!'[72] In this novel, Tynan may avoid portraying the animosities that Francis chooses to dwell on in *Dark Rosaleen*, but the affinities in the authors' viewpoints are readily recognizable: in both texts, no union of the factions within Ireland can be achieved unless the supremacy of Catholicism is acknowledged. If the evidence of her novels can be trusted, Tynan would not change her mind in this regard: the inverse action – a Catholic to Protestant conversion – never occurs in any of her texts, and it was not a course she herself agreed to take.[73]

Tynan's first novel is representative of much of her Irish work which followed it. The overwhelming majority of her Irish novels are romances, and more often than not involve love stories between members of feuding families at odds over the rights to local land. Episodic and anecdotal rather than strategically plotted, these books almost always suggest that regeneration of Irish property cannot be achieved until longstanding prejudices are removed. In some cases, clearing the way for a new generation of Irish reformers – many of whom, in Tynan's texts, have experience of living outside their homeland and are therefore unfettered by local attitudes – involves a significant transformation of the older generation. In a few instances, it involves the death of that generation. The plots of both *The Handsome Brandons* (1899) and *A Girl of Galway* (1902), for example, feature young members of Irish families who have been raised abroad returning to Ireland to mend relations with a landowning grandfather, who incidentally has been mismanaging his property and mistreating his tenants. This attempt at reconciliation in each case meets with failure, and the new generation must instead forge inter-family and inter-cultural alliances in order for peace and well-being to be restored to the Irish homeland.

---

72   Tynan, *The Way of a Maid*, 279.
73   It was in fact Hinkson who converted to Catholicism, but he did not do so until 1919, and then only when he was on his deathbed.

Concurrently, it is the land itself which enacts a 'natural' form of revenge on the immoral older generation.

In *The Handsome Brandons*, a storm swells a bog and the resulting flood sweeps away and drowns both Harry De Lacy's corrupt grandfather and the evil manager of his ancestral estate, the aptly named Castly Angry. The promise for regeneration of the land is thereafter embodied in a pair of alliances which serve to negate old animosities: one between Harry and Esther Brandon, a member of the family with whom the De Lacy's have been feuding; and the other between the old money Aline Brandon and the new money Mr Desmond, the man against whom Aline's late brother, Pierce, held a debilitating grudge. The reason that such alliances can be achieved is succinctly stated by Tynan's young narrator, Hilda Brandon: her generation, she explains, 'had no hereditary hatred in our veins'.[74]

In *A Girl of Galway*, Bertha Grace is the product of a clandestine marriage between Irish parents of differing classes which has caused a seemingly irreparable rift between her father and grandfather. Now an adult, Bertha is sent from England, where she has been raised, to live with her bitter Irish grandfather, Sir Devlin Grace. In this novel, it is a fire that destroys the cursed woods which surround and isolate Bertha in her grandfather's castle. The blaze also kills the cruel and criminally minded manager of the estate and maims Sir Devlin. His injuries lead to a loss of his memory, and thus to the forgetting of the jealousies and enmities that instigated his wicked behaviour, with the result that his friendships and family alliances are renewed immediately prior to his death. The romantic union which is ultimately achieved between Bertha and Hugh Roper subsequently unites the two neighbouring Irish estates which had formerly been at war, and her parents' return to the Irish land is made possible. In both *The Handsome Brandons* and *A Girl of Galway*, legitimacy and responsibility are efficiently restored by the introduction of a nationally and culturally diverse younger generation to Ireland, while the acts of God which rid the land of those who have theretofore governed it cruelly or wrongly effectively eliminate

---

74   Katharine Tynan, *The Handsome Brandons: A Story for Girls* (London: Blackie and Son, 1899), 104.

the need for physical violence or organized rebellion. Forgetting or transcending the legacies of the past is, in each case, an important prerequisite for the rejuvenation of the land and the family.

Tynan's Irish protagonists are invariably reformers, and it is frequently her fictional project to show the means by which her young heroes and heroines achieve absolution for their ancestors, thereby staking rightful claims to both Irish land and the Irish people. In *The Dear Irish Girl* (1899), Maurice O'Hara is descended from a long line of Connaught squires who have 'rack-rented their tenants gaily from father to son'.[75] Rather than repeat the mistakes of the past, Maurice overcomes them through his exposure to an emerging and radically different set of ethics which Tynan represents as specifically maternal in origin. From his biological mother, a member of the worldly La Touche family, Maurice inherits a 'new strain of conscience and responsibility'; through his Celtic Irish foster mother, Nannie, he learns to empathize with 'the people'.[76] With this newfound sense of morality and responsibility, legitimate governance of the land is restored to the O'Hara family, and Maurice is able to wrest the attention and affections of the exiled Biddy O'Connor back from England and the English suitor, John Ayers, who has been vying with him for her allegiance.

In this and similar novels such as *Three Fair Maids* (1900) and *That Sweet Enemy* (1901), issues of rightful ownership of Irish land figure prominently, while religion plays little or no role in the relationship between land and legitimacy. Tynan's advocacy of Irish Ireland values is increasingly evidenced, however, in works such as *Julia* (1904), *The French Wife* (1904) and *Cousins and Others* (1909), in which Catholicism acts as a precondition for the ownership of Irish property. Over the course of these narratives, the law and morality are consistently shown to be at odds as Catholic characters are deprived of land that is rightfully, but not legally, theirs – Tynan's texts thereby prefiguring similar ideas in Emily Lawless's *The Race of Castlebar*. In each case, ownership of property is reinstated to the Catholic family to which it had traditionally belonged, even when such a restoration means

75   Katharine Tynan, *The Dear Irish Girl* (London: Smith, Elder, 1899), 30.
76   Tynan, *The Dear Irish Girl*, 31; 54.

the displacement of those of Protestant descent who have lived on and governed the land for generations, as it does in both *The French Wife* and *Cousins and Others*. These novels represent a significant shift in narrative tone: more assertive in their advocacy of Catholic rights, her narrative themes reflect a newly emboldened political voice – the result, perhaps, of her involvement with *Shan Van Vocht* during the period.

While in *Julia* lands are returned to their rightful Catholic owners through the marriage of Protestant and Catholic characters of common ancestry, Tynan is at pains to emphasize that her Protestant protagonist, Murty O'Kavanagh, has been raised in England and thus away from the taint of Irish Protestant prejudices. There is no equivocation within the text on the matter of blame for religious and racial intolerance in Ireland. For Tynan, it rests squarely on the shoulders of Protestants: 'It is the Anglo-Irish who are the irreconcilables, and not the complaisant and easy-going Celt', she asserts, re-affirming in the process a specifically Irish Protestant culpability for sectarian animosities. She refers derogatorily to the act of proselytism which has served to disinherit the Catholic branch of the O'Kavanagh family, and asserts that 'there may be a Union of Hearts between Celt and Saxon; but to the Anglo-Irishman, more especially if he calls himself Irish, the marriage will be a thing unnatural, impossible'.[77] Through the union, by marriage, of Murty and his distant relation, the Catholic Julia O'Kavanagh, the text reiterates the types of ideas she first broached in *The Way of a Maid* that inter-religious and inter-cultural alliances are beneficial to, and even necessary for, the rehabilitation of Ireland and the restoration of legitimacy of governance to its people. Tynan's text nonetheless reveals a new and vehement sense of menace towards, and apprehension about, Revivalist pursuits and Irish Protestant actions and attitudes (both modern and historic) that linger at the close of the novel.

Julia exemplifies a type of novel Tynan was capable of writing: one in which the endemic racial differences and religious animosities in Ireland form the fulcrum upon which the action of the novel turns. More often, however, and reflecting her own experiences, both positive and negative, of

77   Tynan, *Julia*, 62.

middle class mobility, Tynan's novels figure Ireland as a country in which social boundaries are indistinct to the point of being virtually unrecognizable. Such is the case in *She Walks in Beauty* (1899), in which the Graydons, the 'Quality' family around which the plot centres, are in a steady but largely unlamented financial and social decline, while the Irish community in which they live is characterized as 'a large family' whose diverse members are willing and able to interact freely and affably.[78] In Tynan's fictional evocations of Ireland, it remains the case that 'the good blood is very often in the cottages, and the base blood in the castles', and she deploys this idea regularly to highlight the degree to which eccentricities and inconsistencies thwart attempts to firmly define social categorizations.[79] Tynan's characters rise and fall along the social and economic scale more often on the basis of their own merits and inclinations than through recourse to notions of birth, heredity and family. This is the case in *The House of the Crickets* (1908), in which Hannah Moore is the daughter of an indolent and impoverished Irish farmer. Through her innate poise, singing talent, and the education she is able to pursue because of that talent, Hannah transcends the legacies of her upbringing and the ill-treatment of her puritanical, fatalistic and slovenly father by achieving professional acclaim and marrying into a landed family. Molly De La Poer, the protagonist of 1903's *The Honourable Molly*, is likewise able to move up and down the social spectrum with ease, but opts to make the opposite transition. Despite her status as 'half a peasant', Molly assimilates herself into life with the upper-class half-sisters and aunts with whom she is raised, yet eventually chooses to marry Hugh Sinclair and subsequently settles comfortably and ably into the role of farmer's wife.[80] This blurring of traditional class boundaries – poor and middle class characters rising along the social scale, upper class characters falling, the whole of society mixing cordially – is a common undercurrent in Tynan's

---

78   Katharine Tynan, *She Walks in Beauty* (London: Smith, Elder, 1899), 40.

79   Katharine Tynan, *The Honourable Molly* (London: Smith, Elder, 1903), 206. See also Katharine Tynan, *A Daughter of Kings* (London: Eveleigh Nash, 1905), 67, where Tynan writes that Ireland is a country 'where the good blood is so often in the hut and the base in the Hall'.

80   Tynan, *The Honourable Molly*, 206.

early and mid-career work, in which unification and conciliation of the social classes is represented as an often hard-won, but nevertheless natural and proper, outcome.

Molly de la Poer's descent into the rank of life her chosen partner inhabits highlights what is implicit in a number of Tynan's novels: that for the Irish male, class transitions of any kind are more problematic than they are for women. Whereas Tynan's female characters – through beauty, poise, honour or professional accomplishment – may attract an upper-class man and thereby be raised into the milieu their partner inhabits, working or middle-class male characters regularly remain more class-bound than their female counterparts, and their chosen partners must accept the social decline which inevitably accompanies the marriage. Just as Molly, by marrying Hugh Sinclair, must leave behind the aristocratic home in which she was raised, in *The Story of Cecilia* (1911), Maurice Grace and Cecily Shannon must make their way, after their marriage, on his doctor's wages and live without the companionship of her well-to-do relations. In each case, however, Tynan shows these men achieving a degree of financial and social success which elevates them above their initial status, and the overriding sense is that the notion of class, within Ireland, remains an indistinct and ever-changing concept. At the same time, these narrative preoccupations hint that the existing, restrictive patriarchal system of wealth inheritance is expediting the growth of a more prosperous middle class through the disinheritance of its upper class women.

It is with works such as *A Daughter of the Fields* (1901), however, that Tynan presents her most convincingly complex portraits of characters who range across conventional cultural boundaries, and in which she most effectively evokes a sense of women's fluctuating roles in turn-of-the-century Irish society. Though none qualifies as a New Woman, many of her characters at this juncture are educated and working women who must resolve themselves to ever-altering gender roles, and such is the case with the two central female characters in *A Daughter of the Fields*. In this intricate portrayal of the relationship between gender, class, education and notions of privilege, Tynan constructs two central female characters who embody the class-based and gendered dislocation she herself experienced as an upwardly mobile middle class woman and as the financial head of her household. Meg O'Donoghue, the novel's protagonist, is the child of a small-scale farming family whose father has been ruined in both reputation and livelihood by his alcoholism. Meg's elevation by means of her convent schooling to the hyper-feminized status of 'lady' is achieved against a backdrop in which the mother's physical masculinization and social decline act as the prerequisite for the daughter's rise. Upon Meg's return from school, mother and daughter, more estranged than reconciled by the sacrifices the mother has made and the advantages the daughter has been given, struggle to find metaphorical common ground, yet mirror each other in their displacement and dislocation. Having been educated beyond her station, Meg is neither at home with the landed and financially superior class with whom she has been educated but from whom she senses an inherent social distance, nor does she belong to the working class society from which she emerged. Her mother, meanwhile, after having taken on the heavy physical work of the family farm, no longer occupies a conventionally feminine role. Thus, while Meg finds herself in a position between traditionally defined social classes, her mother is effectively stranded between genders. The resolution of their differences and the difficulties of self-definition in terms of class and gender roles remain problematic even as Tynan struggles to show her characters, at the end of the novel, reconciling themselves to each other and to their newly realized positions within Irish society.

A Daughter of Kings (1905) acts as both companion piece and complement to *A Daughter of the Fields* in centering its action on a similarly complex, yet conversely structured, type of social movement. Anne Daly is a member of the Irish landed gentry forced by financial hardship to seek employment in England. Despite settling readily into working life, she cannot transition as easily into English life, and expresses her distaste for the opulence she perceives in her newfound homeland in culturally specific terms: 'I don't like the – the moneyed people,' she explains. 'It is one of the painful things about living in England. There is so much money. We never suffer from that complaint in Ireland.'[81] Anne is a character who believes firmly in the stratification of society along lines of financial and hereditary

81   Tynan, *A Daughter of Kings*, 126.

privilege, asserting that a culture in which there is 'no aristocracy of wealth, nor refinement, nor birth' is untenable.[82] Her ultimate desire is not for a return to her own position of economic superiority but for a general and renewed sense of the type of civic responsibility she believes was once intrinsic to the Ascendancy in Ireland. Through the act of recognizing, in the self-made Englishman John Corbett, the innate sense of honour she believed was confined to her own class, Anne's prejudices against English *nouveau riche* prosperity are effectively dispelled, yet her nostalgia for a feudalistic type of social hierarchy is never undermined, or even effectively challenged, in the novel.

Anne Daly's views concerning class are in contradiction to those of other affectionately portrayed characters in Tynan's novels, including Mother Joseph in *The House of the Crickets*, who asks, 'What cause could there be for either pride or humility in the mere accident of birth?'[83] Locating Tynan's own opinions in the midst of such divergent characterizations is problematic, yet some patterns of thought are discernible throughout her *oeuvre*. If, for instance, by uniting John Corbett and Anne Daly in *A Daughter of Kings*, Tynan constructs a partnership which on one side of its equation reflects positively on modern society and capitalist economics, it is also in keeping with the sentiment of much of Tynan's fiction that on the other side of that partnership there exists a character who represents all that was honourable about feudalism. 'It was such a golden and pleasant place, Feudal England', Tynan would claim in her 1924 memoir, and her novels written years before suggest that she had long felt just such a nostalgia for old world values.[84] Many of her writings display a sense of equivocation concerning the wholesale trade of feudal values for capitalist ones, and Tynan's novels frequently feature aristocratic characters who aid or guide their bourgeoisie counterparts. The underlying message may remain one of cooperation between classes, races, generations and religions, but the consistent use of aristocratic and upper class characters as a regulatory

---

82   Tynan, *A Daughter of Kings*, 126–127.
83   Tynan, *The House of the Crickets*, 126–127.
84   Tynan, *Memories* (London: Eveleigh Nash and Grayson, 1924), 345.

force is telling in terms of Tynan's own allegiances, and reveals a subtle and surprising but nonetheless perceptible lack of confidence in the new order.

As often as she uses her texts to offer solutions to society's inherent problems, Tynan employs them to trouble or query communal categorizations. In much the same manner that she questions class and gender-based conventions in novels such as *A Daughter of Kings*, in other works she can be seen to disrupt political classifications. Her works feature a number of Irish characters to which conventional Unionist or Nationalist definitions do not apply, and those such as Mrs Brabazon in *Princess Katharine* (1912) are created seemingly for the purpose of confounding expectations of any unambiguous political partisanship within Ireland and of reflecting the shifting loyalties she herself admitted to experiencing due to her long-term residence in England. Echoing the precise sentiments that Tynan ascribes to herself in her 1922 volume of memoirs, Mrs Brabazon suggests that her politic loyalties have a tendency to shift with her geographical location: 'Of course I am [a Unionist] when I'm here [in Ireland],' she explains. 'You should hear me when I'm over there [in England]. I make the hair stand up on their heads with the violence of my rebelly opinions'.[85] Similarly constructed is the character of Lord Carbery in *The Honourable Molly*, who, like his unmistakable real-life counterpart, Emily's Lawless's brother Valentine Frederick Lawless (the fourth Lord Cloncurry), is a reminder of the difficulty of accurately situating the Irish in terms of their political allegiances.[86] In her creation of Carbery, Tynan recognizably draws on what was publicly known about Lawless and his siblings (including his novelist sister), who were avowedly Unionist in their political leanings. Emily Lawless admitted

85 Katharine Tynan, *Princess Katharine* (London, Melbourne, Toronto: Ward, Lock, 1912), 202. In *The Wandering Years*, 135, Tynan writes, 'I was a Sinn Feiner to my English and Scottish friends, and even dared to call myself so', though she admits that her 'Sinn Fein friends' would find her 'sadly lacking'.

86 Ethna Carbery was the pseudonym of Anna Johnston, Tynan's friend and a founder/ publisher of *Shan Van Vocht*. Carbery was the daughter of the Fenian Robert Johnston and an outspoken Nationalist in her own right. The use of her surname is one of several devices Tynan employs to tinge her fictional portrait of the Lawless family with irony.

that she and her brothers were – seemingly incongruously – proud of their grandfather, Valentine Browne Lawless, who had on more than one occasion been imprisoned in the Tower of London for treason.[87] In an echo of their sentiments, Tynan's characters Lord Carbery and his sister Edith are 'staunch Unionists' for whom it is a matter of inordinate pride that there is a 'lawless vein' in their family and that an ancestor was once jailed for treason.[88] With its basis in reality, Tynan's fleeting but noteworthy emphasis on the Carbery family demonstrates her contentions that being 'to some extent anti-Irish […] doesn't involve being pro-English' and exemplifies the degree to which the Irish 'aren't made of a pattern' which can be easily mapped in terms of either-or political distinctions.[89] Her point in creating characterizations such as Carbery is almost certainly revisionary: to defy her reader's expectations and to deconstruct the boundaries of conventional conduct.

This type of tactic serves to elucidate and normalize what might have appeared to her readers to be variant behaviours or identities. So too does another of Tynan's most recognizable fictional missions – that of justifying and defending the Irish to her English readers. Over time Tynan could be seen to expand on such a project, effectively using her texts as warnings to the English to alter their behaviour towards the Irish before trouble ensues – warnings which appear, with hindsight, to be prescient. In *A Union of Hearts*, from 1901, she appropriates for her title a phrase often deployed in political circles to describe the long-standing union between Ireland and England in recognizably ameliorative terms which attempted to redefine it as an alliance based on mutual affection rather than the imposed and uncomfortable position of political dependency that it actually was for Ireland. In her fictional re-envisioning of the English-Irish relationship, Tynan inverts the terms of this union by forcing her well-meaning but misguided English landowner, Rivers, into a state of dependence on the Irish land reformer Aileen Considine, who acts as both his guide and conscience.

87   See Emily Lawless, 'Of the Personal Element in History', *Nineteenth Century* 50/297 (November 1901), 790–798.
88   Tynan, *The Honourable Molly*, 87.
89   Tynan, *The Way of a Maid*, 62 and Tynan, *The Honourable Molly*, 87.

By educating Rivers about the violent 'League days' and cautioning him that 'the Celt is peacable and gentle – till his home or his family is menaced', Aileen manages to convince the Englishman to alter his ways and thus curtails a murderous tenant-led mutiny, saving many lives, including Rivers', in the process.[90]

To the same ends but by very different methods, Tynan uses *A King's Woman* (1902), set during the 1798 Rising, to create characters whose experiences and opinions are recognizably based on real-life Irish counterparts including Lady Lucy Fitzgerald, sister of the insurgent Lord Edward Fitzgerald and love interest of his compatriot Arthur O'Connor, and Lady Sarah Napier, the loyalist whose close relationship to the Fitzgerald family led her to a measure of empathy with the cause of the 1798 rebels. As the tale of *A King's Woman* unfolds, Tynan's first person narrator, Penelope Fayle, views events in Ireland at first hand and, like Lawless's and Francis's English characters who find themselves in similar situations, recognizes the ways in which the Irish are being mistreated by her countrymen. Thereafter, she gradually moves from a steadfastly loyalist stance to one in which she views the Irish insurgents with whom she is forced to live sympathetically. Featuring a picaresque plot in which marital abduction figures and women seize control from their less capable male counterparts in crisis situations, the novel explores similar ideas to those in Lawless's *A Colonel of the Empire* and *The Race of Castlebar*. Like the latter novel, it also ends in a lament for Irish rebels, in this case conveyed through words spoken by Penelope, who remains a steadfast 'king's woman' even as she recognizes the validity of Irish grievances. Penelope's lyrical description of the Irish rebels' final resting place at the close of the novel effectively evokes not only a sense of their heroism, but also of its potential legacies: 'That is the green grave of rebels, the long tongue of grass of too-vivid green, which you shall see stretching out in many a plough-land, sacred for ever, inviolate for ever. For they have long memories here, and they are in love

---

90   Katharine Tynan, *A Union of Hearts* (London: James Nisbet, 1901), 77.

with graves'.[91] Throughout the novel, Penelope's escalating compassion for the Irish and their suffering is made both apparent and understandable, while her final references to 'long memories' and 'too-vivid' graves lend to the text a conspicuous sense of foreboding.

Tynan's most effusive praise is reserved for her fictional Irish conspirators, in all their guises, who wage war against the oppression they face – even when that oppression is not represented by the Crown. These types of characters are ubiquitous in her fiction, but most readily identifiable in the number of her novels which, like *A King's Woman*, use historical episodes as their points of genesis: the Catholic characters who rebel against Protestant oppression in her Tudor-period novel *The Golden Lily* (1902), the Jacobite fighters in *For the White Rose* (1905), and Edward Fitzgerald in *Lord Edward: A Study in Romance* (1916). Conversely, her sharpest criticisms surface in her depictions of those Irish characters resigned to their respective fates. An indication of her steadily altering attitudes towards her countrymen as her time in England lengthened can be glimpsed in the changes in these types of depictions; for, while in her early novels the peasantry are figured largely as the helpless victims of misguided, absentee or willingly cruel landlords, they become over the course of time increasingly complicit in their own victimization through their ready acquiescence to a destructive despair. This is the case in novels such as *The House of the Crickets* and *Heart o' Gold*, in which Tynan laments 'a fatalism, a supineness' to which many of her peasant characters are shown to too readily submit and against which her reforming characters can be powerless.[92]

Equally condemnatory are her depictions of Ascendancy figures unable to adapt to encroaching change. These are often families forced to inhabit increasingly smaller areas of their ancestral homes as those homes crumble around them. Though they may take on the differing names of Castle Angry in *The Handsome Brandons*, Corofin in *A Girl of Galway*, Witch's

---

91   Katharine Tynan, *A King's Woman: Being the Narrative of Miss Penelope Fayle, now Mistress Frobisher, Concerning the Late Troublous Times in Ireland* (London: Hurst and Blackett, 1902), 308–309.

92   Katharine Tynan, *Heart o' Gold, or The Little Princess: A Story for Girls* (London: S. W. Partridge, 1912), 27.

Castle in *A Daughter of Kings*, Castle Finn in *That Sweet Enemy*, Aghadoe Abbey in *The Story of Bawn*, Castle Truagh in *The Adventures of Alicia* (1906), Cappamore in *Heart o' Gold*, Castle Eagle in *The House of the Foxes* (1915), and Castle Kilmorna in *They Loved Greatly* (1923) – these various Big Houses act consistently as the most readily recognizable symbols of their owners' diminishing statuses and by extension as metaphors for their incipient social and economic downfall. Together with Tynan's depictions of decrepit Georgian mansions situated in the midst of a progressively more ghettoized Dublin, these recurring images of Castle Rackrent-type homes act as commentaries upon the illegitimacy of the Pale, while her consistent rebuke of the inert peasantry hints that the rise of the Gael, if the Gael can only be kindled, might be nascent.

Tynan nevertheless regularly creates pitiable Ascendancy figures, poor and elderly widows and spinster sisters most prominent among them. These women, always malnourished and ill, are trapped either in disintegrating Dublin tenements, as are Miss Stasia in *Her Ladyship* (1907) and Miss MacSweeney in *Heart o' Gold* (1912), or victimized by servants in dilapidated country manor homes surrounded by bogs and other desolate landscapes, as is the case with Miss O'Neill in *The House of the Secret* (1910) and Miss Peggy Hamilton in *The House on the Bogs* (1922). The predicaments of these women are often figured as specifically Irish in origin, and consistently and revealingly linked to the activities of the Land League. While repeated images of 'distressed ladies [...] who had suffered during the land agitation' may appear incongruous with the author's own political ethos, particularly her support of Parnell and involvement in the Ladies' Land League, Tynan had with hindsight come to view the League as an 'ugly and sordid, though necessary, revolution' whose precepts ruined 'many a fine family'.[93] Having realized after the fact that the League fell short of her own ideal vision of and for Ireland, Tynan uses her fallen Ascendancy ladies to emphasize her personal disillusionment.

---

93   Katharine Tynan, *Her Ladyship* (London: Smith, Elder, 1907), 57; Tynan, *The Years of the Shadow*, 63; and Tynan, *Heart o' Gold*, 260.

In what is certainly a comment upon the ineffectuality of Irish political
movements of the past, she also increasingly uses her novels to endorse specific policies for the regeneration of Ireland which reflect her own political
philosophies. This tactic is apparent in the manner in which her fictional
Irish politician in *The French Wife*, Sir Gerard Molyneux, promotes anti-
emigration policies of the type that John Redmond, a long-time acquaintance of Tynan's, was advocating at the time of the novel's publication.
Through his experience of visiting Irish slums in New York, Molyneux is
said to have

> learned to appreciate the thing that emigration means to the Irish peasant [...] He
> saw their children dying like flies, themselves familiarised with vice and crime, for-
> getting their religion, contemptuous of their old ideals, the one saving grace left to
> them the desire to return to the old country.[94]

This desire for return is always explicable, for the Ireland that Tynan creates is more often than not a near-idyllic space. She may occasionally peel
back the layers of Irish society far enough to show Dublin's crumbling
tenements and the Irish countryside's poverty-stricken districts, but these
are always anomalies in what is, for her, largely a 'clean and innocent' country.[95] America is characterized in Tynan's novels exclusively by its slums,
poverty and overcrowding, and England becomes in novels such as 1912's
Heart o' Gold a country where even nature has been tainted by the filth of
industry, taking on an almost apocalyptic visage in images of 'the blackness
of the trees in their stems and branches, the blackness of the earth which
seemed to have been mixed with soot; [...] the curious phenomenon that
one could not even pluck a flower without having one's fingers soiled.'[96]
Ireland alone remains a country which is for the most part unsullied, spa-
cious, inhabited by honourable people, and teeming with untapped wealth.
Irish characters in Tynan's novels may mimic their real-life counterparts by
migrating to America and England in search of better lives, but they are

94   Tynan, *The French Wife* (London: F. V. White, 1904), 27.
95   Tynan, *Her Ladyship*, 156.
96   Tynan, *Heart o' Gold*, 246.

doomed to disappointment as these destinations are repeatedly figured as unhealthy and unwelcoming.

More threatening by far, however, are the Indian sub-continent and Africa, as Tynan consistently creates characters only to show them disappearing in these outer reaches of the Empire. The reasons for her narrative bias against these regions can in part be illuminated by evidence from her own life: her first (unrequited) love, Charles Fagan, died in India while attempting to earn the money he needed in order to marry his fiancée, and Jim Alderson, another of her most intimate friends, was killed in a skirmish during the Boer War in South Africa.[97] Offering evidence that these fictional themes have their genesis in her real-life experiences, Tynan can be seen to use her plots as instruments to re-write Fagan's and Alderson's fates, allowing their fictional counterparts more pleasant destinies, even if those destinies are always tainted by a sense of danger and loss. Thus the Fagan-esque Jim Annesley, in *The Dear Irish Girl*, after having endured years of separation from his fiancée Caroline LaTouche in which the personal fortune he has been seeking remains elusive, is able to survive the travails of India and come back to Ireland to marry the woman he loves. Godfrey Barron in *The House of the Secret* likewise is able to return to his Irish homeland in time to rescue his fiancée Maeve Standish from the homicidal servant who has been menacing her, even though the injuries he suffers, identical to those inflicted on Alderson, result in his partial paralysis.[98]

Others of Tynan's wanderers to far-flung regions do not fare as well as Fagan's and Alderson's fictional counterparts, however. Pierce Brandon in

97   See letter from Tynan to Matthew Russell (8 September 1885) regarding Fagan's death and the circumstances leading up to it, Russell Papers J27/73, and Tynan, *Twenty-Five Years*, 347–352, for details about her relationship with Jim Alderson. Alderson was killed by a party of Boers.

98   Before fighting in South Africa, Alderson was sent to India, where he was attacked by a tiger and had 'the muscle torn clean out of' his 'sword-arm', resulting in the loss of use of the arm (Tynan, *Twenty-Five Years*, 348); Godfrey Barron is in India when he is attacked by a knife-wielding native. His fiancée, Maeve Standish, is subsequently told that the 'knife went clean through the muscles of his right arm. He will never hold a sword again'. Katharine Tynan, *The House of the Secret* (London: James Clark, 1910), 157–158.

The Handsome Brandons returns home to Ireland from Africa, penniless and morally compromised, only to die of the fatal disease he has contracted on the dark continent and leave his family of sisters unprovided for and unprotected. Likewise, both Paul Chadwick in *The Story of Cecilia* and Roderick O'Moore in *A Union of Hearts* endure kidnapping by African cannibals and, although they eventually return to Ireland, lose the women they love to other men during their absences. Such diverse but consistently ominous fates suggest that Tynan's intention in creating this litany of characters transcends the personal to reveal an overriding scepticism concerning the efficacy and rectitude of the Imperial project. The implication of each of these stories is clear: remaining in Ireland is not only a far safer option than leaving it, but is also imperative to the maintenance of the country and protection of its people.

It is significant, therefore, that in the same novel in which her anti-emigration themes are first explicitly stated, Tynan can be seen to advocate policies which might give those Irish people who were most inclined to emigrate – the peasantry – a reason to remain. In *The French Wife*, Tynan creates in Gerard Molyneux a virtual clone of George Wyndham, the contemporary politician she most ardently admired and with whom she enjoyed a long-term and cordial correspondence. Wyndham was at the time of the novel's publication Chief Secretary for Ireland, and his Irish Land Purchase Act had been passed by Parliament in 1903, a year before *The French Wife* appeared. Like Wyndham, the fictional Molyneux becomes a Member of Parliament whose political projects culminate with the introduction of a bill for land reform in Ireland. Unlike Wyndham, both Molyneux and his bill suffer defeat, but Tynan's fictional modifications to Wyndham's real-life experiences serve a recognizable political purpose: they strengthen the reader's sense of empathy with Molyneux and his project at a time when Wyndham's own policies were increasingly being subjected to scrutiny.

To similar anti-emigration ends, from the turn of the century onward Tynan would use her novels to advocate policies intended to regenerate the Irish economy. Plots centering on co-operative farming and industry in Ireland – the types of projects that Wyndham and Tynan's close friends Sir Horace Plunkett and A. E. were then espousing – were in particular to become regular features in her fiction. In *The Honourable Molly*, Tynan's heroine works to establish a flower farming co-operative in rural Ireland, while in *The Story of Bawn* the main character defends Arthur Balfour's light railway project by arguing that it has opened up the Irish countryside to commerce, and the successful co-operative farms, creameries and other cottage industries that rapidly spring up around Bawn's rural Irish home soon prove her arguments. The central romance of 1907's *Her Ladyship* is similarly carried out against the backdrop of the weaving and lace-making industries that Irish landowner Lady Anne establishes and nurtures. Tynan would feature comparable plots and analogous business ventures in a number of her novels up to and including 1912's *Heart o' Gold*, in which Cushla MacSweeney and Harry Silvester, both newly returned to Ireland from England, must fight against the fatalism of the peasantry in order to achieve reform on their Irish land.[99] By the end of the novel, Cushla and Harry are united in both marriage and in business. Having together convinced their tenants that 'misfortune is not inevitable, and that God means His children to be happy in this world', they are finally beginning, as the narrative closes, to gain a measure of success with the factory they have built and the local industries they have established.[100]

With its central tale of Cushla MacSweeney, a young girl devoted to her Irish homeland suddenly and unexpectedly relocated to the English town of Tunbridge Wells, *Heart o' Gold* features a migration precisely the opposite to the one its author and her family were to embark upon in the year it was written. Tynan left her home in Southborough, near Tunbridge Wells, in late 1911, and found herself upon her homecoming in an irretrievably 'changed Ireland'.[101] Faced with the unexpected and 'appalling' poverty of Dublin and now occupying a vastly different social stratum to the one she had left – 'we returned to the Anglo-Irish having gone away from the Celts', she later explained – Tynan reacted to the dislocation and disorientation of her renewed residence in Ireland by remaining resolutely silent

99   Tynan, *Heart o' Gold*, 27; 116.
100 Tynan, *Heart o' Gold*, 344.
101 Tynan, *The Years of the Shadow*, 1.

about what confronted her upon her return.[102] Following *Heart o' Gold* and
Princess Katharine, both of which were published in 1912 but largely written while she was resident in England, Tynan took a hiatus from writing
novels set in Ireland. *Molly, My Heart's Delight* (1914), a life of the English
bluestocking artist and writer Mary Granville Delaney who spent her late
life in Co. Down, represented her only Irish-themed output in the years 1913
or 1914.[103] Although she wrote at least six full-length works of fiction with
contemporary settings during that period, not one would feature Ireland.

During her tenure in England, Tynan's fictional vision of Ireland altered
only gradually and subtly. The fact that she did not always appear to be
certain where the boundaries of class and race were drawn in her homeland
did not detract from her optimism for and about her native country, and
in many ways merely aided her in selling to her reading public her vision
of an Ireland whose inherent social and religious divisions could be readily
overcome through mutual sympathy and understanding. English policies
such as Wyndham's had gained her advocacy, and the conciliatory stance
her novels convey even as they advocate for Catholic rights was at odds
with the type of hard-line Nationalism which had been gaining support
in Ireland during her absence. As long as she viewed it from a distance,
Ireland could be imagined as a place that could and would be renovated,
if it were only treated justly and kindly. That she remained, upon her return
to Ireland, silent in her fiction on the subject of her homeland – a topic that
had theretofore preoccupied her regularly – suggests that Tynan's homecoming may have involved a period of reconciliation and re-envisioning
which she could not, or did not want to, work through in the very public
arena of her novels. Her return to Irish fiction did not in fact come until
1915, with *The House of the Foxes* – a novel which, through its representation
of an aristocratic Irish family whose members believe they are doomed to
endlessly repeat historical misfortunes, represents a marked departure from

102   Tynan, *The Years of the Shadow*, 8; 1.
103   Tynan admitted that she rated this novel very highly, and was disappointed that it
      was not nominated for 'the Thousand Guineas Prize in a Hodder and Stoughton
      competition', although she was an enthusiastic admirer of the winner of that prize,
      The Lee Shore by Rose Macaulay. Tynan, *The Years of the Shadow*, 97.

all of her previous work. By this time having already seen the first of her two sons off to the war (the other would follow in 1918), Tynan adopts in this text an outlook which is distinctly more violent and claustrophobic than in any of its predecessors. *The House of the Foxes* is overtly concerned with the ways in which the legacies of the past thwart opportunity and paralyse action in the present. A central relationship in the novel – that between the remaining members of the landed Turloughmore family, a mother and son – in many ways echoes the mutually dependent and reciprocally destructive mother-son alliances in earlier works such as Henrik Ibsen's *Ghosts* (1881) and prefigures those in Kate O'Brien's *The Ante-Room*. The mother's obsessive love of, and smothering fears for, her son mean that he lives a truncated existence, unable to overcome the invalidism which he believes is fated and incurable. Meg Hildebrand, newly recruited to work for the Turloughmores and only recently returned to Ireland from Austria, enters the household to disrupt the injurious bond between mother and son and convince them that 'God is stronger than the devil'.[104] In Meg's assertion that she 'can't believe that God put all that brightness into the world to leave us to the power of darkness', a repudiation of Irish fatalism, which for the first time in Tynan's novels permeates the aristocracy as well as the peasantry, is readily recognizable.[105]

Added to the family's fatalism is the more personal suffering that Ulick Turloughmore endures. Maudlin and self-pitying, Ulick has consistently been afflicted with the 'blue devils' due to his physical disabilities and feels that his life is not worth living.[106] By representing, in condemnatory terms, his ensuing indifference and inertia when he learns that an operation is available in mainland Europe that will either cure or kill him, Tynan can be seen to make her most readily discernible novelistic comment about a specifically Irish form of neutrality: a commentary made more poignant when considered in its mid-war context. In the First World War diary Tynan kept but never published, she had referred to the Irish men she

---

104 Katharine Tynan, *The House of the Foxes* (London: Smith, Elder, 1915), 45.
105 Tynan, *The House of the Foxes*, 46.
106 Tynan, *The House of the Foxes*, 173.

witnessed in Dublin who ignored the call to fight in Europe as 'Shameful! Intolerable! [...] a degradation of the *homo*'.[107] More subtly conveyed in *The House of the Foxes*, Tynan's message remains the same: apathy is reprehensible; action rewarded.

It was not characteristic of Tynan, whose texts so often act as testaments to her enduring faith, to continue to believe in portents of gloom during these first years of the war. The spiritual optimism fuelled by her Catholicism left her, like her character Meg, unable to countenance the 'power of darkness' and incapable, even in this novel written in the midst of the fighting, of maintaining a façade of unflinching cynicism. A year earlier, with the war looming, Tynan had tellingly created a sympathetic character – the admired priest in her English-set novel, *A Shameful Inheritance* – who was a German. Such a tactic served to humanize, rather than demonize, the wartime enemy, and explicit references in *The House of the Foxes* to the numbers of Ireland's Wild Geese who served in Austria, the parallels between Ireland's violent past and that of the Hungarian region of Austria in which Meg has worked, and her compassionate evocation of Meg's former employer, an Austrian Archduchess, serve a similar edifying purpose. These types of textual references lend to this often-ominous tale an overriding sense of humanity's decency, and Tynan's conclusion, in which the Turloughmores are able with Meg's assistance and encouragement to overcome their long-held fears, emotionally and physically healing the family in the process, conveys a significant message about endurance and hope.

When Tynan was accused in his presence of writing 'doctrine' rather than literature, A. E. defended her by suggesting that even the greatest of poets, 'Dante or Milton', have 'many pages where the intellectual anatomy which underlay their fantasy was apparent', adding to this assertion his own editorial comments:

> They appear the greater to our imagination because of this, that they wrote with their whole being and not merely out of part of their being [...] I like Katharine Tynan's poetry best where I find her nature harmonious with my own. Others may take much

107   Tynan, manuscript of *A Woman's Notes in War-Time*, Tynan Papers, Manchester, 13/1, entry for 16 April 1915.

more pleasure in poems whose art I admire but which are born out of emotions I have not shared [...] I was not fortunate enough to be born under a happy star.[108]

Alluding to the faith she shared with the majority of their countrymen, A. E. again refers to the degree to which her Catholicism informed her writing, and particularly the manner in which it inspired that optimism so consistently evidenced in her work. She referred in her poetry to having been 'born under a kind star/In a green world withouten any war', and throughout the first two years of the most terrible war the western world had yet seen, her novels would continue to convey a sense of hopefulness.[109]

Like A. E. – about whom she once wrote, 'One feels inclined to say of him as Lord Henry Fitzgerald said of Lord Edward, "Dear fellow, he is perfect!"' – Tynan was a pluralist as well as a Home Ruler.[110] She admitted that, like her character Mrs Brabazon, her political sympathies had become divided between Ireland and England, her native and adoptive homes. It is unsurprising, given Tynan's enthusiasm for politics and the number of Irish reformers she counted among her many friends, that her novels frequently act to promote the ideals of those who shared her Home Rule values. It is equally unsurprising, considering her fondness for the English homeland she had adopted and only recently relinquished, that the policies she most often and avidly promotes in her novels written to 1916 are ones of compromise and cooperation, on both sides of the Irish-English equation.

Tynan, unable to invest herself unequivocally in the either-or policies of 'Irish Ireland', never fully endorses a Sinn Féin ethos of 'ourselves alone', never actively promotes Douglas Hyde's de-anglicizing mission for Ireland, and only cursorily involves herself in the cultural nationalism of Yeats and his Revivalist colleagues. More often, in fact, her works act to mock or critique the projects that Hyde and Yeats promoted: her character Aileen Considine, in *A Union of Hearts*, openly derides her father's boast that 'Orangemen and Fenians' are equally welcome at his Irish historical

108 A. E., 'Foreword', xii–xiii.
109 Katharine Tynan, 'I was born under a kind star', *Collected Poems by Katharine Tynan*, xiv.
110 Tynan, *The Years of the Shadow*, 83.

society by detailing the infighting she has witnessed there and ironically referring to the ways in which 'a common love of a pursuit or an art unites people', while in *Julia* her Maud Gonne-like character Mary Craven is mockingly referred to as having only very recently discovered that she is Irish, and to be, as a result, 'enthusiastically desirous of learning the language, and something of the literature of [her] late-found country'.[111] As in George Egerton's work, Revivalist pursuits in *The Dear Irish Girl* and *Heart o' Gold* consistently distract characters from more pressing, and far more serious, Irish issues, and with this in mind it is significant to note that, while others of her politically active friends surface as influences on her novelistic themes early and identifiably in her *oeuvre*, neither Yeats's political nor his literary projects appear to have had a significant impact on Tynan's fiction. Yeats makes his first and only appearance in her fiction in *Her Ladyship* in 1907, twelve years after Tynan began publishing novels. When he does emerge, however, his influence on Ireland is readily acknowledged: in the narrative, it is Yeats's poetry that inspires Hugh, a poor tailor, to aid Lady Anne in her co-operative industries and eventually leads him to win her heart.

Otherwise, Yeats is conspicuous for his absence. We might, however, read him into the many and varied tales Tynan constructs in a number of her novels – including *The Way of a Maid*, *The Dear Irish Girl*, *She Walks in Beauty*, *Three Fair Maids*, *That Sweet Enemy*, *A Union of Hearts*, *Julia*, *The Honourable Molly*, *Her Ladyship*, *A Daughter of Kings*, *The Adventures of Alicia*, *The Story of Bawn* and *The Story of Cecilia* – of men who propose marriage but are rejected, as Yeats was by Tynan (and others), and particularly to the number of those spurned suitors who are poetically gifted writers but terrible spellers, as Yeats undoubtedly was.[112] Of these,

---

111   Tynan, *A Union of Hearts*, 17 and Tynan, *Julia*, 187.
112   Tynan herself remained conspicuously silent about the proposal, but members of her family asserted that Yeats did indeed propose marriage to her and was rejected, and historians have become convinced of the veracity of this contention. R. F. Foster conjectures that the proposal occurred in the late 1880s, when Yeats made several extended visits to Whitehall; Peter van de Kamp claims that the proposal occurred on 19 July 1891, at a point when Yeats had recently returned to Ireland after a lengthy

the most significant is the main character of Tynan's novel *John-A-Dreams*, published in September of that all-important year, 1916. The John of the title is, like Yeats, a talented poet who loves the seemingly unattainable Octavia Sweeney. Octavia can be seen to act as a composite of two women central to Yeats's life to that point: her name, pre-existing romantic relationship, and affection for John are reminiscent of the married woman, Olivia Shakespear, with whom Yeats once had a passionate affair, while her stately physical appearance and humanitarian projects are more redolent of the poet's great love, Maud Gonne. Rather than the elusive Octavia, John's family encourage him to marry his dear friend Monica, whom they admire and advocate for John much as the Yeats family admired Katharine Tynan and once advocated her for their son and brother 'Willie'. John at first cannot contemplate proposing to a woman with whom he is not in love, but his opinion soon changes when Monica considers entering a convent, as Tynan herself once did. At that point, John, 'in sudden angry

spell in London and was again staying at Whitehall. The latter date is more likely: it coincides with the first mention in Yeats's correspondence of Harry Hinkson, and, barring the few letters which came to Tynan from Yeats in a flurry immediately after 20 July 1891 and indicate that he left Whitehall in some haste (he wrote to request that she have her brother return the razor, comb and brush he left behind, and informs her that he has been making enquiries about 'Hinckson'), also corresponds with a decline in the frequency of his communications to Tynan. Nora Tynan O'Mahony would recall that her elder sister thought Yeats's offer 'a lovely and suitable thing' but, as Yeats had already met and been rejected by Gonne, it was perhaps considered unsuitable by Tynan because she realized her position as second best in Yeats's affections. It is more likely the case, however, that (as van de Kamp suggests) by 1891 Tynan had already become secretly engaged to Hinkson. See R. F. Foster, *W. B. Yeats: A Life*, I, 105, Van de Kamp, 'Tynan, Katharine (1859–1931)', *Oxford Dictionary of National Biography*, letters from Yeats to Tynan from 24 July to 7 August 1891 in John Kelly and Eric Domville, eds., *The Collected Letters of W. B. Yeats, Volume 1, 1865–1895* (Oxford: Clarendon Press, 1986), and Nora Tynan O'Mahony, interviewed by Austin Clarke ca. 1930, quoted in R. F. Foster, *W. B. Yeats: A Life*, I, 39.

revolt against' what he terms 'her sacrifice', asks her to marry him.[113] She rejects him only because he is not in love with her.[114]

Noting the many ways in which the details of Tynan's novel dovetail with what we now know about her relationship with Yeats, it is conceivable that, into *John-A-Dreams*, Tynan wove at least some of the tale of their friendship. Lending credence to this suggestion, Tynan borrows her title from the nickname, 'Jack o'Dreams', that Yeats gave to the main character of his only published novel, *John Sherman* (1891).[115] In this earlier work, the titular John bears a resemblance to the author himself, while Tynan almost certainly can be glimpsed in the character of John's true love, the plain but honourable Mary Carton. If *John-A-Dreams* does indeed write back to *John Sherman* and was intended as an allegory of Tynan's relationship with the poet, it was an understandable undertaking considering the import of events in the year it was published and the history of their acquaintance. Although their ways had long since parted, Tynan and Yeats had spent much time together in their idealistic youth, had shared an enthusiasm for the 'Young Ireland' ethos of their friend, the '48 man John O'Leary, and had together conjured dreams and visions of a better Ireland. By the time that Tynan was to publish *John-A-Dreams*, those early aspirations for Ireland were being shattered by the violent aftermath of the Easter Rising.

Over the course of the First World War, the tone and subject matter of Tynan's output continued to alter. Perceptibly more melancholy during the war's first two years, it became even more so after the spring of 1916, particularly when its setting was Ireland. The liaison of John and Octavia at the end of *John-A-Dreams* is achieved, but only against the backdrop of a poverty-stricken and disease-ridden Ireland. *Lord Edward: A Study in Romance*, also published in the year of the Rising, is an elegiac biography

113   Katharine Tynan, *John-A-Dreams* (London: Smith, Elder, 1916), 256.
114   For additional information on Tynan and Yeats's relationship, see James J. McFadden, 'William Butler Yeats at Katharine Tynan's Home, Whitehall', in Richard J. Finneran, ed., *Yeats: An Annual of Critical and Textual Studies*, vol. 8 (Ann Arbor: Michigan University Press, 1990), 206–242; Katharine Tynan, *Twenty-Five Years*, 39; and Katharine Tynan, *The Middle Years*, 66.
115   W. B. Yeats, *John Sherman & Dhoya* (Dublin: The Lilliput Press, 1990), 9.

of Edward Fitzgerald suffused with a sense of sadness and a tone of regret, in which Tynan's frequent asides serve to highlight the similarities between the failed 1798 and 1916 Risings: 'Is it 1796 or 1916?' she interrupts the narrative to ask at one point; 'Was not the old wine in new bottles in the Dublin rising of 1916?' she queries at another.[116] Her other novels of the period, *The West Wind* (1916) and *The Rattlesnake* (1917) are, respectively, a tale replete with misalliances, divorce and orphaned children, and one which features a murderous character never suitably punished for his crimes.

A shift in the tone of Tynan's novels would come again in 1922, when she rewrote her 1910 novel *The House of the Secret* as *The House on the Bogs* with noteworthy modifications. In the earlier novel, two female characters are terrorized in an isolated country house by their Irish servants, who are brother and sister. By the end of the narrative, Tynan allows even the more sinister of the siblings, Corney Reardon, a partial redemption when, consumed with remorse and believing he has killed his beloved sister, he drowns himself in a bog. In the latter tale, French rather than Irish siblings intimidate the women, and Tynan's already grim conclusion grows perceptibly grimmer. It is as though, after the Rising, she could not envision an unequivocal happy ending for her Irish characters, and in the midst of Civil War could not bear to imagine a story in which the Irish victimized one another. The servants, Pierre and Margot, continue to be the objects of 'disgust and horror' long after their demise, and remain unforgiven at the close of *The House on the Bogs*.[117] At the same time, it is only those characters who choose to live out their lives away from Ireland who are able to feel 'young and happy again'.[118] Tynan may leave her Irish characters with the possibility of a contented future by suggesting in the novel's final pages that 'the ghosts of the old house should be banished by the happiness of the children', yet even here her use of the modal verb conveys

116   Tynan, *Lord Edward: A Study in Romance*, 242 and 243.
117   Katharine Tynan, *The House on the Bogs* (London and Melbourne: Ward, Lock, 1922), 298.
118   Tynan, *The House on the Bogs*, 298.

a sense of uncertainty, and she must defer her vision of contentment to a future generation.[119]

Tynan's acts of migrating from Ireland to England and back again between 1893 and 1911 had transformed her political views and resulted in divided allegiances, as she would admit in her memoirs: 'I had lived eighteen years in England, I had come to believe that affection for England and love of Ireland could quite well go hand in hand'.[120] She was to find, however, that her relationship to her homeland had been altered in ways she was eventually unable to overcome. Shocked by the British response to the Rising, she would be even more horrified by the subsequent actions of her fellow Irish people. From the point of the outbreak of Ireland's Civil War, the sense of hopefulness would diminish perceptibly from her Irish fiction, and she would admit her disillusionment with her countrymen in personal letters, including one written in 1923, following the assassination of Michael Collins, in which she derided the 'wretched rulers of Ireland & the whole ignominious affair!'[121] She left her homeland permanently in 1924, passing the rest of her days on the European continent and in England. Although she never abandoned her project of pointing out Ireland's difficulties to her readers, she increasingly struggled to achieve adequate resolutions to the problems she portrayed. By the time she was to write her 1930 novel *The Playground*, Dublin had become for her a place of slums and poverty much as America once was, and imbued with the same types of apocalyptic imagery that had once defined her fictional London, but with the added menace of vigilante violence. The playground of Tynan's title acts as a metaphor for an untroubled Ireland, but her final images – of a 'crippled child' sitting by a window and of a 'baby who had leant adoringly over a withered flower in a bottle, talking to it' – instill a sense of melancholy, while her closing thoughts concerning a future when the 'Spirit of Evil should be shut out' of the still unfinished playground are unambiguously about

---

119 Tynan, *The House on the Bogs*, 298.
120 Tynan, *The Years of the Shadow*, 204.
121 Letter from Tynan to Frank Mathew (4 July 1923), Tynan Papers, Manchester, 16/4.

dreams for Ireland which have yet to be realized.[122] She died in Wimbledon in 1931, disappointed to the last in what had transpired after the Free State was formed, and mourning the man, 'Mick' Collins, who was to join the ranks of Lord Edward Fitzgerald, Charles Stewart Parnell and George Wyndham as one of her beloved, fallen Irish heroes.[123]

In many ways these processes of alteration had begun for Tynan years before she left Ireland, and her migration can be seen as an extension of, rather than the sole reason for, her sense of difference from her fellow Irish people. As the daughter of an upwardly mobile farmer, then as a middle class writer moving amongst the cultural and financial elite, and eventually as the Catholic wife of a Protestant husband, Tynan increasingly found herself in a position of economic, social and cultural displacement during the period of her upbringing and early adulthood in Ireland. Her act of leaving her homeland can be seen as a natural response to her already extant outsiderhood. To put it metaphorically, Tynan had always occupied shifting ground. Time, distance and personal circumstances would only widen the gap which already existed between her and her countrymen. In the altering landscapes of her fiction we can trace her altering relationship to her homeland, and the complex and eventually irresoluble political opinions which developed alongside it.

122 Katharine Tynan, *The Playground* (London and Melbourne: Ward, Lock, 1930), 320.
123 Letter from Tynan to Frank Mathew (6 December 1921), Tynan Papers, Manchester, 16/4.

Conclusion: Writing about Ireland; Writing about Problems

> In one of the publisher's notes or announcements attached to this fresh and graceful story, it is remarked, presumably by way of heightening interest or of allaying alarm, that 'Katharine Tynan,' in her new book, does not deal in any way with Irish problems. It is not a compliment, and it is in some ways an injustice. Nobody could write sincerely about Ireland without writing about problems.
>
> — G. K. CHESTERTON, Review of Katharine Tynan's
> *Her Ladyship* (1907)[1]

In 1907, G. K. Chesterton, musing on Katharine Tynan's most recent novel, noted the contradiction inherent in her publishers' affirmation that the book in question did not deal with Irish problems. While Chesterton admitted that *Her Ladyship* was 'a fresh and graceful story' which did not overtly address the 'political problem of Irish nationalism', he also assured his readers that it was preoccupied in no small measure with Irish political issues. In particular, it had much to do with what he deemed a prevalent lack of patriotism among the Irish aristocracy, and with the subject of those numerous Big House owners who had failed in their duties to Ireland by remaining loyal to the Union. 'Had [the Irish aristocracy] been true to nationalism', Chesterton conjectured, 'the Irish would have followed their lords; they might even have followed their tyrants. The deepest offence of the great Irish peers is not that they are tyrants, but that they are traitors.'[2] Whether Chesterton came to these conclusions as a result of reading

---

1   G. K. Chesterton, 'A Book of the Day: The Irish Aristocrat', *Daily News* (London) (30 October 1907), 11.

2   Chesterton, 'A Book of the Day: The Irish Aristocrat', 11.

Tynan's novel, or whether the reading of it acted merely to confirm and distil suppositions he had arrived at independently of her text, his stance was unequivocal: *Her Ladyship* was a novel intended to enlighten and even persuade its readers on a subject of political import to Ireland. As a book which dealt earnestly with its Irish subject matter, it was also and by necessity, he asserted, centrally concerned with the troubles that afflicted Ireland, for no one 'could write sincerely about Ireland without writing about problems'.[3]

Her Ladyship is, indeed, a narrative set in an Ireland replete with difficulties. Its elderly aristocratic women, left with no money and no recourse to employment, are shown starving and freezing in Dublin tenements, its peasant children are forced to act as 'missionaries' of industry to combat their parents' overriding 'squalor and laziness' and its young land reformers are criticized for their capitalist ethics and hindered in their plans for improvements by a society in thrall to its traditions.[4] Most notably, the novel abounds with positive images of manufacturing and commerce, particularly through its portrayal of a peasant population raised out of its torpor by work provided to them through new business and agricultural initiatives, which range from the harvesting of blackberries and the draining of bogs to cottage lace-making industries and the mining of natural resources. The romantic entanglements with which the story is supposed to be centrally concerned often read as the subtext to Tynan's reformist message for Ireland in the novel, and *Her Ladyship* confirms that its author believed herself to be writing about a country struggling to find the means to care for its people of all classes and creeds because it remained resistant to change: 'it was an inevitable law, people could not stand still,' she asserted in the narrative, 'to stand still was to decay'.[5]

The caveat that Tynan's publishers felt it incumbent to attach to *Her Ladyship* assuring its readers of its apolitical status also indicates their collusion in the prevailing Redmondite tactic of avoiding 'the

3   Chesterton, 'A Book of the Day: The Irish Aristocrat', 11.
4   Tynan, *Her Ladyship*, 179.
5   Tynan, *Her Ladyship*, 93.

uncomfortable reality of Home Rule'.[6] Not only Smith and Elder but also the *Irish Monthly* – which, in praising the novel, drew primary attention to the fact that it managed to tell its tale 'without an allusion to the unwholesome problems' besetting Ireland at the time – hint that the combination of Ireland and politics was, just then, a subject best avoided.[7] Yet it is difficult, viewed with hindsight, to surmise how anyone might have read the novel without recognizing its political significance. That both Tynan's English publishers and her Irish reviewers did so indicates the degree to which Irish politics had by the time of the novel's publication become synonymous with a narrowly defined form of Irish nationalism with which Tynan's narrative vision is at odds. *Her Ladyship* enacts a process of fictionally regenerating what is presented as an economically stagnated Ireland by industrializing the Irish countryside and unifying Irish and English interests on Irish land, a fictional project which would have found ready favour with the Empire-worshipping British public in the post-Boer War period. Yeats's poetry may figure into Tynan's narrative, and her fictional projects for reform may also suggest the influence of A. E.'s opinions on her text, but her vision of an ideal Ireland is far from a return to the 'mythic west' so beloved by the visionaries of the Celtic Twilight. *Her Ladyship* eschews Revivalist sentiments, overt references to Home Rule and nationalist rhetoric. Its most admirable character is a class-blind, improving and modernizing landlord who happens to be a woman, and who chooses to marry the tailor she loves rather than the aristocrat who loves her. As such, it spoke to its readership about Ireland in a liberal but implicitly upper class and English idiom, and, because it did so, its political biases were not only tolerated, but completely overlooked, by some commentators.

Tynan's long period of exile can be glimpsed in this novelistic merging of Irish and English viewpoints. Her earliest Irish novels had neither been so subtle in their politics nor so deeply enamoured of industrialization: but then, Tynan had lived in England for fourteen years by the time *Her Ladyship* was written. An extended period of exile had, it seems, acted at

---

6   *The Times* (London) (20 February 1905), 7.
7   'Notes on New Books', *Irish Monthly* 35/414 (December 1907), 704.

the very least to alter her fictional tactics – she had learned over the course of her residency in Britain how to address her English readers in a manner that would engage their interests without offending their cultural sensibilities. The evidence of Tynan's personal papers and memoirs suggests that this stance was not merely a process of posturing for popularity's sake: over time, she appears to have remained a constitutional Home Ruler rather than a nationalist in the Republican sense of the term.

Emily Lawless's Irish works indicate that her narrative approach underwent a similar transformation. Coming to her subject matter with a unionist sensibility, she would enact a shift precisely the opposite to Tynan's. The backlash in Ireland against *Hurrish* and its narrative preoccupation with extant political concerns would have demonstrated to her the necessity of adopting a more clandestine approach towards issues of current political import to Ireland in her texts. As evidence that this was indeed the case, from 1890 onwards, she consistently tackled the subject of Ireland from a position of remove. Thereafter, she frequently employed historical rather than contemporary settings in her fiction, occasionally visualized Ireland through a child's (or a child-like character's) perspective, and always assumed the viewpoint of a foreigner to, or exile from, Ireland to tell her Irish tales. If her work was of no less political significance as a result of these modifications, she would manage, by taking this more nuanced approach to the subject of Ireland, to make her texts increasingly palatable to a nationalist readership. The altering attitudes towards her novels among the Irish press confirm that this change of literary tactic had, in at least some nationalist quarters, met with distinct approval. Just four years after *Hurrish* was published to widespread condemnation in Ireland, the *Nation* was suggesting about Lawless and *With Essex* that '[n]o writer has ever sounded the depths of that horror [British misrule in Ireland] so completely, or depicted the tragedy in such an effective way'.[8] In asserting the power and veracity of Lawless's vision of Elizabethan Ireland, the *Nation* also admitted, without

---

8   'The Romance of Butchery', the *Nation* (27 September 1890), 2.

rancour or remorse, to being swayed by the author's vision of a 'noble' English conqueror.[9]

Exile played an equally defining role in the texts of L. T. Meade, which often featured emigrant characters and the clash of English and Irish cultures. In her schoolgirl texts, Irish girls who arrive in England to be educated are demonstrated to be variant in their manners, behaviour, morals and attitudes towards education, yet what remains consistent about them is the degree to which they reflect the differing values of the country from which they come and the country in which they come to live. In her Irish novels written for an adult readership, English characters similarly and just as regularly misunderstand their Irish counterparts to the detriment of those on both sides of the international relationship. The narrative devices Meade employed in both her children's and adult works may have acted to advocate English tolerance of Irish idiosyncrasies, but novels such as *Light o' the Morning* and *The Stormy Petrel* affirm that the converse was also true. Conspicuously critical of English attitudes and behaviour towards the Irish while finding significantly less fault on the Irish side of things, these texts indicate that Meade understood the reasons for Ireland's drive towards separatism as much as she did the need for English forbearance.

Francis's Irish texts would feature female revolutionaries and Irish communities distrustful of English law, women who managed their Irish lands more capably than their male counterparts and innocent Irish women victimized by corrupt English and intolerant Northern Irish societies. In the earliest of her Irish texts, her country's political landscape is subordinated to the machinations of plot, yet politics would come increasingly to the fore as her period of exile in England lengthened. By the time she was to write *Dark Rosaleen* in the run-up to the Easter Rising, Ireland's political landscape had become her central concern. *Dark Rosaleen* is a novel which, despite its heavy-handed deployment of allegory and obvious Catholic bias, must be ranked among the most forthright works of Irish political literature to emerge during the 1910s. Through its portraits of a violently riven Derry and the microcosmic version of that city's society enacted within

---

9   'The Romance of Butchery', the *Nation*, 2.

Hector and Norah's household, it offered its readers both a personal and communal viewpoint on the Protestant-Catholic and north-south divides which presciently revealed the kinds of misconceptions and animosities that would, in the years following its publication, lead to increasingly bitter struggles in Northern Ireland.

Egerton's and Thurston's texts stand apart from those of the other authors covered in this study by privileging gendered politics over national or nationalist issues, but it is arguably in the novels written by these women that the spectre of exile looms most ominously. In their works, limited in number though they may be, the moral stringency of Irish Catholic society and the lack of economic opportunity for women in Ireland is central to their female characters' fates: the motivations for Mary Desmond's retreat into an all-female community in England at the close of *The Wheel of God*, Clodagh Asshlin's need to transcend the legacies of her Irish heritage in *The Gambler* and Isabel Costello's doomed rebellions against convention in *The Fly on the Wheel* can all be traced to the narrowness of prospects for women within Irish society. According to the terms on which an Irishwoman's life must be lived in Egerton's and Thurston's texts, escape by any means becomes a necessity.

The actions that each of these six authors would take in their own lives serve to corroborate Egerton's and Thurston's narrative vision of Ireland as a place in which women were denied opportunities for personal fulfilment and economic progress. The correspondence, autobiographical writings and prolific output of Meade, Francis and Tynan attest to the desire for economic independence that instigated and/or perpetuated their literary careers, and Egerton's letters to her publisher John Lane likewise confirm that, increasingly as her career progressed, her writing projects were undertaken to fill a financial void.[10] Lawless, too, seems to have been seeking to make a financial break from, or alleviate the economic concerns of, her family through her literary efforts. Although her relatively modest output

10   See letter from Egerton to John Lane (10 November 1896), in which Egerton agrees to make changes that Lane has requested to her manuscript of *Symphonies* because, she tells him, 'I have not a shilling in my purse'. Bright Papers, Princeton 2/17.

suggests that her writing career was not undertaken due to any form of extreme economic need, this fact does not preclude the notion that she may have wanted to achieve something for and by herself, independently of family funds and influences, through her writing. What little of her correspondence survives – that to Lecky and to her publisher Alexander Macmillan most notably – substantiates the idea that she viewed writing as a profession rather than a pastime, her letters to Lecky indicating the degree of attention she paid to the accuracy of historical detail in her novels, those to Macmillan evidencing her assiduous management of her career. These letters also confirm that she took actions which served to increase her own income, and was not averse to pitting publishers against one another in bidding for the copyrights to her novels.[11] Thurston's career alone among the group was not initiated as a result of a desire for financial independence, yet it is apparent that her economic concerns grew over time, and by the point at which her final novel was published she was privately admitting her anxieties about its success and her hopes of the financial rewards it might bring.[12] The fact that these women's careers were, in every case, pursued outside of Ireland strongly suggests that the prospects for publishing success there – as Tynan's references to the demoralized state of the Dublin publishing industry indicate – were extremely limited.

All of these writers also already occupied an ambivalent position in their homeland prior to leaving Ireland permanently. Emily Lawless was the sister of an evicting landlord whose family's status as landowners was being threatened by debt and agrarian violence. L. T. Meade's position as a Protestant in the extreme south of Ireland was already an anomaly prior to the death of her mother, at which point she felt she had become an outsider even in her own family. George Egerton's romantic entanglements placed her in a position of moral remove from her extended Catholic relations,

11   See, in particular, letter from Lawless to Alexander Macmillan (23 September 1891), Macmillan Archive, Add. 54966, British Library, London and undated letter from Lawless to Lecky, Lecky Correspondence, MSS 18827, Manuscript 2482, Trinity College Dublin.
12   See letter from Thurston to Gavin (17 September 1910), Thurston Papers, NLS 11378/12.

and Katherine Cecil Thurston's marriage to a Protestant man and eventual divorce had similar consequences. As an elite Catholic living in rural Ireland, M. E. Francis was born into a family placed at a distance, socially, from her immediate neighbours, and the middle class and Catholic Katharine Tynan's entry into the predominantly Protestant circle of the Dublin literati had the effect of dislocating her in social terms which were exacerbated by her marriage to a Protestant man. In a similar manner to their actively nationalist female contemporaries – who were largely excluded from membership in, or sidelined from activities on behalf of, political organizations – literary women with an interest in Revivalist pursuits (Lawless, Francis and Tynan among their number) were for the most part barred from prominent roles in, or recognition from the main actors in, that movement. In each case, a sense of outsiderhood in Ireland preceded and to some degree instigated these women's respective decisions to leave the country, and the evidence provided in this study confirms that most left Ireland for reasons complementary to those of male literary exiles past and present: because Ireland was not a space where their creative intellect could be nurtured and prioritized. Perhaps the most damning indictment of the opportunities Ireland offered to its women is the fact that, once they had left their homeland for England, not one of these authors was willing to make a permanent return. Tynan stands alone among the group in having attempted to live in Ireland once again, but her repatriation would in fact last less than a decade. Along with the wider dispersal of noteworthy females from Ireland – the writer Hannah Lynch to France, the novelist and journalist Beatrice Grimshaw on travels across the world, and the activist and non-fiction author Anna Parnell to England, to name only a few – these findings suggest that there was a trend of long-term or permanent self-exile among some of the most prominent members of what can accurately be termed the Irish female intelligentsia which warrants further research.

Chesterton's review indicates that the process Stephen Brown would later refer to – that of highlighting a 'contrast of temperaments' between the Irish and English rather than addressing the subject of Home Rule directly – was at work in Tynan's *Her Ladyship*. That Chesterton found a verification of the improprieties he attached to the Irish aristocracy in what others believed to be a politically innocuous work also suggests the degree to which Brown may have been correct in his assumption that the popular novel could act as an effective form of surreptitious political propaganda. It is evident that not only Tynan, but Lawless, Meade, Egerton, Thurston and Francis all believed the novel to be a viable forum for airing political views, and, despite the fact that some would publicly profess otherwise, did not consider their gender to disqualify them from adding their own voices to the debates surrounding the Irish and Woman Questions. Did these women use their texts to point out the differences which existed between the Irish and English and use their 'power to observe' the politics of nation and of gender to inform and illuminate their readers? The answer is unequivocally yes. The regularity with which their works address the political landscape of their homeland (and of women in their homeland) in fact suggests that, when Ireland was their subject matter, they felt compelled or even obliged to deal with Irish problems. Among those texts which have too long been overlooked in assessments of the literature of the post-Parnell and pre-Easter Rising era, Lawless's *Grania*, Egerton's *The Wheel of God*, Thurston's *The Fly on the Wheel* and Francis's *The Story of Mary Dunne* must rank among those which are most unfairly neglected, and each of these works has compelling and unique ideas to convey about the politics, gendered or national, of its author's homeland. Despite the efforts of a growing group of researchers to reclaim Irish women's literature of the period, a broader definition of what constitutes 'national literature' than the one to which Daniel Corkery pointed ('national' as synonymous with 'nationalist') is still required.

What impact these texts and others like them may have made on the political attitudes of their reading public is impossible to quantify, but evidence suggests that the novels written by Lawless, Meade, Egerton, Thurston, Francis and Tynan reached a far more extensive audience than did, for instance, the poetry of Hyde or Yeats.[13] In some cases, too, the ideas conveyed by these authors are potentially as politically inflammatory as those expressed by their more overtly nationalist compatriots. Despite its

13 For a study of reading trends in Ireland, see J. C. McWalter, 'The Dublin Libraries', *Irish Times* (29 September 1910), 5.

Celticist stereotypes, Lawless's *Maelcho*, for example, graphically depicts atrocities committed by British troops on Irish soil and is openly and vehemently critical of English misrule in Ireland. *Maelcho* could indeed be seen to harbour the potential, as one commentator suggested, to 'make rebels' of its Irish readers.[14] Similar seditious possibilities may be glimpsed in Meade's *The O'Donnells of Inchfawn*, Tynan's *A King's Woman*, Francis's *Miss Erin* and *Dark Rosaleen* and Thurston's *The Gambler*. The greater majority of these texts, however, performed an ameliorative function by addressing their English readers in what was, so to speak, their own language. Whatever approach the author chose to take, few of these novels would portray the Irish situation without simultaneously tackling English misconceptions of it. In seeking to elucidate, these authors were not only entering into the political debates surrounding Home Rule, they were actively attempting to alter hearts and minds.

These writers were not – did not choose to be – influential in the way that the Revivalists were: none of their texts actively advocates Irish nationalism or offers a straightforward depiction of Irish heroism; in them there is no ready idealization or mythologizing of the west, no glorification of blood sacrifice. From his retrospective viewpoint, Yeats saw the rebellion of 1916 as the closing event of Ireland's rebirth. The views of the women writers covered here extend much further. In their portrayals of the economic problems which beset Ireland, of sectarian animosities and longstanding resentments, and in their repeated emphasis on the value of compromise and mutual comprehension not only between the Irish and the English, but among the Irish themselves, they foresaw that Ireland's rebirth, in whatever form it was to take, would be a painful and protracted process.

14   Clipping from *Irish Daily Independent* (5 November 1894), n.p., Lawless Papers.

Bibliography

Archive Sources

Emily Lawless Papers, Marsh's Library, Dublin.
Gladstone Papers, British Library, London.
Horace Plunkett Papers, The Plunkett Foundation, Woodstock, Oxfordshire.
John Dunne/George Egerton Papers, National Library of Ireland, Dublin.
Katherine Cecil Thurston Papers, National Library of Scotland, Edinburgh.
Lecky Correspondence, Trinity College Dublin.
Macmillan Archive, British Library, London
Papers of Father Matthew Russell, S. J., Jesuit Archive, Dublin.
Papers of Katharine Tynan, John Rylands Library, Manchester.
Papers of Mary Sweetman Blundell, Private Collection of Mark Blundell, Crosby
    Hall Estate, Little Crosby.
Selected Papers of Mary Chavelita Bright, Department of Rare Books and Special
    Collections, Princeton University Library, Princeton, New Jersey.
Seumas O'Sullivan Correspondence, Trinity College Dublin.
Yeats Correspondence, National Library of Ireland, Dublin.

Electronic Sources

Irish Independent Online <http://www.independent.ie>.
The Oxford Dictionary of National Biography (Oxford: Oxford University Press, 2004)
    <http://www.oxforddnb.com>.

Published Sources

A. E., 'Foreword', in Katharine Tynan, *Collected Poems by Katharine Tynan* (London: Macmillan, 1930), vii–xiv.

Akenson, Donald Harman, *Small Differences: Irish Catholics and Irish Protestants: 1815–1922* (Dublin: Gill and MacMillan, 1988).

'America', *Daily News* (London) (7 October 1868), 5.

Annat, Aurelia Louisa Spottiswoode, *Imaginable Nations: Constructions of History and Identity and the Contribution of Selected Irish Women Writers 1891–1945*, (D.Phil thesis, University of Oxford, St. Hugh's College, 2009).

'An Appeal Against Female Suffrage', *Nineteenth Century* 25/148 (June 1889).

Archibald, Douglas, 'John Butler Yeats', in David Holdeman and Ben Levitas, eds., *W. B. Yeats in Context* (Cambridge: Cambridge UP), 109–118.

Bartlett, Thomas et al., *The 1798 Rebellion: An Illustrated History* (Boulder, Colorado: Roberts Rinehart, 1998).

Belanger, Jacqueline, ed., *The Irish Novel in the Nineteenth Century: Facts and Fictions* (Dublin: Four Courts Press, 2005).

Bergin, Alan Thomas, 'Masquerade, Self-Invention and the Nation: uncovering the fiction of Katherine Cecil Thurston (PhD thesis: NUI Galway, 2014).

Bielenberg, Andy, 'Irish Emigration to the British Empire, 1700–1914', in Andy Bielenberg, ed., *The Irish Diaspora*, 215–234.

——, *The Irish Diaspora* (Harlow: Pearson, 2000).

'Births, Marriages and Deaths', *Freeman's Journal* (25 September 1879), 1.

'Births, Deaths, Marriages and Obituaries', *Standard* (London) (28 April 1882), 1.

Black, Helen C., *Pen, Pencil, Baton and Mask: Biographical Sketches* (London: Spotiswood, 1896).

Blind, Karl, 'An Irish Martyr', *National Observer*, 7/166 (1892), 246–247.

Blundell, Brian Whitlock, 'Blundell, Francis Nicholas Joseph (1880–1936), *Oxford Dictionary of National Biography* (Oxford: Oxford University Press, 2004) <http://oxforddnb.com/view/article/65565>.

Blundell, Margaret, *An Irish Novelist's Own Story* (Dublin: Catholic Truth Society, n.y.).

——, 'M. E. Francis', *Catholic World* 134/804 (March 1932), 684–691.

—— and M. E. Francis, *Wood Sanctuary* (London: G. Allen & Unwin, 1930).

Boucicault, Dion, *The Colleen Bawn; Or, The Brides of Garryowen* (London: Lacy's Acting Edition, 1865).

Bourke, Angela et al., eds., *The Field Day Anthology of Irish Writing Volumes iv and v: Irish Women's Writing and Traditions* (Cork: Cork University Press, 2002).

Boyd, Ernest, *Ireland's Literary Renaissance* (London: Grant Richards, 1923 [1916]).

'The British Covenant for Ulster: Women's Signatures', *The Times* (London) (10 March 1914), 8.

Brown, Stephen J., 'The Catholic Novelist and His Themes', *Irish Monthly* 63/745 (July 1935), 432–444.

——, *Ireland in Fiction: A Guide to Irish Novels, Tales, Romances, and Folk-Lore* (Dublin and London: Maunsel, 1916).

——, 'Novels of the National Idea', *Irish Monthly* 48/563 (May 1920), 254–262.

——, 'The Question of Irish Nationality', *Studies: An Irish Quarterly Review* 1/4 (December 1912), 634–654.

Cadogan, Mary and Patricia Craig, *You're a Brick, Angela: A New Look at Girls' Fiction from 1839 to 1975* (London: Victor Gollancz, 1976).

Chesterton, G. K., 'A Book of the Day: The Irish Aristocrat', *Daily News* (London) (30 October 1907), 11.

'Civil War Imminent', *Irish Independent* (21 March 1914), 5.

Clairmonte, E., *The Africander: A Plain Tale of Colonial Life* (London: T. Fisher Unwin, 1896).

Clark, Samuel, 'The Importance of Agrarian Classes: Agrarian Class Structure in Nineteenth-Century Ireland', *British Journal of Sociology* 29/1 (March 1978), 22–40.

Clarke, Austin, *A Penny in the Clouds* (Dublin: Moytura Press, 1990).

Cloyne, George, 'Thursday's Child', *The Times* (London) (19 November 1959), 15.

Connolly, L. W., *George Bernard Shaw and Barry Jackson* (Toronto: University of Toronto Press, 2002).

Copeland, Caroline, 'An Oasis in the Desert: The Transatlantic Publishing Success of Katherine Cecil Thurston', *Edinburgh Bibliographical Society* 1/2 (2007), 23–41.

——, 'The Sensational Katherine Cecil Thurston: an investigation into the life and publishing history of a "New Woman" author', (PhD thesis: Edinburgh Napier University, 2007).

Corkery, Daniel, *Synge and Anglo-Irish Literature* (Cork: Cork University Press, 1931).

Costello, Peter, *The Heart Grown Brutal: The Irish Revolution in Literature, from Parnell to the Death of Yeats, 1891–1939* (Dublin: Gill and Macmillan, 1977).

'The Country and Mr Parnell', *Freeman's Journal* (12 December 1890), 6.

Daily News (London) (23 November 1894), 7.

Daly, Dominic, *The Young Douglas Hyde: The Dawn of the Irish Revolution and Renaissance 1874–1893* (Totowa, NJ: Rowman and Littlefield, 1974).

'A Daughter of the Soil', *The Times* (London) (26 April 1895), 13.

De Bhaldraithe, Eoin, 'Mixed Marriages and Irish Politics: The Effect of "Ne Temere"', *Studies: An Irish Quarterly Review* 77/307 (Autumn 1988), 284–299.

De Vere White, Terence, *A Leaf from the Yellow Book: The Correspondence of George Egerton* (London: The Richards Press, 1958).

——, 'A Strange Lady', *Irish Times* (26 February 1983), 12.

Derrick, Francis [Frances E. M. Notley], *Forgotten Lives, Englishwoman's Domestic Magazine* 119 (1 November 1874), 226–231.

Doak, Naomi, 'Ulster Protestant Women Authors: Olga Fielden's *Island Story', Irish Studies Review* 15/1 (2007), 37–49.

Dooley, Terence, 'The Mortgage Papers of St Patrick's College, Maynooth. 1871–1923', *Archivium Hibernicum* 59 (2005), 106–136.

Egerton, George, *Fantasias* (London and New York: John Lane/The Bodley Head, 1898).

——, *Flies in Amber* (London: Hutchinson, 1905).

——, *Keynotes and Discords* (London: Virago, 1993 [1893/1894]).

——, *Rosa Amorosa* (London: Grant Richards, 1901).

——, *Symphonies* (London and New York: John Lane/The Bodley Head, 1897).

——, *The Wheel of God* (London: Grant Richards, 1898).

Ellmann, Richard, *James Joyce* (Oxford: Oxford University Press, 1959).

'Emigrants-Beware!', *Freeman's Journal* (5 December 1857), 1.

'The Evicted Tenants Commission', (10 March 1893), *Freeman's Journal*, 5.

Fallon, Ann Connerton, *Katharine Tynan* (Boston: Twayne, 1979).

Fawcett, Millicent Garrett, 'Employment for Girls: The Civil Service', *Atalanta* 1/3 (1887), 174–176.

——, L. L. D., *Women's Suffrage: A Short History of a Great Movement* (New York: Dodge Publishing, 1911).

Finneran, Richard J., ed., *Yeats Annual No. 2* (London and Basingstoke: Macmillan, 1983).

——, ed., *Yeats: An Annual of Critical and Textual Studies*, vol. 8 (Ann Arbor: Michigan University Press, 1990).

Fitzpatrick, William John, *Life, Times, and Contemporaries of Lord Cloncurry* (Dublin: James Duffy, 1855).

Foster, Frederick, 'The City of Mobile Passengers', *Freeman's Journal* (9 September 1857), 1.

Foster, John Wilson, *Irish Novels 1890–1940: New Bearings in Culture and Fiction* (Oxford: Oxford UP, 2008).

Foster, R. F., *Modern Ireland 1600–1972* (London: Penguin, 1988).

——, *Paddy and Mr Punch* (London: Allen Lane/Penguin, 1993).

——, *W. B. Yeats: A Life, I: The Apprentice Mage. 1865–1914* (Oxford and New York: Oxford University Press, 1997).

——, *W. B. Yeats: A Life, II: The Arch-Poet. 1915–1939* (Oxford and New York: Oxford University Press, 1997).

Foster, Vere, 'Morality on Shipboard: To the Editor of the New York Tribune', *Freeman's Journal* (9 October 1857), 1.

'The Fountain of Beauty. By L. T. Meade', *Freeman's Journal* (29 May 1909), 5.

Francis, M. E., *Cousin Christopher* (London: T. Fisher Unwin, 1925).

——, *Dark Rosaleen* (New York: P. J. Kennedy, 1917[1915]).

——, *A Daughter of the Soil* (London and New York: Harper Brothers, 1900).

——, *Dorset Dear* (London: Longmans, 1905).

——, *Fiander's Widow* (New York and Bombay: Longmans, Green, 1901).

——, 'Flowers in Fiction', *Academy* 1717 (1 April 1905), 361–363.

——, *In a North Country Village* (Wigan: Northwest Catholic History Society, 2008 [1893]).

——, *A Maid o' Dorset* (London: Cassell, 1917).

——, *Miss Erin* (New York, Cincinnati, Chicago: Benziger Brothers, 1898).

——, *Molly's Fortunes* (London: Sands, 1913).

——, *Napoleon of the Looms* (London: Hutchinson, 1925).

——, *Pastorals of Dorset* (London: Longmans, 1901).

——, *The Story of Dan* (Boston and New York: Houghton and Mifflin, 1894).

——, *The Story of Mary Dunne* (London: John Murray, 1913).

——, *The Things of a Child* (London: Collins, 1918).

——, *Whither?* (London: Griffith and Farran, 1892).

——, *Wild Wheat: A Dorset Romance* (London: Longmans, 1905).

Friedrichs, Hulda, 'A Peep at the Pioneer Club', *Young Woman* 4 (1896), 302–306.

'Funerals', *The Times* (London) (12 October 1912), 9.

G. M. S. [Gertrude Sweetman], 'M. E. Francis', *Irish Monthly* 8/683 (May 1930), 229–239.

Garner, Les, *Stepping Stones to Women's Liberty: Feminist Ideas in the Women's Suffrage Movement 1900–1918* (Cranbury, New Jersey: Associated University Presses, 1984).

Garriock, Jean Barbara, 'Late Victorian and Edwardian Images of Women and their Education in the Popular Press with Particular Reference to the Work of L. T. Meade' (University of Liverpool: PhD Thesis, 1997).

Gaskell, Elizabeth, *Cranford* (London: Chapman & Hall, 1853).

Gladstone, W. E., 'Notes and Queries on the Irish Demands', *Special Aspects of the Irish Question: A Series of Reflections in and since 1886. Collected from Various Sources and Reprinted* (London: J. Murray, 1892).

Gonne MacBride, Maud, *A Servant of the Queen: Her Own Story* (Dublin: Golden Eagle, 1938).

Gould, Warwick, ed., *Yeats Annual No. 4* (Houndmills, Basingstoke: Macmillan, 1986).

Graves, Clo, 'Employment for Girls: Chromo-Lithography', *Atalanta* 1/8 (1888), 474.

Greenwood, James, *The Seven Curses of London* (Boston: Fields, Osgood, 1869).

Gregory, Lady Augusta, *Lady Gregory's Journals: Volume Two, Books 30–44, 21 February 1925–1929 May 1932*, ed. Daniel J. Murphy (Gerrards Cross: Colin, Smythe, 1987).

——, *Our Irish Theatre: A Chapter of Autobiography* (New York and London: G. P. Putnam's Sons, The Knickerbocker Press, 1913).

Griffin, Daniel, *The Life of Gerald Griffin, By His Brother* (Dublin, 1872).

Griffin, Gerald, *The Collegians: A Tale of Garryowen* (New York: D. and J. Sadlier, 1843).

H-R-N [pseud. of John J. Dunne], *Here and There Memories* (London: T. Fisher Unwin, 1896).

Hammond, Mary, 'Readers and Readerships' in Joanne Shattock, ed., *The Cambridge Companion to English Literature 1830–1914*, 30–49.

Hansson, Heidi, *Emily Lawless, 1845–1913: Writing the Interspace* (Cork: Cork University Press, 2007).

——, ed., *New Contexts: Re-Framing Nineteenth-Century Irish Women's Prose* (Cork: Cork University Press, 2008).

——, 'Patriot's Daughter, Politician's Wife: Gender and Nation in M. E. Francis's *Miss Erin*' in Heidi Hansson, ed., *New Contexts: Re-Framing Nineteenth-Century Irish Women's Prose*, 109–124.

——and James H. Murphy, eds., *Fictions of the Irish Land War* (Oxford: Peter Lang, 2014).

Hardy, Thomas, *Tess of the d'Urbervilles* (London: Osgood, McIlvaine, 1891).

Hepburn, A. C., *Ireland 1905–1925: Volume 2, Documents and Analysis* (Newtownards: Colourpoint, 1998).

Herron, Tom, ed., *Irish Writing London, Volume 1: Revival to the Second World War* (London: Bloomsbury, 2013).

Hickman, Mary J. and Bronwen Walter, 'Deconstructing Whiteness: Irish Women in Britain', *Feminist Review* 50 (Summer 1995), 5–19.

Hinkson, Pamela, *The Ladies' Road* (London: Victor Gollancz, 1932).

Hogan, Robert, ed., *Dictionary of Irish Literature* (London: Aldwych Press, 1996).

Holdeman, David and Ben Levitas, eds., *W. B. Yeats in Context* (Cambridge: Cambridge UP, 2010).

Holdsworth, Carolyn, '"Shelley Plain": Yeats and Katharine Tynan' in Richard J. Finneran, ed., *Yeats Annual No. 2*, 59–92.

Huntley, Edith, M. D., 'Employment for Girls: Medicine', *Atalanta* 1/11 (1888), 655.

'Hurrish', the *Nation* (20 February 1886), 3.

Hussey de Burgh, U. H., *The Landowners of Ireland* (Dublin: Hodges, Foster and Figgis, 1878).

'In Fiction', *Southern Star* (Cork) (8 April 1905), 1.

'Ireland', *The Times* (London) (24 January 1888), 10.

'Ireland', *The Times* (London) (28 August 1888), 6.

'Ireland, Limerick City Assizes, July 25: Horrible Murder', *The Times* (London) (4 August 1820), 3.

'The Irish Crisis', *The Times* (London) (15 December 1890), 6.

Irish Independent (18 April 1910), 4.

'Irish Writer: Mrs Katherine Cecil Thurston Dies', *Sunday Independent* (10 September 1911), 8.

Jackson, Pauline, 'Women in Nineteenth-Century Irish Emigration', *International Migration Review* 18/4 (Winter 1984), 1004–1020.

Johnson, Edith M., 'Members of the Irish Parliament, 1784–1787', *Proceedings of the Royal Irish Academy. Section C: Archaeology, Celtic Studies, History, Linguistics, Literature* 71 (1971), 139–246.

Jordan, Ellen, '"Making Good Wives and Mothers"? The Transformation of Middle-Class Girls' Education in Nineteenth-Century Britain', *History of Education Quarterly* 1/4 (1991), 439–462.

Jordan, Donald, 'Merchants, "Strong Farmers" and Fenians: The Post-Famine Political Elite and the Irish Land War', in C. H. E. Philpin, ed., *Nationalism and Popular Protest in Ireland*, 321–348.

Kelly, John and Eric Domville, eds., *The Collected Letters of W. B. Yeats, Volume 1, 1865–1895* (Oxford: Clarendon Press, 1986).

Kickham, Lisbet, *Protestant Women Novelists and Irish Society 1879–1922* (Helgona-backen, Sweden: Department of English, Lund University, 2004).

Kirkpatrick, Kathryn, ed., *Border Crossings: Irish Women Writers and National Identities* (Tuscaloosa and London: The University of Alabama Press, 2000).

Kolloen, Ingar Sletten, *Knut Hamsun: Dreamer and Dissenter*, trans. Deborah Dawkin and Erik Skuggerik (New Haven, Yale UP, 2009).

'The Late Lord Cloncurry. The Inquest', *Freeman's Journal* (6 April 1869), 4.

Lawless, Emily, *The Book of Gilly: Four Months out of a Life* (London: Smith, Elder, 1906).

——, *A Chelsea Householder* (London: Sampson Low, 1882).

——, *A Colonel of the Empire* (New York: D. Appleton, 1895).

——, *A Garden Diary: September 1899–September 1900* (London: Methuen, 1901).

——, *Grania: The Story of an Island* (2 vols) (London: Smith, Elder, 1892).

——, *Hurrish* (Belfast: Appletree Press, 1992 [1886]).

——, *The Inalienable Heritage and Other Poems* (London: Privately Printed, 1914).

——, *Ireland: The Story of the Nations* (London: T. Fisher Unwin, 1887).

——, *Maelcho: A Sixteenth-Century Narrative*, (2 vols) (London: Smith, Elder, 1894).

——, *Major Lawrence, F. L. S.* (London: John Murray, 1887).

——, *A Millionaire's Cousin* (London: Macmillan, 1885).

——, 'Of the Personal Element in History', *Nineteenth Century* 50/297 (November 1901), 790–798.

——, *Traits and Confidences* (London: Garland Publishing, 1979).

——, *With Essex in Ireland* (London: Smith, Elder, 1890).

——, *With the Wild Geese* (London: Isbister, 1902).

—— and Shan F. Bullock, *The Race of Castlebar* (London: John Murray, 1913).

Lecky, William Edward Hartpole, 'Noticeable Books: *With Essex in Ireland*', *Nineteenth Century* 28/162 (August 1890), 236–251.

——, *History of England in the Eighteenth Century* (8 vols) (London: Longmans, Green, 1878–1890).

Ledger, Sally, *The New Woman: Fiction and Feminism at the Fin de Siècle* (Manchester: Manchester University Press, 1997).

——, 'The New Woman and Feminist Fictions', in Gail Marshall, ed., *The Cambridge Companion to the Fin de Siècle*, 153–168.

Liebgrits, Peter and Wimm Tigges, eds., *Beauty and the Beast: Christina Rossetti, Walter Pater, R. L. Stevenson and Their Contemporaries* (Amsterdam and Atlanta: Editions Rodolpi, 1996).

Linn, William J., 'George Egerton', in Robert Hogan, ed., *Dictionary of Irish Literature*, 404.

Lloyd's Weekly Newspaper (20 June 1886), 1.

Loeber, Rolf and Magda Stouthamer Loeber, 'Literary Absentees: Irish Women Authors in Nineteenth-Century England' in Jacqueline Belanger, ed., *The Irish Novel in the Nineteenth Century*, 167–186.

'Lord Cloncurry and His Murroe Tenants', *Freeman's Journal* (6 March 1882), 8.

M. B. [Mary Blundell], 'Through the Bars', *Irish Monthly* 7 (1879), 639–649.

MacCurtain, Margaret, et al., 'An Agenda for Women's History in Ireland, 1500–1900', *Irish Historical Studies* 28/109 (May 1992), 1–37.

MacNeill, J. G. Swift, Q. C. M. P., *Titled Corruption* (London: T. Fisher Unwin, 1894).

'The Making of a Novelist', *The Ladies' Realm* 17 (1904–1905), 658.

Marshall, Gail, ed., *The Cambridge Companion to the Fin de Siècle* (Cambridge: Cambridge University Press, 2007).

Matthews, Ann, *Renegades: Irish Republican Women 1900–1922* (Cork: Mercier Press, 2010).

Maume, Patrick, 'Emily Lawless's *Maelcho* and the Crisis of Imperial Romance', *Eire-Ireland* 41/3–4 (2007), 245–266.

McCormack, Declan, 'The Butterfly on the Wheel, *Irish Independent Online* (24 September 2000) <http://www.independent.ie/unsorted/features/the-butterfly-on-the-wheel-26256539.html> accessed 1 September 2014.

McFadden, James J., 'William Butler Yeats at Katharine Tynan's Home, Whitehall', in Richard J. Finneran, ed., *Yeats: An Annual of Critical and Textual Studies* 8, 206–242.

McHugh, Roger, ed., *W. B. Yeats: Letters to Katharine Tynan* (Dublin: Clonmore and Reynolds, 1953).

McLaughlin, J. B., 'Katharine Tynan', *Ampleforth Journal* 18 (1913), 277–295.

McMahon, Sean, *A Short History of Ireland* (Dublin: Mercier Press, 1996).

McWalter, J. C., 'The Dublin Libraries', *Irish Times* (29 September 1910), 5.

McWilliams, Ellen, *Women and Exile in Contemporary Irish Fiction* (Houndmills, Basingstoke: Palgrave Macmillan, 2013).

Meade, L. T., 'Appreciation of the late Rev. Benjamin Waugh', *The Times* (London) (14 March 1908), 7.

——, *Ashton-Morton, or Memories of My Life* (London: T. Cautley Newby, 1866).

——, *The Autocrat of the Nursery* (London: Hodder and Stoughton, 1884).

——, *Bashful Fifteen* (London: Cassell, 1892).

——, 'Children Past and Present', *Parents' Review* 6/12 (1896), 881–887.

——, *Daddy's Boy* (London: Hatchards, 1887).

——, *The Daughter of a Soldier* (London: Chambers, 1915).

——, 'Girls' Schools of To-day I – Cheltenham College', *Strand Magazine* 9 (1895), 457–462.

——, *Great St. Benedict's: A Tale* (London: John F. Shaw, 1876).

——, *The Home of Silence* (London: Sisley's, 1890).

——, 'How I Began', *Girls' Realm* 3 (1900), 57–64.

——, *Kitty O'Donovan* (London: Chambers, 1912).

——, *Lettie's Last Home* (London: John F. Shaw, 1875).

——, *Light o' the Morning: The Story of An Irish Girl* (London: Chambers, 1899).

——, *The O'Donnells of Inchfawn* (London: Hatchard, 1887).

——, *The Passion of Kathleen Duveen* (London: Modern Publishing, 1913).

——, *Peggy from Kerry* (London: Chambers, 1912).

——, 'The Queen of Girls'-Book Makers', *The Saturday Review of Politics, Literature, Science and Art* 102/2669 (1906), 774.

——, *The Rebel of the School* (London: Chambers, 1902).

——, 'Red Letter Days', *Sunday Magazine* (June 1899), 406–410.

——, *Scamp and I* (London: John F. Shaw, 1877).

——, *The Stormy Petrel* (London: Hurst and Blackett, 1909).

——, *A Wild Irish Girl* (London: Chambers, 1910).

——, *Wild Kitty* (London: Chambers, 1897).

——, *A World of Girls: The Story of a School* (London: Cassell, 1886).

——, and Clifford Halifax, 'Stories from the Diary of a Doctor', *Strand Magazine* (1893), 91–102.

Meaney et al., *Reading the Irish Woman: Studies in Cultural Encounter* (Liverpool: Liverpool UP, 2013).

Meaney, Gerardine, 'Decadence, Degeneration and Revolting Aesthetics: The Fiction of Emily Lawless and Katherine Cecil Thurston', *Colby Quarterly* 36/2 (2000), 157–175.

'A Mid-Victorian Home in Ireland', *Saturday Review of Politics, Literature and Art*, 125/3268 (15 June 1918), 535.

Mitchell, Sally, *The New Girl: Girls' Culture in England, 1880–1915* (New York: Columbia University Press, 1995).

'Monthly Report of the Wholesale Book Trade', *Bookman* 7/39 (December 1894), 74.

'Mr F. E. Smith & Civil War Cry', *Freeman's Journal* (2 May 1914), 9.

'Mr Parnell', *Freeman's Journal* (11 December 1890), 5.

'Mr Parnell in Ireland', *Daily News* (London) (11 December 1890), 5.

'Mrs L. T. Meade at Home', *Sunday Magazine* (September 1894), 615–620.

Murphy, James H., *Catholic Fiction and Social Reality in Ireland, 1873–1922* (Westport, Connecticut: Greenwood Press, 1997).

——, *Irish Novelists and the Victorian Age* (Oxford: Oxford UP, 2011).

——, '"Things Which Seem to You Unfeminine": Gender and Nationalism in the Fiction of Some Upper Middle Class Catholic Women Novelists, 1880–1910', in Kathryn J. Kirkpatrick, ed., *Border Crossings: Irish Women Writers and National Identities*, 58–78.

Murray, Tony, *London Irish Fictions: Narrative, Diaspora and Identity* (Liverpool: Liverpool University Press, 2012).

'The National Council. Boycott of Non-Irish Goods', *Irish Independent* (29 November 1904), 5.

Nenagh Guardian (2 June 1880), 3.

Nenagh Guardian (4 June 1881), 4.

'New Writers', *Bookman* 23/138 (March 1903), 227.

Nicoll, Sir William Robertson, 'New Writers', *Bookman* 6/35 (August 1894), 138–139.

'Notes on New Books', *Irish Monthly* 22/250 (April 1894), 221–224.

'Notes on New Books', *Irish Monthly* 35/414 (December 1907), 701–707.

'Novels in Brief', *Athenaeum* 4706 (9 July 1920), 52.

O'Brien, Kate, *The Ante-Room* (London: Virago, 1988 [1934]).

O'Connor, Ulick, *Celtic Dawn: A Portrait of the Irish Literary Renaissance* (Dublin: Town House and Country House, 1999).

O'Neill, Ciaran, *Catholics of Consequence: Transnational Education, Social Mobility, and the Irish Catholic Elite 1850–1900* (Oxford: Oxford University Press, 2014).

O'Neill, Marie, 'Katharine Tynan Hinkson: A Dublin Writer', *Dublin Historical Record* 40/3 (June 1987), 83–93.

O'Toole, Tina, *The Irish New Woman* (London: Palgrave Macmillan, 2013).

'Obituary: Captain J. J. Dunne', *The Times* (London) (8 February 1910), 11.

Oliphant, M. A., 'A Noble Lady', *New Review* 14/82 (March 1896), 241–247.

'Our London Correspondence', *Glasgow Herald* (17 January 1894), 7.

'Outstanding Novels, No. XXXVII, *Wood Sanctuary*', *Tablet* (12 April 1930), 486.

Parker, Percy L., 'Katharine Tynan at Home', *Woman's Signal* 2 (11 January 1894), 17.

Pašeta, Senia, *Irish Nationalist Women, 1900–1918* (Cambridge: Cambridge UP, 2013).

'People, Places and Things', *Hearth and Home* 150 (1894), 649.

'People, Places and Things', *Hearth and Home* 154 (1894), 814.

Philpin, C. H. E., ed. *Nationalism and Popular Protest in Ireland* (Cambridge: Cambridge UP, 1987).

Pierse, Mary S., *Irish Feminisms: 1810–1930* (5 vols) (Routledge: London and New York, 2010).

Plunkett, Sir Horace Curzon, *Ireland in the New Century* (London: John Murray, 1905).

Pugh, Edwin, 'Four Novels', *Bookman* 49/289 (October 1915), 24–25.

'The Queen of Girls'-Book Makers', *Saturday Review of Politics, Literature, Science and Art* 102/2669 (1906), 774.

R. M. [Rosa Mulholland], 'Wanted An Irish Novelist', *Irish Monthly* 19/217 (1891), 368–373.

Reimer, Mavis Barkman, 'Tales out of School: L. T. Meade and the School Story' (University of Calgary: PhD Thesis, 1993).

'Remarkable Demonstration in Dublin. English Rowdyism Smartly Punished', *Southern Star* (Cork) (7 July 1900), 3.

'Results of Prize Competitions: The Six Most Popular Living Writers for Girls', *Girl's Realm* 1/4 (1899), 431.

'Review. *The Story of Dan*. By M. E. Francis.', *Saturday Review of Politics, Literature, Science and Art* 78/2038 (17 November 1894), 543.

'The Right Hon. The Lord Mayor and Lord Cloncurry', *Freeman's Journal* (14 March 1867), 1.

Rodgers, Beth, 'Irishness, Professional Authorship and the "Wild Irish Girls" of L. T. Meade', *English Literature in Transition* 56/2 (2013), 146–166.

'The Romance of Butchery', the *Nation* (27 September 1890), 2.

Rose, Marilyn Gaddis, *Katharine Tynan* (Lewisburg: Bucknell University Press, 1974).

Russell, Matthew, 'The Literary Output of Three Irish-Women', *Irish Monthly* 39/442 (April 1910), 200–202.

——, 'Notes on New Books', *Irish Monthly* 18/209 (November 1890), 612–616.

——, 'Poets I Have Known. No. 5: Katharine Tynan', *Irish Monthly* 31/359 (May 1903), 250–267.

——, 'A Word about Irish Catholic Literature', *Irish Monthly* 40/468 (June 1912), 311–312.

Ryan, William Patrick, *The Irish Literary Revival* (New York: Lemma, 1970 [1894]).

'A Sad Story', *Freeman's Journal* (5 September 1857), 1.

Sayles, G. O., 'Contemporary Sketches of the Members of the Irish Parliament in 1782', *Proceedings of the Royal Irish Academy. Section C: Archaeology, Celtic Studies, History, Linguistics, Literature* 56 (1953/1954), 227–286.

Shattock, Joanne, ed., *The Cambridge Companion to English Literature, 1830–1914* (Cambridge: Cambridge University Press, 2010).

'She-Notes by Borgia Smudgiton', *Punch* (10 March 1894), 109.

'She-Notes by Borgia Smudgiton', *Punch* (17 March 1894), 130.

Showalter, Elaine, 'Twenty Years On: A Literature of Their Own Revisited', *NOVEL: A Forum on Fiction* 31/3 (Summer 1998), 399–413.

Sichel, Edith, 'Emily Lawless', *Nineteenth Century and After* 76/449 (July 1914), 80–100.

Southern Star (Cork) (15 January 1898), 2.

Standlee, Whitney, 'The "Personal Element" and Emily Lawless's Hurrish (1886)' in Heidi Hansson and James H. Murphy, eds., *Fictions of the Irish Land War* (Oxford: Peter Lang, 2014), 19–40.

——, '"A World of Difference": London and Ireland in the Works of Katharine Tynan' in Tom Herron, ed., *Irish Writing London, Volume 1: Revival to the Second World War* (London: Bloomsbury, 2013), 70–83.

Stetz, Margaret Diane, '"George Egerton": Woman and Writer of the Eighteen Nineties' (Harvard University: PhD Thesis, 1982).

Stutfield, Hugh E. M., 'Tommyrotics', *Blackwood's Edinburgh Magazine* 157/956 (June 1895), 833–845.

Synge, J. M., *The Playboy of the Western World* (Dublin: Maunsel, 1907).

Taylor, R. W., 'M. E. Francis: An Appreciation', in M. E. Francis, *In a North Country Village* (Wigan: Northwest Catholic History Society, 2008), v–xvi.

'The Threatened Civil War', *Irish Independent* (20 January 1914), 6.

'Through Irish London', the *Nation* (2 May 1891), 4.

Thurston, Ernest Temple, *The Apple of Eden* (London: Dodd, Mead, 1905).

Thurston, Katherine Cecil, *The Circle* (Edinburgh and London: William Blackwood, 1903).

——, *The Fly on the Wheel* (London: Virago, 1987 [1908]).

——, *The Gambler* (London: Hutchinson, 1906).

——, *John Chilcote, M. P.* (Edinburgh and London: William Blackwood, 1904).

——, *Max* (London: Hutchinson, 1910).

Tighe, J. J., 'God Save the Queen', *Irish Times* (29 June 1897), 6.

The Times (London) (20 February 1905), 7.

'To Investors – Wanted', *Morning Post* (London) (19 July 1884), 8.

'To-Day's Tittle Tattle', *Pall Mall Gazette* (1 July 1889), 6.

Tracy, Dominick, 'Squatting the Deserted Village: Idyllic Resistance in Griffin's *The Collegians*' in Jacqueline Belanger, ed., *The Irish Novel in the Nineteenth Century: Facts and Fictions*, 94–109.

'Trial of Sir J. Piers', *Morning Post* (London) (24 February 1807), n.p.

Tynan, Katharine, *The Adventures of Alicia* (London: F. V. White, 1906).

——, *Collected Poems by Katharine Tynan* (London: Macmillan, 1930).

——, *Cousins and Others* (London: T. Werner Laurie, 1909).

——, *A Daughter of Kings* (London: Eveleigh Nash, 1905).

——, *A Daughter of the Fields* (Chicago: A. C. McClurg, 1901).

——, *The Dear Irish Girl* (London: Smith, Elder, 1899).

——, *The French Wife* (London: F. V. White, 1904).

——, *A Girl of Galway* (London, Glasgow and Dublin: Blackie and Son, 1902).

——, *The Handsome Brandons: A Story for Girls* (London, Glasgow, Dublin, Bombay: Blackie and Son, 1899).

——, *Heart O' Gold or The Little Princess: A Story for Girls* (London: S. W. Partridge, 1912).

——, *Her Ladyship* (London: Smith, Elder, 1907).

——, *The Honourable Molly* (London: Smith, Elder, 1903).

——, *The House of the Crickets* (London: Smith, Elder, 1908).

——, *The House of the Foxes* (London: Smith, Elder, 1915).

——, *The House of the Secret* (London: James Clarke, 1910).

——, *The House on the Bogs* (London and Melbourne: Ward, Lock, 1922).

——, *John-A-Dreams* (London: Smith, Elder, 1916).

——, *Julia* (London: Smith, Elder, 1904).

——, *Katharine Tynan: Letters 1884–1885* (n.pl.: Apex One, 1973).

——, *A King's Woman: Being the Narrative of Miss Penelope Fayle, Now Mistress Frobisher, Concerning the Late Troublous Times in Ireland* (London: Hurst and Blackett, 1902).

——, *Lord Edward: A Study in Romance* (London: John Murray, 1916).

——, *Louise de la Vallière and Other Poems* (London: Kegan, Paul, Trench, 1886).

——, *Memories* (London: Eveleigh Nash and Grayson, 1924).

——, *The Middle Years* (London: Constable, 1916).

——, *Molly, My Heart's Delight* (London: Smith, Elder, 1914).

——, *Mrs Pratt of Paradise Farm* (London: Smith, Elder, 1913).

——, *A Nun, Her Friends and Her Order: Being A Sketch of the Life of Mother Mary Xaveria Fallon* (London: Kegan Paul, Trench, Trübner, 1891).

——, *Paradise Farm* (New York: Duffield, 1911).

——, *The Playground* (London and Melbourne: Ward, Lock, 1930).

——, *Princess Katharine* (London, Melbourne, Toronto: Ward, Lock, 1912).

——, *The Rattlesnake* (London, Melbourne and Toronto: Ward, Lock, 1917).

——, *A Rose of the Garden* (London: Constable, 1912).

——, *A Shameful Inheritance* (London, New York, Toronto and Melbourne: Cassell, 1914).

——, *She Walks in Beauty* (London: Smith, Elder, 1899).

——, *The Story of Bawn* (London: Smith, Elder, 1906).

——, *The Story of Cecilia* (London: Smith, Elder, 1911).

——, *That Sweet Enemy* (London: Archibald Constable, 1901).

——, *They Loved Greatly* (London: Eveleigh Nash and Grayson, 1923).

——, *Three Fair Maids or the Burkes of Derrymore* (London, Glasgow and Bombay: Blackie and Son, 1900).

——, *Twenty-Five Years: Reminiscences* (New York: Devin Adair, 1913).

——, *A Union of Hearts* (London: James Nisbet, 1901).

——, *The Wandering Years* (London: Constable, 1922).

——, *The Way of a Maid* (London: Lawrence and Bullen, 1895).

——, *The West Wind* (London: Constable, 1916).

——, *The Years of the Shadow* (London: Constable, 1919).

Tynan Hinkson, Katharine, *For the White Rose* (New York, Cincinnati, Chicago: Benziger Brothers, 1905).

——, *The Golden Lily* (New York, Cincinnati, Chicago: Benziger Brothers, 1902).

Tynan O'Mahony, Nora, 'Katharine Tynan's Girlhood', *Irish Monthly* 59/696 (June 1931), 358–363.

Van de Kamp, Peter, 'Tynan, Katharine (1859–1931)', *Oxford Dictionary of National Biography* (Oxford: Oxford University Press, 2004) <http://www.oxforddnb.com/view/article33887> accessed 1 September 2014.

——, 'Some Notes on the Literary Estate of Pamela Hinkson', in Warwick Gould, ed., *Yeats Annual No. 4*, 181–188.

——, 'Wrapped in a Dream: Katharine Tynan and Christina Rossetti', in Peter Liebgrits and Wimm Tigges, eds., *Beauty and the Beast: Christina Rossetti, Walter Pater, R. L. Stevenson and Their Contemporaries*, 59–98.

Walker, Nano Harris, *T. P.'s Weekly* 18/463 (22 September 1911), 356.

Weekes, Ann Owens, *Irish Women Writers: An Uncharted Tradition* (Lexington: University Press of Kentucky, 1990).

——, *Unveiling Treasures: The Attic Guide to the Published Works of Irish Women Literary Writers* (Dublin: Attic Press, 1993).

Whitaker's Peerage, Baronetage, Knightage and Companionage for the Year 1906 (London: Whitaker's, 1907).

Woods, G. S., 'Thurston, Katherine Cecil (1875–1911)', rev. Sayoni Basu, *Oxford Dictionary of National Biography*, Oxford University Press, 2004 <http://www.oxforddnb.com/view/article/36521> accessed 28 July 2014.

Woolf, Virginia, *A Room of One's Own/Three Guineas* (London: Penguin, 1993).

Yeats, W. B., *The Celtic Twilight* (London: A. H. Bullen, 1902).

——, *John Sherman & Dhoya* (Dublin: The Lilliput Press, 1990).

——, *Uncollected Prose*, John P. Frayne, ed. (London: Macmillan, 1970).

——, *The Wanderings of Oisin* (London: Kegan Paul, 1889).

——and Lionel Johnson, *Poetry and Ireland: Essays by W. B. Yeats and Lionel Johnson* (Dundrum: Cuala Press, 1908).

Zimmern, Alice, 'Girls' Book Lists', *The Leisure Hour: An Illustrated Magazine for Home Reading* (February 1901), 333–337.

Index

Reimagining Ireland

Series Editor: Dr Eamon Maher, Institute of Technology, Tallaght

The concepts of Ireland and 'Irishness' are in constant flux in the wake of an ever-increasing reappraisal of the notion of cultural and national specificity in a world assailed from all angles by the forces of globalisation and uniformity. Reimagining Ireland interrogates Ireland's past and present and suggests possibilities for the future by looking at Ireland's literature, culture and history and subjecting them to the most up-to-date critical appraisals associated with sociology, literary theory, historiography, political science and theology.

Some of the pertinent issues include, but are not confined to, Irish writing in English and Irish, Nationalism, Unionism, the Northern 'Troubles', the Peace Process, economic development in Ireland, the impact and decline of the Celtic Tiger, Irish spirituality, the rise and fall of organised religion, the visual arts, popular cultures, sport, Irish music and dance, emigration and the Irish diaspora, immigration and multiculturalism, marginalisation, globalisation, modernity/post-modernity and postcolonialism. The series publishes monographs, comparative studies, interdisciplinary projects, conference proceedings and edited books.

Proposals should be sent either to Dr Eamon Maher at eamon.maher@ittdublin.ie or to ireland@peterlang.com.

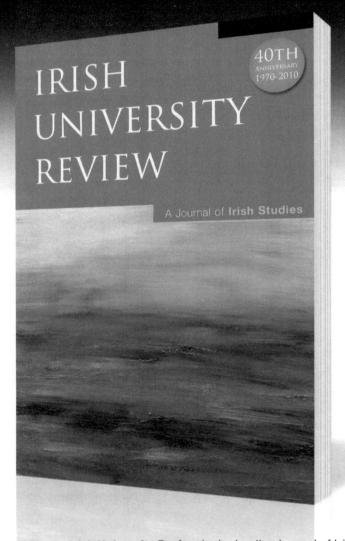